Robert Byron was born in 1905 and educated at Eton and
Merton College, Oxford. Among his other books are *The Station*
(1928), *The Byzantine Achievement* (1929) and *First Russia,
Then Tibet* (1933). He died when his ship was torpedoed in the
Mediterranean in 1941.

Robert Byron

The Road to Oxiana

Introduction by Bruce Chatwin

PICADOR
published by Pan Books

First published 1937 by Macmillan and Co. Ltd
This Picador edition published 1981 by Pan Books Ltd
Cavaye Place, London sw10 9pg
© The Estate of Robert Byron 1937
Introduction © Bruce Chatwin 1981
isbn 0 330 26445 1
Printed in Great Britain by
Richard Clay (The Chaucer Press) Ltd, Bungay, Suffolk

Contents

ENTRIES

Part II

Part III

Introduction

Anyone who reads around the travel books of the thirties must, in the end, conclude that Robert Byron's *The Road to Oxiana* is the masterpiece. Byron was a gentleman, a scholar and an aesthete, who drowned in 1941 when his ship to the Mediterranean was torpedoed. In his short life he travelled as far as China and Tibet, and to most of the countries nearer home. In 1928 he published *The Station*, an account of a visit to the monasteries of Mount Athos, and followed it up with two pioneering volumes on Byzantine civilization, which, at that time, received scant consideration from academic circles. He had some lively prejudices. Among the targets of his abuse were the Catholic (as opposed to the Orthodox) Church; the art of Classical Greece; the paintings of Rembrandt; Shakespeare – and when his Intourist guide protested that the plays could never have been written by a grocer from Stratford-upon-Avon, he murmured, 'They are exactly the sort of plays I would expect a grocer to write.' In 1932, attracted by the photo of a Seljuk tomb-tower on the Turkoman steppe, he set out on a quest for the origins of Islamic architecture. And if it is fair to place his earlier books as the work of a dazzlingly gifted young amateur, it is equally fair to rank *The Road to Oxiana* as a work of genius.

I write as a partisan, not as a critic. Long ago, I raised it to the status of 'sacred text', and thus beyond criticism. My own copy – now spineless and floodstained after four journeys to Central Asia – has been with me since the age of fifteen. Consequently, I am apt to resent suggestions that it is a 'lost book' or in need of being 'rescued from the library shelves'. By a stroke of luck, it was never lost on me.

Because I felt the death of Robert Byron so keenly, I sought out his friends and pestered them for their reminiscences. 'Very cross,' they said. 'An awful tease.' 'Surprisingly tough.' 'Abrasive.' 'Incredibly funny.' 'Fat.' 'Rather hideous ... eyes like a fish.' 'Wonderful imitation of Queen Victoria.' By the time I was twenty-two, I had read everything I could – by and about him – and that summer set out on my own journey to Oxiana.

In 1962 – six years before the Hippies wrecked it (by driving educated Afghans into the arms of the Marxists) – you could set off to Afghanistan with the anticipations of, say, Delacroix off to Algiers. On the streets of Herat you saw men in mountainous turbans, strolling hand in hand, with roses in their mouths and rifles wrapped in flowered chintz. In Badakhshan you could picnic on Chinese carpets and listen to the bulbul. In Balkh, the Mother of Cities, I asked a fakir the way to the shrine of Hadji Piardeh. 'I don't know it,' he said. 'It must have been destroyed by Genghiz.'

Even the Afghan Embassy in London introduced you to a world that was hilarious and strange. Control of the visa section rested with a tousle-haired Russian emigré giant, who had cut the lining of his jacket, so that it hung, as a curtain, to hide the holes in the seat of his pants. At opening time, he'd be stirring up clouds of dust with a broom, only to let it settle afresh on the collapsing furniture. Once, when I tipped him ten shillings, he hugged me, lifted me off the floor and bellowed: 'I hope you have a very ACCIDENT-FREE trip to Afghanistan!'

No. Our journeys were never quite accident-free: the time a soldier lobbed a pick-axe at the car; the time our lorry slid, with gentle resignation, over the cliff (we had time to jump off); the time we were whipped for straying into a military area; the dysentery; the septicaemia; the hornet sting; the fleas – but, mercifully, no hepatitis.

Sometimes, we met travellers more high-minded than ourselves who were following the tracks of Alexander or Marco Polo: for us, it was far more fun to follow Robert Byron. I still have notebooks to prove how slavishly I aped both his itinerary and – as if that were possible – his style. Take this entry of mine for 5 July 1962 and compare it with his for 21 September 1933:

In the afternoon we called on Mr Alouf the art dealer. He took us to an apartment filled with french-polished 'French' furniture, most of it riddled with worm and upside down. He had recently converted to Catholicism and, on showing us a signed photograph of Pope Pius XII, crossed himself fervently and rattled his dentures.

From a cupboard he produced the following:

A Roman gold pectoral set with blue glass pastes. A forgery.

A Neolithic marble idol with an erect phallus, on an accompanying perch. The perch was genuine, the idol not.

Thirty Syro-Phoenician funerary bone dolls.

A 'Hittite' figure, bristling with gold attributes, perhaps the one Byron saw in 1933. A fake.

Various worrying gold objects.

A collection of Early Christian glasses (genuine). 'I have many glasses,' said Mr Alouf, crossing himself, 'covered with crosses. But they are in the bank.'

Finally, a marble head of Alexander the Great. 'I have refuse twenty-thousand dollars for this piece. TWENTY THOUSAND DOLLARS! All archaeologists agree mine is the only genuine head of Alexander: Look! The neck! The ears!' Perhaps – but the face was entirely missing.

From the Levant we would go on to Teheran. There was more money about than in Byron's day and many more Europeans after it. But the Shah was a pale copy of his father and already he, too, looked pretty silly, and the men around him, queasy. One day we went to see HE Amir Abbas Hoveyda in his office at the Iranian Oil Company (he was not yet Prime Minister): 'A man with big eyes and despairing gestures. He seemed trapped behind the enormity of his desk. He offered us the use of his helicopter in case we should need it.'

Once Byron gets to Iran, his search for the origins of Islamic architecture really gets under way. But to construct, out of stone and brick and tile, a prose that will not only be readable but carry the reader to a pitch of excitement requires talents of the highest calibre. This is Byron's achievement. His paean of praise for the Sheikh Lutf'ullah Mosque in Isfahan must put him at least in the rank of Ruskin. One afternoon, to see how it was done, I took *The Road to Oxiana* into the mosque and sat, cross-legged, marvelling both at the tilework and Byron's description of it.

Now the 'experts' will carp that, while Byron may have had lyrical powers of description, he was not a scholar – and, of course, in their sense he wasn't. Yet, time and again, he scores over sound scholarship with his uncanny ability to gauge the morale of a civilization from its architecture, and to treat ancient buildings and modern people as two facets of a continuing story.

Already in *The Byzantine Achievement*, written at twenty-five, there is a haunting passage that tells in four sentences as much about the schism of the Western and Eastern Churches as any number of portentous volumes:

The existence of St Sophia is atmospheric; that of St Peter's, overpoweringly, imminently substantial. One is a church to God; the other a salon for his agents. One is consecrated to reality, the other, to illusion. St Sophia, in fact, is large, and St Peter's is vilely, tragically small.

On the subject of Iran, he is even more clairvoyant. On reading *The Road to Oxiana* you end up with the impression that the Iranian plateau is a 'soft centre' that panders to megalomaniac ambitions in its rulers without providing the genius to sustain them.

As is well known, the late Shah-in-Shah saw in the ruins of Persepolis a mirror image of his own glory and, for that reason, held his coronation binge about a mile from the site, in tents designed by Jansen of Paris, where a riffraff of royalty could dine with the ghosts of his *soi-disant* predecessors.

Read, therefore, Byron's comments on Persepolis in the light of the pretensions and downfall of the Pahlevi Dynasty:

The stone, owing to its extreme hardness, has proved impervious to age; it remains a bright smooth grey, as slick as an aluminium saucepan. This cleanness reacts on the carving like sunlight on a fake old master; it reveals, instead of the genius one expected, a disconcerting void... My involuntary thought as Herzfeld showed us the new (newly excavated) staircase was: 'How much did this cost? Was it made in a factory? No, it wasn't. Then how many workmen for how many years chiselled and polished these endless figures?' Certainly, they are not mechanical figures; nor are they guilty of elaboration for their own sake; nor are they cheap in the sense of lacking technical skill. But they are what the French call *faux bons*. They have art, but not spontaneous art... Instead of mind or feeling, they exhale a soulless refinement, a veneer adopted by the Asiatic whose own artistic instinct has been fettered and devitalized by... the Mediterranean.

Now if you pursue this vein, you will find that, under the bravura passages, Byron is expounding a very serious thesis – and one of crucial importance for understanding our own time. All he finds most admirable in Persian art – the tower at Gumbad-i-Kabus, the Seljuk Mosque in Isfahan, the incomparable mausoleum of the Mongol Khan Uljaitu, or the buildings of Gohar Shad – results from a fusion (one could say, a chemical explosion) between the old Iranian civilization and the peoples of nomad stock from the Oxus Basin and beyond. You even feel that Byron's favourite character, Shir Ahmad Khan, the Afghan Ambassador to Teheran, belongs among these first-rate monuments: in other words, genius visits Iran from the north-east.

Certainly – in Byron's day, and mine – to cross the Afghan frontier, after the lowering fanaticism of Meshed, was like coming up for air. 'Here at last,' he wrote of Herat, 'is Asia without an inferiority complex.' And it is this moral superiority of the Afghans, together with a fear of the centrifugal forces spinning in Central Asia, that has scared the Russians and the bunch of seedy traitors who have sold their country. (May they boil in Gehenna!) So when I read that the Heratis have been sending women's dresses and cosmetics to the cowards of Kandahar, I think back to a dress I once saw flapping in the old clothes bazaar in Herat – a gown of flamingo crêpe with sequined butterflies on the hips and the label of a boutique in Beverley Hills.

Even in Kabul, the unlikely was always predictable: the sight of the King's cousin Prince Daud at a party, the old 'Mussolini' blackshirt, with his muddy smile and polished head and boots, talking to – who? – Duke Ellington, who else? The Duke in a white-and-blue spotted tie and a blue-and-white spotted shirt: he was on his last big tour. And we know what happened to Daud – shot, with his family, in the palace he usurped.

I can guess what's happened to the crippled Nuristani boy, who brought us our dinner from his village up the mountain. We had camped by the river, and he came down the rock face, swinging his crutch and his withered leg and, somehow, hanging on to the dish and a lighted firebrand. He sang while we ate – but they have bombed the village and used gas on the inhabitants.

I can guess, too, what happened to Wali Jahn. He took me to safety when I got blood-poisoning. He carried me on his back through the river, and bathed my head, and made me rest under the ilexes. But when we came back, five years later, he was coughing, deep retching coughs, and had the look of someone going down to the cold.

But what have they done to Gul Amir the Tadjik? He was ugly as sin with an unending nose and silver earrings. You never saw anyone so devout. Every time he wanted a rest, 'There was no God but God . . .' but as he bowed his face to Mecca, he would squint out sideways and, when I fell in the river trying to cast a trout fly, God was forgotten in a peal of girlish giggles.

Where is now the Hakim of Kande? We stayed in his summerhouse under a scree of shining schist and watched the creamy clouds coming over the mountain. In the evening we saw a girl in red creeping out of a maize field: 'The corn is high,' he said. 'In nine months there will be many babies.'

What's become of the trucker who admired my ear-lobes? We left him in the middle of the road. His carburettor had clogged and his hashish pipe had clogged, and the pieces were all mixed up, on the road, and we were in a hurry.

Or the houseboy at the Park Hotel in Herat? He wore a rose-pink turban and, when we asked for lunch, said:

'Yessir! Whatyoulike? Everything!'

'What you got?'

'No drink. No ice. No bread. No fruit. No meat. No rice. No fish. Eggs. One. Maybe. Tomorrow. YES!'

Or the man in Tashkurgan who took me to his garden? It was a very hot and dusty afternoon and Peter was looking for traces of the Bactrian Greeks. 'Go and find your Greeks,' I said. 'Give me your Marvell and I'll find a garden' – where I really did stumble on melons as I passed and had green thoughts in a green shade.

Or the mad woman in Ghazni at the Tomb of Mahmud? She was tall and lovely and she stared gloomily at the ground and rattled her bracelets. When they opened the doors, she flung herself on the wooden balustrade, and flapped her crimson dress and cawed like a wounded bird. Only when they let her kiss the tomb did she fall silent. And she kissed the inscription, as if each white marble letter contained the cure for her sickness.

How could she know what Byron wrote of it? 'I have enjoyed many examples of it [kufic lettering] in the last ten months. But none can compare with these tall rhythmic ciphers, involved with dancing foliage, which mourn the loss of Mahmud, the conqueror of India, Persia and Oxiana, nine centuries after his death in the capital where he lived.'

This is the year – of all years – to mourn the loss of Robert Byron, the arch-enemy of Appeasement, who said, 'I shall have warmonger put on my passport,' when he saw what the Nazis were up to. Were he alive today, I think he would agree that, in time (everything in Afghanistan takes time), the Afghans will do something quite dreadful to their invaders – perhaps awaken the sleeping giants of Central Asia.

But that will not bring back the things we loved: the high, clear days and the blue icecaps on the mountains; the lines of white poplars fluttering in the wind, and the long white prayer-flags; the fields of asphodels that followed the tulips; or the fat-tailed sheep brindling the hills above Chakcharan, and the ram with a tail so big they had to strap it to a cart. We shall not lie on our backs at the Red Castle and watch the vultures wheeling over the valley where they killed the grandson of Genghiz. We will not read Babur's Memoirs in his garden at Istalif and see the blind man smelling his way around the rose bushes. Or sit in the Peace of Islam with the beggars of Gazar Gagh. We will not stand on the Buddha's head at Bamiyan, upright in his niche like a whale in a dry-dock. We will not sleep in the nomad tent, or scale the Minaret of Jam. And we shall lose the tastes – the hot, coarse, bitter bread; the green tea flavoured with cardamoms; the grapes we cooled in the snow-melt; and the nuts and dried mulberries we munched for altitude sickness. Nor shall we get back the smell of the beanfields; the sweet, resinous smell of deodar wood burning, or the whiff of a snow leopard at 14,000 feet. Never. Never. Never.

Bruce Chatwin
    August 1980

Books by Robert Byron

Europe in the Looking Glass (1927)

The Station (Duckworth, 1928; John Lehmann, 1949)

The Byzantine Achievement (Routledge, 1929)

The Birth of Western Painting (Routledge, 1930)

An Essay on India (Routledge, 1931)

The Appreciation of Architecture (Wishart, 1932)

First Russia, Then Tibet (Macmillan, 1933)

The Road to Oxiana (Macmillan, 1937; John Lehmann, 1950; Jonathan Cape, 1966)

Four Studies in Loyalty by Christopher Sykes (Collins, 1950) contains an essay on Byron

Part I

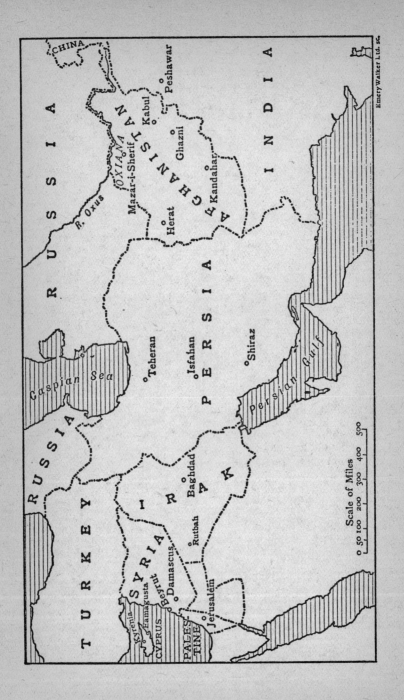

Venice, 20 August 1933   Here as a joy-hog: a pleasant change after that pension on the Giudecca two years ago. We went to the Lido this morning, and the Doge's Palace looked more beautiful from a speed-boat than it ever did from a gondola. The bathing, on a calm day, must be the worst in Europe: water like hot saliva, cigar-ends floating into one's mouth, and shoals of jellyfish.

Lifar came to dinner. Bertie mentioned that all whales have syphilis.

Venice, 21 August   After inspecting two palaces, the Labiena, containing Tiepolo's fresco of Cleopatra's Banquet, and the Pappadopoli, a stifling labyrinth of plush and royal photographs, we took sanctuary from culture in Harry's Bar. There was an ominous chatter, a quick-fire of greetings: the English are arriving.

In the evening we went back to Harry's Bar, where our host regaled us with a drink compounded of champagne and cherry brandy. 'To have the right effect,' said Harry confidentially, 'it must be the worst cherry brandy.' It was.
Before this my acquaintance with our host was limited to the hunting field. He looked unfamiliar in a green beach vest and white mess jacket.

Venice, 22 August   In a gondola to San Rocco, where Tintoretto's *Crucifixion* took away my breath; I had forgotten it. The old visitors' book with Lenin's name in it had been removed. At the Lido there was a breeze; the sea was rough, cool, and free from refuse.

We motored out to tea at Malcontenta, by the new road over the lagoons beside the railway. Nine years ago Landsberg found Malcontenta, though celebrated in every book on Palladio, at the point of ruin, doorless and windowless, a granary of indeterminate farm-produce. He has made it a habitable dwelling. The proportions of the great hall and staterooms are a mathematical paean. Another man would have filled them with so-called Italian furniture, antique-dealers' rubbish, gilt. Landsberg has had the furniture made of plain wood in the local village. Nothing is 'period' except the candles, which are necessary in the absence of electricity.

Outside, people argue over the sides and affect to deplore the back. The front asks no opinion. It is a precedent, a criterion. You can analyse it – nothing could be more lucid; but you cannot question it. I stood with Diane on the lawn below the portico, as the glow before dusk defined for one moment more clearly every stage of the design. Europe could have bid me no fonder farewell than this triumphant affirmation of the European intellect. 'It's a mistake to leave civilization,' said Diane, knowing she proved the point by existing. I was lost in gloom.

Inside, the candles were lit and Lifar danced. We drove back through a rainstorm, and I went to bed with an alarm clock.

SS Italia, *26 August* The moustachio'd and portly gondolier attached to the palace was waiting for me at five. All towns are the same at dawn; as even Oxford Street can look beautiful in its emptiness, so Venice now seemed less insatiably picturesque. Give me Venice as Ruskin first saw it – without a railway; or give me a speed-boat and the international rich. The human museum is horrible, such as those islands off the coast of Holland where the Dutch retain their national dress.

The departure of this boat from Trieste was attended by scenes first performed in the Old Testament. Jewish refugees from Germany were leaving for Palestine. On the one hand was a venerable wonder-rabbi, whose orthodox ringlets and round beaver hat set the fashion for his disciples down to the age of eight; on the other, a flashy group of boys and girls in beach clothes, who stifled their emotions by singing. A crowd had assembled to see them off. As the boat unloosed, each one's personal concerns, the lost valise, the misappropriated corner, were forgotten. The wonder-rabbi and his attendant patriarchs broke into nerveless, uncontrollable waving; the boys and girls struck up a solemn hymn, in which the word Jerusalem was repeated on a note of triumph. The crowd on shore joined in, following the quay to its brink, where they stood till the ship was on the horizon. At that moment Ralph Stockley, ADC to the High Commissioner in Palestine, also arrived on the quay, to find he had missed the boat. His agitation, and subsequent pursuit in a launch, relieved the tension.

*

A northerly wind flecks the sapphire sea with white, and has silenced those exuberant Jews below. Yesterday we sailed past the Ionian Islands. The familiar shores looked arid and unpeopled, but invincibly beautiful through the rosy air. At the south-west corner of Greece we turned east, passed Kalamata in its bay, and came to Cape Matapan, which I last saw from Taygetus outlined by the distant sea as though on a map. The rocky faces turned to ruddy gold, the shadows to a gauzy blue. The sun sank, Greece became a ragged silhouette, and the southernmost lighthouse of Europe began to wink. Round the corner, in the next bay, twinkled the electricity of Gytheion.

Stockley recounted an anecdote of his Chief, who was shot in the legs during the Boer War and left for thirty-six hours before help came. Others had been shot likewise, for the Boers had fired low. Some were dead, and the vultures collected. So long as the wounded could move, however feebly, the birds kept off. When they could not, their eyes were pecked out while still alive. Stockley's Chief had described his feelings at the prospect of this fate, while the birds were hovering a few feet above him.

This morning the double peaks of Santorin cut across a red dawn. Rhodes is in sight. We reach Cyprus at midday tomorrow. I shall have a week to myself there before the Charcoal-Burners arrive at Beyrut on 6 September.

CYPRUS: Kyrenia, 29 August   History in this island is almost too profuse. It gives one a sort of mental indigestion. At Nicosia, a new Government House has replaced that which the riots destroyed in 1931. Outside it stands a cannon presented by Henry VIII of England to the Order of St John of Jerusalem in 1527. This bears the Tudor arms. But the coinage, struck to commemorate the jubilee of British rule in 1928, bears the arms of Richard Coeur-de-Lion, who conquered the island and married there in 1191. I landed at Larnaca. A few miles off, in AD 45, landed Paul and Barnabas. Lazarus is buried at Larnaca. So are two nephews of Bishop Ken, Ion and William, who died in 1693 and 1707. Dates begin with an Egyptian notice of 1450 BC. Fame arrived at the end of the twelfth century, with the rule and culture of the Lusignans: to King Peter I, authors so various as Boccaccio and St Thomas Aquinas dedicated books. In 1489 Queen Catherine Cornaro surrendered her sovereignty to the Venetians, and eighty years later the last Venetian commander was flayed alive by the Turks. The three centuries of oblivion that followed were ended by the Treaty of Berlin, which leased the island to the English. In 1914 we annexed it.

The affinity of the landscape is with Asia rather than the other Greek islands. The earth is bleached to whiteness; only a green patch of vines or a flock of black and tawny goats relieves its arid solitude. Trees were planted along the immaculate tarmac road that brought me from Larnaca to Nicosia, casuarinas and cypresses. But the wind has defeated them, a furious hot blast which gets up off the sea every afternoon and turns the countless water-wheels. These gaunt iron skeletons stand in groves on the outskirts of the towns; their choral creaking is the island's chief song. In the distance are always mountains. And over the whole scene hangs a peculiar light, a glaze of steel and lilac, which sharpens the contours and perspectives, and makes each vagrant goat, each isolated carob tree, stand out from the white earth as though seen through a stereoscope.

The prospect is beautiful in the abstract, but violent and forbidding as the home of man. Even flowers are lacking, at this season, but for a small asphodel, *grey* in colour, whose nod is the nod of a ghost. The Greeks call it 'candle-flower'. The north face of the mountains, between Nicosia and the coast, is more hospitable. Here, the earth is red, as though more nourishing, and the terraced fields are dotted with carob trees. The carob harvest was in full swing as I passed: men bashing down the fruit with long poles; women loading it into sacks and loading them on to donkeys. The carob is exported to make cattle-food. It looks like a shrivelled banana and tastes, I found, like a glucose doormat.

I called on the Archbishop in Nicosia, to ask him for a letter to the clergy of Kiti. His attendants were disobliging; for the Church leads the opposition to the English, and they could hardly have known I had spoken for their cause in the English press. But the Archbishop, though old and deaf, seemed pleased to have a visitor, and caused the letter to be typewritten by a secretary. When it was done, they brought him a pen ready dipped in red ink, and with this he signed it, in virtue of a privilege granted by the Emperor Zeno in the fifth century: ' + Cyril of Cyprus'. The secular Governors of the island have since usurped this privilege. The Turkish ones did so to annoy, the English to be picturesque.

I went to Bella Paese this morning, to see the abbey. My chauffeur went to see his fiancée, who lives in the adjacent village. She and her aunt gave me coffee and a preserve of sugared walnuts. We sat on a balcony, surrounded as ever by pots of basil and carnations, and looking down across the village roofs to the sea. The aunt's son, aged two, kept pushing chairs about and yelling, 'I'm a steamer, I'm a motor-car.' When the real motor-car, with me in it, left, he broke into a howl of disappointment, which followed me down the mountain.

This afternoon, at the castle, a gentleman wearing a white topee and white beard was pointed out to me as Mr Jeffery. Since he was responsible for the antiquities of the island, I introduced myself. He recoiled. I tried to make amends by mentioning his book on the sieges of Kyrenia. 'I've written many things,' he replied. 'I can't possibly remember what. But sometimes, you know, I read them, and I find them *quite interesting*.'

We proceeded to the castle, where we found some convicts engaged in desultory excavation. As we appeared, they threw down their spades, threw off their clothes, and ran out of a side door into the sea for their afternoon swim. 'A pleasant life,' said Mr Jeffery. 'They only come here when they want a rest.' He produced a plan of the thirteenth-century foundations, as revealed by the convicts' digging. But exposition made him dry, and we went to the office for a drink of water. 'The worst of water is,' he said, 'it makes you so thirsty.'

Kyrenia, 30 August Mounted on a chocolate-coloured donkey with ears eighteen inches long, I rode up to St Hilarion's Castle. At the walls we tethered the donkey, and also its fellow brute, a grey mule bearing cold water in a massive clay amphora stopped with carob leaves. Precipitous paths and flights of steps led up through chapels, halls, cisterns, dungeons, to the topmost platform and its sentinel tower. Below the gleaming silver crags and stunted green-feathered pines, the mountain fell three thousand feet to the coastal plain, an endless panorama of rusty red speckled with myriads of little trees and their shadows, beyond which, sixty miles away across the blue sea, appeared the line of Asia Minor and the Taurus Mountains. Even sieges must have had their compensations when solaced by such a view.

Nicosia (500 ft), 31 August 'Mishap necessitates delay one week so arriving Beyrut fourteenth have informed Christopher stop car not plant at fault.'

This gives me an extra week. I shall spend it in Jerusalem. 'Plant', I suppose, means the charcoal apparatus. Considering the cost of telegraphing, I can only assume this doesn't work. Otherwise, why bother to deny it?

Long ago, at the Greek Legation in London, I was introduced to a nervous boy in a long robe, who was holding a glass of lemonade. This was His Beatitude Mar Shimun, Patriarch of the Assyrians; and since he is now an exile in Cyprus, I went to call on him this morning at the Crescent Hotel. A sturdy bearded figure in flannel trousers greeted me in accents peculiar to the English universities (Cambridge in his case). I offered my condolences. He turned to recent events: 'As Ai toeld Sir Francis Humphreys, the paepers in Baghdad had been proeclaeming a Jehad against us for months. Ai asked him if he could guarantee our saefety, he said he could, and soe on and soe forth. They put me in prison four months agoe – even then he did nothing, though every one knew what was coming. From here I shall goe to Geneva to plead our cause and soe on and soe forth. They took me away by aeroplane against my will, but what will become of may poor people, raeped, shot down bay machine-guns and soe on and soe forth, Ai doen't knoew.' And so on and so forth.

Another landmark in the Betrayal Era of British foreign policy. Will it never stop? No doubt the Assyrians were intractable. But the point Mar Shimun made, which I believe to be true, is that the British authorities knew, or had ample means of knowing, what the Irakis were intending, and took no steps to prevent it.

Famagusta, 2 September There are two towns here: Varosha, the Greek, and Famagusta, the Turkish. They are joined by an Anglo-residential suburb, which contains the offices of the administration, the English club, a public garden, numerous villas, and the Savoy Hotel where I live. Famagusta is the old town; its walls flank the port.

If Cyprus were owned by the French or Italians, as many tourist boats would visit Famagusta as now go to Rhodes. Under English rule, the visitor is thwarted by a deliberate philistinism. The Gothic nucleus of the town is still completely walled. That this nucleus can still be defaced by any building that anyone likes to put up; that the squalor of the old houses is excelled by that of the new; that the churches are tenanted by indigent families; that the bastions are daily carpeted with human excrement; that the citadel is a carpenter's shop belonging to the Public Works Department; and that the palace can only be approached through the police station – these manifestations of British care, if inartistic, have at least the advantage of defence against the moribund atmosphere of a museum. The absence of guides, postcard-sellers, and their tribe is also an attraction. But that, in the whole of the two towns, there should be only one man who knows even the names of the churches, and he a Greek schoolmaster of such diffidence as to make rational conversation impossible; that the one book, by Mr Jeffery, which can acquaint the visitor with the history and topography of the place, should be on sale only at Nicosia forty miles away; that every church, except the cathedral, should be always locked and its keys kept, if their whereabouts can be traced at all, by the separate official, priest, or family to whose use it has been consigned, and who is generally to be found, not in Famagusta, but in Varosha; these manifestations were too much even for me, who, though speaking some Greek – which most visitors cannot do – entirely failed in three whole days to complete a tour of the buildings. The spectacle of such indifference has an interest of its own, to students of the English commonwealth. But it is not the kind of interest to draw shiploads of profitable sightseers. For them there is only one gratification, 'Othello's Tower', an absurd fiction which dates from the English occupation. Not only cab-drivers uphold this fiction. There is an official placard on the building, as though it were 'Teas' or 'Gentlemen'. This placard is the sole direction which the authorities, or anyone else, can vouchsafe.

I stand on the Martinengo bastion, a gigantic earthwork faced with cut stone and guarded by a rock-hewn moat forty feet below, into which the sea once flowed. From the bowels of this mountainous fortification two subterranean carriage-drives debouch into the daylight at my feet. To the right and left stretch the parapets of the encircling walls, interrupted by a succession of fat round towers. The foreground is waste; across it moves a string of camels led by a Turk in baggy trousers. A small depression is occupied by two Turkish women, cooking something beneath a fig tree. Beyond them starts the town, a medley of little houses, some of mud, some of stones ravished from the monuments, some of new white stucco roofed in red. There is no plan, no regard for amenity. Palms stand up among the houses; allotments surround them. And out of this confusion tower the crockets and buttresses of a Gothic cathedral, whose orange-coloured stone cuts across the distant union of sky and sea, turquoise and sapphire. A range of lilac mountains continues the coastline on the left. A ship steams out of harbour towards it. A bullock-cart emerges from the ground at my feet. The camels lie down. And a lady in a pink frock and picture-hat is gazing sentimentally in the direction of Nicosia from the top of the next tower but one.

Larnaca, 3 September The hotel here is not up to standard. Elsewhere they are clean, tidy, and above all cheap. The food is not delicious; but even English occupation has been unable to change Greek cooking for the worse. There are some good wines. And the water is sweet.

I drove out to Kiti, eight miles away, where the priest and sacristan, both wearing baggy trousers and high boots, received the Archbishop's letter with respect. They took me to the church, whose mosaic is a beautiful work; its technique seems to me of the tenth century, though others ascribe it to the sixth. The Virgin's robe is smoky mauve, almost charcoal-coloured. The angels beside her wear draperies of white, grey, and buff; and the green of their peacock wings is repeated on the green globes they hold. Faces, hands, and feet are done in smaller cubes than the rest. The whole composition has an extraordinary rhythm. Its dimensions are small, not more than life-size, and the church is so low that the vault containing it can be examined from as near as ten feet.

*

SS Martha Washington, *4 September*   I found Christopher on the pier, adorned with a kempt but reluctant beard five days old. He has heard nothing from the Charcoal-Burners, but welcomes the prospect of Jerusalem.

There are 900 passengers on board. Christopher took me a tour of the third-class quarters. Had their occupants been animals, a good Englishman would have informed the RSPCA. But the fares are cheap; and being Jews, one knows they could all pay more if they wanted. The first class is not much better. I share a cabin with a French barrister, whose bottles and fopperies leave no room for another pin. He lectured me on the English cathedrals. Durham was worth seeing. 'As for the rest, my dear sir, they are mere plumbing.'

At dinner, finding myself next an Englishman, I opened conversation by hoping he had had a fine passage.

He replied: 'Indeed we have. Goodness and mercy have followed us throughout.'

A tired woman struggled by, leading an unruly child. I said: 'I always feel so sorry for women travelling with children.'

'I can't agree with you. To me, little children are as glints of sunshine.'

I saw the creature later, reading a Bible in a deck-chair. This is what Protestants call a missionary.

PALESTINE: Jerusalem (2800 ft), 6 September   A Nicaraguan leper would have fared better with the port authorities of a British Mandate than we did yesterday. They came on board at 5 a.m. After waiting two hours in a queue, they asked me how I could land without a visa and when my passport was not even endorsed for Palestine. I said I could buy a visa, and explained that the system of endorsement was merely one of the cruder forms of dishonesty practised by our Foreign Office, which had no real bearing on the validity of a passport. Another busybody then discovered I had been to Russia. When? and why? Oh, for pleasure was it? Was it pleasurable? And where was I going now? To Afghanistan? Why? Pleasure again, indeed. I was on a pleasure-trip round the world, he supposed. Then they grew so absorbed with Christopher's diplomatic visa that they forgot to give him a card of disembarkation.

A frenzied crowd seethed round the head of the gangway. Physically, Jews can look the best or the worst bred people in the world. These were the worst. They stank, stared, shoved, and shrieked. One man, who had been there five hours, began to weep. When his rabbi failed to comfort him, Christopher offered him a whisky and soda out of the bar window. He refused it. Our luggage, by degrees, was handed into a boat. I followed it. Christopher had to go back for his card of disembarkation. There was a heavy swell, as we negotiated the surf-bound reef which constitutes the 'port' of Jaffa. A woman was sick over my hand. Her husband nursed their child, while supporting in his other arm a tall plant of veronica in a pot.

'Upstairs, please!' The sweating, malformed mob divided into two queues. After half an hour I reached the doctor. He apologized for delay, and gave me a medical certificate without an examination. Downstairs the boatmen were clamouring for money. The transport of ourselves and luggage cost £1 2s. 'Do you write books?' asked the customs officer, scenting an author of dutiable obscenities. I said I was not Lord Byron, and suggested he should get on with his business. At length we found a car, and putting the hood down in compliment to the Holy Land, set out for Jerusalem.

The King David Hotel is the only good hotel in Asia this side of Shanghai. We treasure every moment spent in it. The general decoration is harmonious and restrained, almost severe. But you might not think so from this notice which hangs in the hall:

NOTICE FOR THE INTERIOR DECORATION OF
THE KING DAVID HOTEL, JERUSALEM

The object was to evoke by reminiscence of ancient Semitic styles the ambience of the glorious period of King David.

A faithful reconstruction was impossible, so the artist tried to adopt to modern taste different old Jew styles.

Entrance hall: Period of King David (Assyrian influence).
Main lounge: Period of King David (Hittite influence).
Reading-room: Period of King Salomon.
Bar: Period of King Salomon.
Restaurant: Greek-Syrian style.
Banquet hall: Phenician style (Assyrian influence), etc.

G. A. HUFSCHMID
Decorator, OEV & SWB
Geneva

The beauty of Jerusalem in its landscape can be compared with that of Toledo. The city stands in the mountains, a scape of domes and towers enclosed by crenellated walls and perched on a table of rock above a deep valley. As far as the distant hills of Moab the contours of the country resemble those of a physical map, sweeping up the slopes in regular, stratified curves, and casting grand shadows in the sudden valleys. Earth and rock reflect the lights of a fire-opal. Such an essay in urban emplacement, whether accidental or contrived, has made a work of art.

In detail, even Toledo offers no comparison with the steep winding streets, cobbled in broad steps and so narrow that a single camel causes as much disturbance as a motor coach in an English lane. Jostling up and down King David Street, from dawn to sunset, the crowd is still a picture of 'the East', immune as yet from the tide of lounge suits and horn spectacles. Here comes the desert Arab, furiously moustached, sailing by in his voluminous robes of gold-worked camel hair; the Arab woman, with her face tattooed and her dress embroidered, bearing a basket on her head; the priest of Islam, trim of beard and sporting a neat white turban round his fez; the Orthodox Jew, in ringlets, beaver hat, and black frock coat; the Greek priest and Greek monk, bearded and bunned beneath their tall black chimney-pots; priests and monks from Egypt, Abyssinia, and Armenia; the Latin father in brown robe and white topee; the woman of Bethlehem, whose backward-sloping head-dress beneath a white veil is said to be a legacy of the Norman kingdom; and among them all, as background of the essential commonplace, the occasional lounge suit, the cretonne frock, the camera-strapped tourist.

Yet Jerusalem is more than picturesque, more than shoddy in the style of so many Oriental towns. There may be filth, but there is no brick or plaster, no crumbling and discolourment. The buildings are wholly of stone, a whitish cheese-like stone, candid and luminous, which the sun turns to all tones of ruddy gold. Charm and romance have no place. All is open and harmonious. The associations of history and belief, deep-rooted in the first memories of childhood, dissolve before the actual apparition. The outpourings of faith, the lamentations of Jew and Christian, the devotion of Islam to the holy Rock, have enshrouded the *genius loci* with no mystery. That spirit is an imperious emanation, evoking superstitious homage, sustained thereby perhaps, but existing independently of it. Its sympathy is with the centurions rather than the priests. And the centurions are here again. They wear shorts and topees, and answer, when addressed, with a Yorkshire accent.

Set in this radiant environment, the Church of the Holy Sepulchre appears the meanest of churches. Its darkness seems darker than it is, its architecture worse, its cult more degraded. The visitor is in conflict with himself. To pretend to detachment is supercilious; to pretend to reverence, hypocritical. The choice lies between them. Yet for me that choice has been averted. I met a friend in the doorway, and it was he who showed me how to cope with the Holy Places.

My friend was a black-robed monk, wearing short beard, long hair, and a tall cylindrical hat.

'Hail,' said I in Greek. 'You come from Mount Athos?'

'I do,' he replied, 'from the monastery of Docheiariou. My name is Gabriel.'

'You are the brother of Aristarchus?'

'I am.'

'And Aristarchus is dead?'

'He is. But who could have told you?'

I have described Aristarchus in another book. He was a monk at Vatopedi, the richest of the Athonite monasteries, whither we arrived, after five weeks on the Holy Mountain, tired and underfed. Aristarchus looked after us. He had once been a servant on an English yacht, and he called us every morning with the question: 'What time would you like lunch today, sir?' He was young, efficient, and material, entirely unsuited to the monastic vocation and determined, if he could, to save enough money to take him to America. He hated the older monks, who humiliated him.

One day, a year or two after our visit, he acquired a revolver and shot a couple of these venerable bullies. So the story goes. What is certain is that he then committed suicide. A saner man, externally, than Aristarchus never existed, and the Athonite community was filled with shame and reticence at the tragedy.

'Aristarchus was cracked in the head,' said Gabriel, tapping his own. Gabriel, I knew – for Aristarchus had told me – was happy in his vocation and could see in his brother's violence only an aberration. 'Is this your first visit to Jerusalem?' he continued, changing the subject.

'We arrived this morning.'

'I'll show you round. Yesterday I was in the Tomb itself. Tomorrow I go in again at eleven. This way.'

We were now in a broad circular chamber as high as a cathedral, whose shallow dome was supported on a ring of massive piers. In the middle of the empty floor stood the shrine, a miniature church resembling an old-fashioned railway engine.

'When were you last on Mount Athos?' asked Gabriel.

'In 1927.'

'I remember. You came to Docheiariou.'

'Yes. And how is my friend Synesios?'

'Very well. But he's too young yet to be an Elder. Come in here.'

I found myself in a small marble chamber, carved in the Turkish baroque style. The way to the inner sanctuary was blocked by three kneeling Franciscans.

'Whom else do you know at Docheiariou?'

'I know Frankfort. Is he well?'

'Frankfort?'

'Frankfort, Synesios's cat.'

'Ah! his cat... Don't mind those men; they're Catholics. It's a black cat—'

'Yes, and jumps.'

'I know. Now here we are. Mind your head.'

Stepping through the Franciscans as though they were nettles, Gabriel dived into a hole three feet high, from which came a bright light. I followed. The inner chamber was about seven feet square. At a low slab of stone knelt a Frenchwoman in ecstasy. By her side stood another Greek monk.

'This gentleman has been to Mount Athos,' announced Gabriel to his crony, who shook hands with me across the body of the Frenchwoman. 'It was six years ago and he remembers Synesios's cat... This is the Tomb' – pointing to the slab of stone – 'I shall be in here all day tomorrow. You must come and see me. There's not much room, is there? Let's go out. Now I'll show you the other places. This red stone is where they washed the body. Four of the lamps are Greek, the others Catholic and Armenian. Cavalry's upstairs. Ask your friend to come up. This is the Greek part, that the Catholic. But these are Catholics at the Greek altar, because Calvary was there. Look at the inscription over the cross. It's in real diamonds and was given by the Tsar. And look at this image. Catholics come and give these things to her.'

Gabriel pointed to a glass case. Inside I beheld a wax Virgin, draped in a pawnbroker's stock of chains, watches, and pendants.

'My friend here is a Catholic,' I informed Gabriel maliciously.

'Oh, is he? And what are you? Protestant? Or nothing at all?'

'I think I shall be Orthodox while I'm here.'

'I shall tell God that. You see these two holes? They put Christ in them, one leg in each.'

'But is that in the Bible?'

'Of course it's in the Bible. This cave is the place of the Skull. That's where the earthquake split the rock. My mother in Samos had thirteen children. Now only my brother in America, my sister in Constantinople, and myself are left. That there is Nicodemus's tomb, and that the tomb of Joseph of Arimathaea.'

'I thought Joseph of Arimathaea was buried in England.'

Gabriel smiled, as though to say, 'Tell that to the marines.'

'Here,' he continued, 'is a picture of Alexander the Great visiting Jerusalem, and being received by one of the prophets – I can't remember which.'

'But did Alexander ever visit Jerusalem?'

'Certainly. I only tell you the truth.'

'I'm sorry. I thought it might be a legend.'

We emerged at last into the daylight.

'If you come and see me the day after tomorrow, I shall be out of the tomb again. I come out at eleven, after being in all night.'

'But won't you want to sleep?'

'No. I don't like sleeping.'

The other holy sites are the Weeping Wall and the Dome of the Rock. Nodding and ululating over their books, squeezing their heads into crevices of the enormous masonry, the Jewish mourners are not more attractive than the performers in the Sepulchre. But at least it is light; the sun shines, and the Wall itself is comparable to the walls of the Incas. The Dome of the Rock shelters an enormous crag, whence Mohammad the Prophet took off on his ride up to Heaven. And here at last, apart from its associations, is a monument worthy of Jerusalem. A white marble platform, several acres in extent and commanding a view of the city walls and the Mount of Olives, is approached on different sides by eight flights of steps announced by lines of arches. In the middle of the platform, dwarfed by the space around it, stands a low octagon spangled with blue tiles and supporting a blue-tiled drum, whose breadth is about one-third of the octagon's. On top of the drum is a dome, faintly bulbous and powdered with ancient gilt. To one side stands another miniature octagon, as it were a child of the larger, resting on pillars and sheltering a fountain. The inside has a Greek impress: the marble pillars uphold Byzantine capitals, and the vaults of gold mosaic, adorned with twirling arabesques, must be the work of Greek craftsmen. Iron screens commemorate a Christian interlude, when the Crusaders turned the place into a church. As a mosque, it was founded in the seventh century. But many ages have contributed to its present form. Quite lately, the Byzantine capitals have been too brightly regilded. They will tone down in time.

When we first saw the mosque, it was too late to go in; but we could just get a glimpse of it from the entrance at the bottom of King David Street. An Arab planted himself in our way and began to be informative. I said I would rather *see* the mosque for the moment, and hear about it tomorrow; would he be so kind as to move to one side? To this he answered: 'I am an Arab and I shall stay where I please. This mosque belongs to me, not you.' So much for Arab charm.

This evening we went to Bethlehem. It was already dusk, and we could hardly distinguish the magnificent rows of columns which support the basilica. The guides were almost more tiresome than at the Sepulchre. I left Christopher to see the manger, or whatever it is they show, by himself.

Jerusalem, 7 September As I was sitting beneath an olive tree in the court of the Dome of the Rock, an Arab boy came to share the shade and repeat his lessons out loud. They were English lessons. 'Gulfs and promòntories, gulfs and promòntories, gulfs and promòntories,' he reiterated.

'It's not promòntories,' I interrupted, 'but pròmontories.'

'Gulfs and pròm-òntories, gulfs and pròm-òntories, gulfs and pròm-òntories. Deliver Mosul, deliver Mosul, deliver Mosul. Gulfs and . . .' He said he was first in his drawing class, and hoped to go to Cairo, where he could study to be an artist.

Stockley gave a dinner-party last night, at which two Arab guests proved good company. One of them, who used to be in the Turkish Foreign Office, knew Kemal and his mother in the old days. The War found him consul at Salonica, whence he was deported by Sarrail to Toulon – an unnecessary hardship since the Turkish frontier was so near, and one which lost him all his furniture and possessions. Talk turned on the Arlosorov, the Jewish leader, who was shot on the sands of Jaffa while walking with his wife. The murderers are supposed to have been Jewish revisionists, an extreme party that want to be rid of the English and set up a Jewish state. I don't know how long they think the Arabs would suffer a single Jew to exist once the English went.

This morning we went to Tel Aviv as the guests of Mr Joshua Gordon, chief showman of the Jewish agency. At the municipality, where Christopher was received as the son of his father, the walls were hung with portraits of the apostles of Zionism: Balfour, Samuel, Allenby, Einstein, Reading. A map showed the development of the place by years, from a struggling Utopia of only 3000 people to a bursting community of 70,000. Over Jaffa hock in the Palestine Hotel, I tried the Arab arguments on Mr Gordon. He was contemptuous. A commission had been set up to look after landless Arabs. It could only find a few hundred. Meanwhile, the Arabs of Transjordania were begging the Jews to go there and develop the country.

I asked if it might not pay the Jews to placate the Arabs, even at inconvenience to themselves, with a view to peace in the future. Mr Gordon said no. The only possible basis of an Arab-Jewish understanding was joint opposition to the English, and this the Jewish leaders would not countenance. 'If the country is to be developed, the Arabs must suffer, because they don't like development. And that's the end of it.' The sons of the desert have had enough apologists lately. I find it more refreshing to contemplate an expanding budget – the only one in the world at the moment – and congratulate the Jews.

The Italians were another snake in Mr Gordon's grass. Some time ago, he and others had tried to start an Anglo-Palestinian shipping line, which might carry the mails instead of Italian boats. They failed, for lack of English cooperation. The Italians offer free education in Rome to all Palestinians, with reduced fares thrown in. Admittedly, only about 200 a year go. But Mr Gordon grew bitter when he considered the difficulties encountered by any student who wishes to finish his education in London, even at his own cost.

After visiting the orange-belt and the opera-house, we went to bathe. Suddenly, out of the crowd on the sea-front, stepped Mr Aaranson of the *Italia*. 'Hello, hello – you here too? Jerusalem's so dead at this time of year, isn't it? But I may look in tomorrow. Goodbye.'

If Tel Aviv were in Russia, the world would be raving over its planning and architecture, its smiling communal life, its intellectual pursuits, and its air of youth enthroned. But the difference from Russia is that instead of being still only a goal for the future, these things are an accomplished fact.

Jerusalem, 10 September Yesterday we lunched with Colonel Kish. Christopher entered the room first. But the Colonel made for me with the words: 'You, I can see, are Sir Mark Sykes's son' – the implication being, we supposed, that no Englishman of such parentage could possibly wear a beard. During lunch our host informed us of King Feisal's death in Switzerland. On the wall hung a fine painting of Jerusalem by Rubin, whom Mr Gordon had meant us to visit in Tel Aviv if he had not been away.

I went to swim at the YMCA opposite the hotel. This necessitated paying two shillings, the waiving of a medical examination, changing among a lot of hairy dwarves who smelt of garlic, and finally having a hot shower accompanied by an acrimonious argument because I refused to scour my body with a cake of insecticide soap. I then reached the bath, swam a few yards in and out of a game of water-football conducted by the Physical Director, and emerged so perfumed with antiseptic that I had to rush back and have a bath before going out to dinner.

We dined with the High Commissioner, most pleasantly. There were none of those official formalities which are very well at large parties, but embarrass small ones. In fact, but for the Arab servants, we might have been dining in an English country house. Did Pontius Pilate remind his guests of an Italian squire?

*

There was a dance at the hotel when we got back. Christopher met a school friend in the bar, who begged him, in the name of Alma Mater, to remove his beard. 'I mean to say, Sykes, you know, daffinitely, no I don't like to say it, well I mean, daffinitely, never mind, I'd rather not say daffinitely, you see old boy it's like this, I mean daffinitely I should take off that beard of yours if I were you, because people daffinitely think you know, I mean, no honestly I won't say it, no daffinitely I can't, it wouldn't be fair, daffinitely it wouldn't, well then if you really want to know, you've pressed me for it haven't you, daffinitely, it's like this, I mean people might think you were a bit of a cad you know, daffinitely.'

When everyone had gone to bed, I walked to the old town. The streets were shrouded in fog; it might have been London in November. In the church of the Holy Sepulchre, an Orthodox service was in progress at the Tomb, accompanied by a choir of Russian peasant women. Those Russian chants changed everything; the place grew solemn and real, as the white-bearded bishop in his bulbous diamond crown and embroidered cope emerged from the door of the shrine into the soft blaze of candles. Gabriel appeared, and after the service shoved me into the sacristy to have coffee with the old man and the treasurer. It was half-past three when I got home.

SYRIA: Damascus (2200 ft), 12 September Here is the East in its pristine confusion. My window looks out on a narrow, cobbled street, whose odour of spiced cooking has temporarily vanished in a draught of cool air. It is dawn. People are stirring, roused by the muezzin's unearthly treble from a small minaret opposite, and the answer of distant others. The clamour of vendors and the clatter of hoofs will soon begin.

I regret having left Palestine. It is refreshing to find a country endowed with great natural beauty, with a capital whose appearance is worthy of its fame, with a prosperous cultivation and a prodigiously expanding revenue, with the germ of an indigenous modern culture in the form of painters, musicians, and architects, and with an administration whose conduct resembles that of a benevolent Lord of the Manor among his dependants. There is no need to be a Zionist to see that this state of things is due to the Jews. They are pouring in. Last year permission was given for 6000: 17,000 arrived, the extra 11,000 by frontiers which cannot be guarded. Once in Palestine, they throw away their passports, and so cannot be deported. Yet there appear to be means of supporting them. They have enterprise, persistence, technical training, and capital.

The cloud on the horizon is Arab hostility. To a superficial observer it seems that the Government, by deferring to the susceptibility of the Arabs, is encouraging their sense of aggrievement, while obtaining none of their goodwill. The Arabs hate the English, and lose no opportunity of venting their ill-manners on them. I cannot see why this should support their case in the eyes of the Government. They have not the Indian excuse, the colour-bar.

At dinner here last night Christopher was talking of Persia, when he noticed a party at the same table gazing at us. Suddenly he heard them talking Persian. He tried to recall, in whispers to me, if he had said anything derogatory to the Shah or his country. We seem to be approaching a medieval tyranny of modern sensibilities. There was a diplomatic incident when Mrs Nicolson told the English public she could buy no marmalade in Teheran.

Damascus, 13 September The Omayad Mosque, though much restored after a fire in 1893, dates from the eighth century. Its grand arcade, with gallery above, is as well proportioned, and proceeds with as stately a rhythm, in its bare, Islamic way, as the Sansovino Library in Venice. Originally, its bareness was clothed in a glitter of mosaics. Some remain: the first landscapes of the European tradition. For all their Pompeian picturesqueness, their colonnaded palaces and crag-bound castles, they are real landscapes, more than mere decoration, concerned inside formal limits with the identity of a tree or the energy of a stream. They must have been done by Greeks, and they foreshadow, properly enough, El Greco's landscapes of Toledo. Even now, as the sun catches a fragment on the outside wall, one can imagine the first splendour of green and gold, when the whole court shone with those magic scenes conceived by Arab fiction to recompense the parched eternities of the desert.

Beyrut, 14 September To come here, we took two seats in a car.

Beside us, at the back, sat an Arab gentleman of vast proportions, who was dressed like wasp in a gown of black and yellow stripes and held between his knees a basket of vegetables. In front was an Arab widow, accompanied by another basket of vegetables and a small son. Every twenty minutes she was sick out of the window. Sometimes we stopped; when we did not, her vomit flew back into the car by the other window. It was not a pleasant three hours.

The post has brought newspaper cuttings describing the departure of the Charcoal-Burners. Even *The Times* has half a column. The *Daily Express* writes:

Five men left a West End hotel last night on a secret expedition. It may prove to be the most romantic expedition ever undertaken.

They left London for Marseilles and the Sahara Desert. After that, few men know what their destination will be.

A PREMATURE ANNOUNCEMENT MIGHT ENTAIL SERIOUS POLITICAL CONSEQUENCES...

These five men will travel by two lorries driven by portable gas plants. The fuel used is ordinary charcoal, and refuelling is necessary only every fifty or sixty miles. It is the first time this new invention has been used, but it is probable that it will be universally utilized for road transport in the future.

It is a nuisance to find one's name associated with such rot.

We now await the *Champollion*, with cars and party on board.

Beyrut, 16 September   My forebodings have come true.

I went on board the *Champollion* at daybreak. Goldman? Henderson? Deux camions? No one had heard of them. But Rutter was there, with a tale of disaster and absurdity.

The cars broke down at Abbeville. They might have continued on petrol, but have been secretly returned to England, where the invention is to be further perfected and a new start is to be made, this time unknown to the press, in a month or so. Lest I also should return and give the failure away by my presence in London, Rutter has been sent on ahead to expedite me safely into Persia. In fact I am gratuitously invested with the powers and character of a blackmailer.

*

We have spent most of the day in the sea, recovering from shock, and have booked places in the Nairn bus for Baghdad on Tuesday.

Mr Nairn himself came in for a drink this evening, inquisitive about the charcoal cars. Having known of the invention for many years, or others like it, he was sceptical, and with the best will in the world we could not oppose much faith to his doubts. All Syria is excited by the pictures of his new Pullman bus, which is to arrive in November.

Damascus, 18 September Since our arrival on these coasts, Christopher and I have learned that the cost of everything from a royal suite to a bottle of soda water can be halved by the simple expedient of saying it must be halved. Our technique was nicely employed in the hotel at Baalbek.

'Four hundred piastres for *that* room? *Four hundred* did you say? Good God! Away! Call the car. Three hundred and fifty? *One* hundred and fifty you mean. Three hundred? Are you deaf, can't you hear? I said a hundred and fifty. We must go. There are other hotels. Come, load the luggage. I doubt if we shall stay in Baalbek at all.'

'But, sir, this is first-class hotel. I give you very good dinner, five courses. This is our best room, sir, it has bath and view of ruins, very fine.'

'God in heaven, are the ruins yours? Must we pay for the very air? Five courses for dinner is too much, and I don't suppose the bath works. You still say three hundred? Come down. I say, come down a bit. That's better, two hundred and fifty. I said a hundred and fifty. I'll say two hundred. You'll have to pay the other fifty out of your own pocket, will you? Well *do*, please. I shall be delighted. Two hundred then? No? Very good. (*We run downstairs and out of the door.*) Goodbye. What? I didn't hear. Two hundred. I thought so.

'And now a whisky and soda. What do you charge for that? Fifty piastres. Fifty piastres indeed. Who do you think we are? Anyhow you always give too much whisky. I'll pay *fifteen* piastres, not fifty. Don't laugh. Don't go away either. I want exactly this much whisky, no more, no less; that's only half a full portion. Thirty, you say? Is thirty half fifty? Can you do arithmetic? Soda water indeed. Twenty now. No *not* twenty-five. Twenty. There is all the difference, if you could only realize it. Bring the bottle at once, and for heaven's sake don't argue.'

During the five-course dinner, we complimented the man on some succulent birds.

'Partridges, sir,' he replied, 'I make them fat in little houses.'

Admission to the ruins costs five shillings per person per visit. Having secured a reduction of this charge by telephoning to Beyrut, we walked across to visit them.

'Guide, monsieur?'
Silence.
'Guide, monsieur?'
Silence.
'Qu'est-ce que vous désirez, monsieur?'
Silence.
'D'où venez-vous, monsieur?'
Silence.
'Où allez-vous, monsieur?'
Silence.
'Vous avez des affaires ici, monsieur?'
'Non.'
'Vous avez des affaires à Baghdad, monsieur?'
'Non.'
'Vous avez des affaires à Téhéran, monsieur?'
'Non.'
'Alors, qu'est-ce que vous faites, monsieur?'
'Je fais un voyage en Syrie.'
'Vous êtes un officier naval, monsieur?'
'Non.'
'Alors, qu'est-ce que vous êtes, monsieur?'
'Je suis homme.'
'Quoi?'
'HOMME.'
'Je comprends. Touriste.'

Even 'voyageur' is obsolete; and with reason: the word has a complimentary air. The traveller of old was one who went in search of knowledge and whom the indigènes were proud to entertain with their local interests. In Europe this attitude of reciprocal appreciation has long evaporated. But there at least the 'tourist' is no longer a phenomenon. He is part of the landscape, and in nine cases out of ten has little money to spend beyond what he has paid for his tour. Here, he is still an aberration. If you can come from London to Syria on business, you must be rich. If you can come so far without business, you must be very rich. No one cares if you like the place, or hate it, or why. You are simply a tourist, as a skunk is a skunk, a parasitic variation of the human species, which exists to be tapped like a milch cow or a gum tree.

At the turnstile, that final outrage, a palsied dotard took ten minutes to write out each ticket. After which we escaped from these trivialities into the glory of Antiquity.

Baalbek is the triumph of stone; of lapidary magnificence on a scale whose language, being still the language of the eye, dwarfs New York into a home of ants. The stone is peach-coloured, and is marked in ruddy gold as the columns of St Martin-in-the-Fields are marked in soot. It has a marmoreal texture, not transparent, but faintly powdered, like bloom on a plum. Dawn is the time to see it, to look up at the Six Columns, when peach-gold and blue air shine with equal radiance, and even the empty bases that uphold no columns have a living, sun-blest identity against the violet deeps of the firmament. Look up, look up; up this quarried flesh, these thrice-enormous shafts, to the broken capitals and the cornice as big as a house, all floating in the blue. Look over the walls, to the green groves of white-stemmed poplars; and over them to the distant Lebanon, a shimmer of mauve and blue and gold and rose. Look along the mountains to the void: the desert, that stony, empty sea. Drink the high air. Stroke the stone with your own soft hands. Say goodbye to the West if you own it. And then turn, *tourist*, to the East.

We did, when the ruins closed. It was dusk. Ladies and gentlemen in separate parties were picnicking on a grass meadow, beside a stream. Some sat on chairs by marble fountains, drawing at their hubble-bubbles; others on the grass beneath occasional trees, eating by their own lanterns. The stars came out and the mountain slopes grew black. I felt the peace of Islam. And if I mention this commonplace experience, it is because in Egypt and Turkey that peace is now denied; while in India Islam appears, like everything else, uniquely and exclusively Indian. In a sense it is so; for neither man nor institution can meet that overpowering environment without a change of identity. But I will say this for my own sense: that when travelling in Mohammadan India without previous knowledge of Persia, I compared myself to an Indian observing European classicism, who had started on the shores of the Baltic instead of the Mediterranean.

Yesterday afternoon at Baalbek, Christopher complained of lassitude and lay on his bed, which deferred our going till it was dark and bitterly cold on top of the Lebanon. On reaching Damascus, he went to bed with two quinine tablets, developed such a headache that he dreamt he was a rhinoceros with a horn, and woke up this morning with a temperature of 102, though the crisis is past. We have cancelled our seats in the Nairn bus for tomorrow, and booked them for Friday instead.

Damascus, 21 September   A young Jew has attached himself to us. This happened because there is a waiter in the hotel who is the spit of Hitler, and when I remarked on the fact the Jew, the manager, and the waiter himself broke into such paroxysms of laughter that they could hardly stand.

As Rutter and I were crossing a bit of dusty ground left waste by the French bombardment, we saw a fortune-teller making marks on a tray of sand, while a poor woman and her emaciated child awaited news of the child's fate. Near by was a similar fortune-teller, unpatronized. I squatted down. He put a little sand in my palm and told me to sprinkle it on the tray. Then he dabbed three lines of hieroglyphics in the sand, went over them once or twice as though dealing out patience cards, paused in thought before making a sudden deep diagonal, and spoke these words, which Rutter, who once spent nine months in Mecca disguised as an Arab, may be supposed to have translated with sufficient accuracy:
     'You have a friend of whom you are fond and who is fond of you. In a few days he will send you some money for the expenses of your journey. He will join you later. You will have a successful journey.'
     My blackmailing powers, it seems, are working of their own accord.

The hotel is owned by M. Alouf, whose children inhabit the top floor.

One evening he led us into an airless cellar lined with glass cases and a safe. From these he took the following objects:

A pair of big silver bowls, stamped with Christian symbols and a picture of the Annunciation.

A document written on mud-coloured cloth, between three and four feet long and eighteen inches broad, purporting to be the will of Abu Bakr, the first Caliph, and said to have been brought from Medina by the family of King Hussein in 1925.

A Byzantine bottle of dark-blue glass as thin as an egg-shell, unbroken, and about ten inches high.

A gold Hellenistic head, with parted lips, glass eyes, and bright blue eyebrows.

A gold mummy in a trunk.

And a silver statuette nine and a half inches high, which, for lack of anything to compare it with, M. Alouf called Hittite. This object, if genuine, must be one of the most remarkable discoveries of recent years in the Near East. The figure is that of a man, with broad shoulders and narrow hips. On his head he wears a pointed cap as tall as his own body. His left arm is broken; his right carries a horned bull in its crook and holds a sceptre. Round the waist are bands of wire. This wire, the sceptre, the tail and horns of the bull, and the cap are all of gold. And the gold is so pliable that M. Alouf gaily bent the sceptre at a right-angle and put it straight again. No persuasions could induce him to let me photograph the object. One wonders when and how it will be rescued from that cellar.

Christopher got up on Wednesday, and Rutter took us to tea with El Haj Mohammad ibn el Bassam, an old man of seventy or more, dressed in Bedouin clothes. His family befriended Doughty and he is a famous figure to Arabophils. Having made a fortune out of camels in the War, he lost £40,000 after it by speculating in German marks. We had tea at a marble table, which the height of the chairs just enabled us to touch with our chins. The noise of the Arabic conversation, punctuated by gurks and gulps, reminded me of Winston Churchill making a speech.

The Arabs hate the French more than they hate us. Having more reason to do so, they are more polite; in other words, they have learnt not to try it on, when they meet a European. This makes Damascus a pleasant city from the visitor's point of view.

*

IRAK: Baghdad (115 ft), 27 September If anything on earth could have made this place attractive by contrast, it was the journey that brought us here. We travelled in a banana-shaped tender on two wheels, which was attached to the dickey of a two-seater Buick and euphemistically known as the aero-bus. A larger bus, the father of all motor-coaches, followed behind. Hermetically sealed, owing to the dust, yet swamped in water from a leaky drinking-tank, we jolted across the pathless desert at forty miles an hour, beaten upon by the sun, deafened by the battery of stones against the thin floor, and stifled by the odour of five sweating companions. At noon we stopped for lunch, which was provided by the company in a cardboard box labelled 'Service with a Smile'. It will be Service with a Frown if we ever run transport in these parts. Butter-paper and egg-shells floated away to ruin the Arabian countryside. At sunset we came to Rutbah, which had been surrounded, since I lunched there on my way to India in 1929, by coolie lines and an encampment: the result of the Mosul pipe-line. Here we dined; whiskies and sodas cost six shillings each. At night our spirits lifted; the moon shone in at the window; the five Irakis, led by Mrs Mullah, sang. We passed a convoy of armoured cars, which were escorting Feisal's brothers, ex-King Ali and the Emir Abdullah, back from Feisal's funeral. Dawn discovered, not the golden desert, but mud, unending mud. As we neared Baghdad, the desolation increased. Mrs Mullah, till now so coy, hid her charms in a thick black veil. The men brought out black forage-caps. And by nine o'clock we could have imagined ourselves at the lost end of the Edgware Road, as the city of the Arabian Nights unfolded its solitary thoroughfare.

It is little solace to recall that Mesopotamia was *once* so rich, so fertile of art and invention, so hospitable to the Sumerians, the Seleucids, and the Sasanids. The prime fact of Mesopotamian history is that in the thirteenth century Hulagu destroyed the irrigation system; and that from that day to this Mesopotamia has remained a land of mud deprived of mud's only possible advantage, vegetable fertility. It is a mud plain, so flat that a single heron, reposing on one leg beside some rare trickle of water in a ditch, looks as tall as a wireless aerial. From this plain rise villages of mud and cities of mud. The rivers flow with liquid mud. The air is composed of mud refined into a gas. The people are mud-coloured; they wear mud-coloured clothes, and their national hat is nothing more than a formalized mud-pie. Baghdad is the capital one would expect of this divinely favoured land. It lurks in a mud fog; when the temperature drops below 110, the residents complain of the chill and get out their furs. For only one thing is it now justly famous: a kind of boil which takes nine months to heal, and leaves a scar.

Christopher, who dislikes the place more than I do, calls it a paradise compared with Teheran. Indeed, if I believed all he told me about Persia, I should view our departure tomorrow as a sentence of transportation. I don't. For Christopher is in love with Persia. He talks like this as a well-bred Chinaman, if you ask after his wife, will reply that the scarecrow of a bitch is not actually dead – meaning that his respected and beautiful consort is in the pink.

The hotel is run by Assyrians, pathetic, pugnacious little people with affectionate ways, who are still half in terror of their lives. There is only one I would consign to the Baghdadis, a snappy youth called Daood (David), who has put up the prices of all cars to Teheran and referred to the arch of Ctesiphon as 'Fine show, sir, high show.'

This arch rises 121½ feet from the ground and has a span of 82. It also is of mud; but has nevertheless lasted fourteen centuries. Photographs exist which show two sides instead of one, and the front of the arch as well. In mass, the ill-fired bricks are a beautiful colour, whitish buff against a sky which is blue again, now that we are out of Baghdad. The base has lately been repaired; probably for the first time since it was built.

The museum here is guarded, not so that the treasures of Ur may be safe, but lest visitors should defile the brass of the show-cases by leaning on them. Since none of the exhibits is bigger than a thimble, it was thus impossible to see the treasures of Ur. On the wall outside, King Feisal has erected a memorial tablet to Gertrude Bell. Presuming the inscription was meant by King Feisal to be read, I stepped up to read it. At which four policemen set up a shout and dragged me away. I asked the director of the museum why this was. 'If you have short sight, you can get special leave,' he snapped. So much, again, for Arab charm.

We dined with Peter Scarlett, whose friend, Ward, told a story of

Feisal's funeral. It was a broiling day and a large Negro had made his way into the enclosure reserved for the dignitaries. After a little time he was removed. 'God damn,' yelled the Commander of the English troops, 'they've taken away my shade.'

Money was waiting for me here, as the fortune-teller promised.

Part II

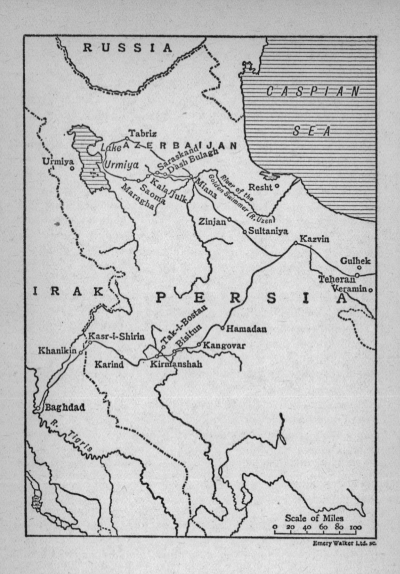

PERSIA: Kirmanshah (4900 ft), 29 September We travelled for twenty hours yesterday. The effort was more in argument than locomotion.

A burning dust-storm wafted us along the road to Khanikin. Through the murk loomed a line of hills. Christopher grasped my arm. 'The ramparts of Iran!' he announced solemnly. A minute later we breasted a small incline and were on the flat again. This happened every five miles, till an oasis of sour green proclaimed the town and frontier.

Here we changed cars, since Persia and Irak refuse admission to one another's chauffeurs. Otherwise our reception was hospitable: the Persian officials offered us their sympathy in this disgusting business of customs, and kept us three hours. When I paid duty on some films and medicines, they took the money with eyes averted, as a duchess collects for charity.

I remarked to Christopher on the indignity of the people's clothes: 'Why does the Shah make them wear those hats?'

'Sh. You mustn't mention the Shah out loud. Call him Mr Smith.'

'I always call Mussolini Mr Smith in Italy.'

'Well, Mr Brown.'

'No, that's Stalin's name in Russia.'

'Mr Jones then.'

'Jones is no good either. Hitler has to have it now that Primo de Rivera is dead. And anyhow I get confused with these ordinary names. We had better call him Marjoribanks, if we want to remember whom we mean.'

'All right. And you had better write it too, in case they confiscate your diary.'

I shall in future.

At Kasr-i-Shirin we stopped another hour, while the police gave us a permit for Teheran. Then indeed the grandeur of Iran unfolded. Lit from behind by the fallen sun, and from in front by the rising moon, a vast panorama of rounded foothills rolled away from the Sasanian ruins, twinkling here and there with the amber lights of villages; till out of the far distance rose a mighty range of peaks, the real ramparts at last. Up and down we sped through the fresh tonic air, to the foot of the mountains; then up and up, to a pass between jagged

51

pine-tufted pinnacles that mixed with the pattern of the stars. On the other side was Karind, where we dined to the music of streams and crickets, looking out on a garden of moon-washed poplars and munching baskets of sweet grapes. The room was hung with printed stuffs depicting a female Persia reposing in the arms of Marjoribanks, on whom Jamshyd, Artaxerxes, and Darius looked down approvingly from the top of the arch at Ctesiphon.

Teheran (3900 ft), 2 October   At Kirmanshah the chauffeur gave way to temperament. He did not wish to spend the night at Hamadan; he wished to sleep at Kazvin. Why, he could not say – and I doubt if he knew; he was like a child who wants one doll rather than another. To stop the argument, which had begun to involve the whole staff of the hotel, I went off to Tak-i-Bostan for the morning. It thus became impossible for us to go further than Hamadan that day.

More than one sculptor must have worked in the grottoes at Tak-i-Bostan. The angels over the arch have Coptic faces, and their drapery is as low and delicate as a Renascence bronze medal. The side panels inside the arch are in higher relief, but themselves differ; for while that on the left is exquisitely finished and modelled, its fellow opposite was never finished, being carved in a series of flat planes which look as though they had accrued to the rock instead of come forth from it. Then at the back, in violent contrast to these mobile, cinematograph-like scenes of hunt and court, stands the giant figure of a mounted king whose empty ruthlessness reminds one of a German war memorial. This is typically Sasanian. It is hard to believe that the other artists were Persian at all.

The grottoes are cut in the base of a huge mountain escarpment, and are reflected in a reservoir. Beside them stands a tumble-down pleasure house, in which, at this moment, a party of ladies were having a picnic. The romance of the place was completed when they were joined by a hatchet-faced gentleman wearing a soiled shirt with the tails outside, lilac sateen plus-fours, and cotton stockings upheld by lilac suspenders.

Bisitun delayed us a minute, with its great cuneiform inscription cut like the pages of a book on the blood-coloured rock; and also

Kangovar, a ruinous little place which boasts the wreck of a Hellenistic temple and a tribe of children who threw bricks at us. At Hamadan we eschewed the tombs of Esther and Avicenna, but visited the Gumbad-i-Alaviyan, a Seljuk mausoleum of the twelfth century, whose uncoloured stucco panels, puffed and punctured into a riot of vegetable exuberance, are yet as formal and rich as Versailles – perhaps richer considering their economy of means; for when splendour is got by a chisel and a lump of plaster instead of the wealth of the world, it is splendour of design alone. This at last wipes the taste of the Alhambra and the Taj Mahal out of one's mouth, where Mohammadan art is concerned. I came to Persia to get rid of that taste.

The day's journey had a wild exhilaration. Up and down the mountains, over the endless flats, we bumped and swooped. The sun flayed us. Great spirals of dust, dancing like demons over the desert, stopped our dashing Chevrolet and choked us. Suddenly, from far across a valley, came the flash of a turquoise jar, bobbing along on a donkey. Its owner walked beside it, clad in a duller blue. And seeing the two lost in that gigantic stony waste, I understand why blue is the Persian colour, and why the Persian word for it means water as well.

We reached the capital by night. Not a glimmer of light on the horizon warned us of it. Trees, then houses, suddenly enveloped us. By day it is a Balkan sort of place. But the Elburz mountains, which usurp half the sky, give a surprising interest to the streets that face them.

Teheran, 3 October At the English club we found Krefter, Herzfeld's assistant at Persepolis, deep in conversation with Wadsworth, the American First Secretary. Their secret, which both were too excited to contain, was that in Herzfeld's absence abroad, Krefter had dug up a number of gold and silver plaques which record the foundation of Persepolis by Darius. He calculated their positions by abstract mathematics; and there they lay, in stone boxes, when the holes were dug. Rather unwillingly he showed us photographs of them; archaeological jealousy and suspicion glanced from his eyes. Herzfeld, it seems, has turned Persepolis into his private domain, and forbids anyone to photograph there.

*

This afternoon I called on Mirza Yantz, a courteous diminutive old gentleman. We sat in his study, overlooking a round pool and a garden of geraniums and petunias which he had planted with his own hand. He is deputy for the Armenian colony of Julfa outside Isfahan, and has translated *The Corsair* into Armenian, since Byron is cherished by the national sentiment for his notice of the Armenian monastery at Venice. We talked of the War, when most Persians had their money (literally as well as metaphorically) on the Central Powers. Having no conception of sea-power, they could not imagine what injury England could inflict on Germany, 200 farsakhs away. Mirza Yantz was more far-sighted:

'I used to tell people the following story. I was travelling once from Basra to Baghdad, and stayed with a sheikh for a few days, who did his best to entertain me. He was a rich man, and he gave me to ride a beautiful grey mare, which danced and bucked, while he himself paced sedately by my side on a black mare of no spirit. So I asked him: "Why do you give me this fine animal, when you keep for yourself only that slow black mare who goes along with her head between her legs?"

'"Do you think she is slow?" said the sheikh. "Let us have a race."

'For the first quarter of a mile I drew ahead. Then I looked round. "Go on, go on," motioned the sheikh with his hand, like this. I went on. After a little while I was aware that the black mare was approaching. I spurred my horse. It was useless. The black mare passed me, still as it seemed without spirit, still with her head between her legs.

'I used to tell people that the grey mare was Germany, and the black mare England.'

Gulhek (4500 ft), 5 October   A lazy morning. Trees dappling the rush blinds of the loggia. Mountains and blue sky through the trees. A stream from the hills rippling into a blue-tiled pool. *The Magic Flute* on the gramophone.

This is the Simla of Teheran.

The bag has come up this fortnight from Baghdad in charge of an Air Force officer, who helped evacuate the Assyrians. He said that if he and his fellow officers had been ordered to bomb the Assyrians, as was mooted, they would have resigned their commissions. The aerodrome where they landed near Mosul was strewn with bodies, mostly shot in the genitals; they, the British, had to bury them. From the windward of the village also came a frightful stench, which reminded the older officers of the War. They took photographs of the bodies, but these were confiscated on return to Baghdad, and orders were given that nothing was to be said of what they had seen. He was furiously indignant, as anyone might be when it comes to saving British face by the concealment of atrocities.

At lunch we met Mr Wylie, an American big-game hunter, who has been after wild ass near Isfahan. Conversation turned on the Caspian tiger and seal, the wild horse and the Persian lion. Tiger and seal are quite common. A horse is alleged to have been shot by a German two years ago; but unfortunately his servants ate not only its flesh but its skin, so that no one else ever saw it. The last lion was seen in the War near Shustar.

The mountains looked very beautiful, as we rode out through gardens and orchards on to the bare foothills: clear and affirmative as a voice calling. A lonely cap of snow on the east was Demavend. The sun declined. Our shadows lengthened, merging into one huge shadow over the whole plain. The lower hills were engulfed; the upper; the peaks themselves. Still Demavend knew the sun, a pink coal in the darkling sky. And then, as we turned the horses, the transformation was reversed and repeated; for the sun had set behind a bank of cloud and now reappeared beneath it. Demavend was in shadow, while the foothills were in light. Quicker this time, the shadow ascended. The range darkened. The pink coal glowed again – for but one minute. And the stars came out of hiding.

News arrived this evening that Teimur Tash died in prison at ten o'clock the night before last, after he had been deprived of all comforts, including his bed. Even I, who was in Moscow during his reception there in 1932, find it sad; those who knew and liked him as the all-powerful vizier are much affected. But justice here is royal and personal; he might well have been kicked to death in public. Marjoribanks rules this country by fear, and the ultimate fear is that of the royal boot. One can argue that this is to his credit in an age of weapons that deal death from a distance.

*

Teheran, 7 October With a view to facilitating my journeys, I called on various people, including Jam, the Minister of the Interior, Mustafa Fateh, Distribution Manager of the Anglo-Persian Oil Company, and Farajollah Bazl the epigraphist. Then to tea with Mirza Yantz, where the conversation was in English, Greek, Armenian, Russian, and Persian. The chief guest was Emir-i-Jang, brother of Sardar Assad the Minister of War, and one of the great Bakhtiari chiefs. He had brought a present to Mirza Yantz's daughter of gilt doll's furniture upholstered in plush. This sent the party into raptures, everyone exclaiming 'Bha! Bha!'

Shir Ahmad, the Afghan Ambassador, looks like a tiger dressed up as a Jew. I said: 'If Your Excellency gives me permission, I am hoping to visit Afghanistan.'

'Hoping to visit Afghanistan? (*Roaring*) OF COURSE you will visit Afghanistan.'

According to him, there really is a road from Herat to Mazar-i-Sherif.

Teheran, 10 October There is a fluted grave-tower at Ray about six miles off, whose lower part is Seljuk; and another at Veramin further on, which is more graceful but less monumental. This one has a roof, and was tenanted by an opium fiend who looked up from cooking his lunch to tell us that it was his home and 3000 years old. The mosque at Veramin dates from the fourteenth century. From a distance, it resembles a ruined abbey, Tintern for example; but has a dome instead of a steeple, which rises from an octagonal middle storey above the square sanctuary chamber at the west end. The whole is of plain, café-au-lait brick, strong, unpretentious, and well-proportioned; it expresses the idea of content, as Moorish and Indian façade architecture never does. Inside is a stucco mihrab of the same technique as the Gumbad-i-Alaviyan at Hamadan; but the design, being later, is coarse and confused.

A man looking like a decayed railway porter – as most Persians do under the present sumptuary laws – joined us in the mosque. On his wrist perched a speckled grey-and-white falcon wearing a leather hood. He had taken it from the nest.

*

We dined with Hannibal, who is descended, like Pushkin, from Peter the Great's Negro, and is thereby cousin to certain English royalties. Having escaped from the Bolsheviks, he had become a Persian subject, and now lives in a style more Persian than the Persians. A servant carrying a paper lantern three feet high conducted us to his house through the labyrinths of the old bazaar. The other guests were a Kajar prince, son of Firman Firma, and his wife, who had been brought up in Hongkong. They, being more English than the English, were disconcerted at having to eat off the floor. The house was tiny; but its miniature wind-tower and sunken court gave it an air. Hannibal is busy instituting a Firdaussi library in honour of the poet's millennium next year.

Zinjan (5500 ft), 12 October We have been trying, and still are, to reach Tabriz by lorry. So far the journey has not gone according to plan. The lorry was due to leave at four. At half past four the garage sent us in a cab to another garage outside the Kazvin Gate. At five this garage tried to send us off in a broken-down bus, revealing at the same time that there had never been any lorry at all. We therefore hired a car, but resolved before starting to make the first garage disgorge our deposits. This caused a riot. Meanwhile a lorry had become available, at which the driver of the car threatened to go to the police if we forsook him. We did not.

In Kazvin next morning we hired another car, whose driver refused to lower the hood. When, therefore, he took a dip at forty miles an hour and my forehead came crack against a wooden strut, I gave him a sharp prod in the back. The car stopped dead. We bade him go on. He did so, at ten miles an hour. We bade him go faster. He did so for a little, then slowed down again.

Christopher: 'Faster! Faster!'
Driver: 'How can I drive if you all hit me?'
R.B.: 'Go on!'
Driver: 'How can I drive if the aga doesn't like me?'
Christopher: 'Drive carefully. We don't dislike you, but we hate dangerous driving.'
Driver: 'Alas, how can I drive? The aga hates me. My times are bitter.'

Christopher: 'The aga does like you.'
Driver: 'How can he if I have broken his head?'

And so on for miles, till we came to a police post. Here he stopped dead, saying he must register a complaint. There was only one thing to do: complain first. We jumped from the car and strode towards the office. This alarmed the man; for it was evident that if we sought the police with such alacrity they must be on our side instead of his. He suggested going on instead. We agreed.

The incident was an illustration, and a warning, of the acute horror which Persians feel towards even the pretence of physical violence.

Mile after mile we pursued a straight line between parallel ranges of mountains. The dome of Sultaniya loomed over the desert. To reach it we had to break down a whole irrigation system. There we found a different Persia. Though but a few miles off the main road, the modern Pahlevi hat was replaced by the old helm-shaped cap that appears in the reliefs at Persepolis. Most of the villagers spoke Turkish. Securing a bowl of curds and a flap of bread as big as a tent from the tea-house, we entered the mausoleum.

This remarkable building was finished by the Mongol prince Uljaitu in 1313. An egg-shaped dome about 100 feet high rests on a tall octagon, and is enclosed by a stockade of eight minarets which stand on the parapet of the octagon at the corners. The brick is pinkish. But the minarets were originally turquoise, and trefoils of the same colour, outlined in lapis, glitter round the base of the dome. Against the flat desert, pressed about by mud hovels, this gigantic memorial of the Mongol Empire bears witness to that Central Asian virility which produced, under the Seljuks, Mongols, and Timurids, the happiest inspirations of Persian architecture. Certainly, this is façade architecture: the prototype of the Taj and a hundred other shrines. But it still breathes power and content, while its offspring achieve only scenic refinement. It has the audacity of true invention; the graces are sacrificed to the idea, and the result, imperfect as it may be, represents the triumph of the idea over technical limitations. Much great architecture is of this kind. One thinks of Brunelleschi.

The inn here is labelled 'Grand Hotel – Town Hall'. We have not been wholly dependent on it, since Hussein Mohammad Angorani, the local agent of the Anglo-Persian Oil Company, invited us to supper. He received us in a long white room with a brilliantly painted ceiling; even the doors and windows were covered with white muslin. The furniture consisted of two brass bedsteads appointed with satin bolsters, and a ring of stiff settees, upholstered in white, before each of which stood a small white-covered table bearing dishes of melon, grapes, and sweets. In the middle of the floor, which was covered with two layers of carpets, stood three tall oil lamps, unshaded. A grey-bearded steward in a buff frock-coat, whom our host addressed as 'aga', attended us.

Our letter of introduction had said we wished to visit Sultaniya. If we returned this way, said our host, he would take us in his car. A trouble? He visited Sultaniya every day, for business or sport. In fact he had a house there, in which he could entertain us. In my innocence I believed these courtesies. But Christopher knew better. After an enormous meal, which we ate with out hands, the steward led us back to our bare cubicle in the Grand Hotel – Town Hall.

I am sitting in the street outside it; for the morning sun is the only available warmth. A pompous old fellow in check tweeds, who looks like Lloyd George, has just come up and announced himself as the Reis-i-Shosa. This means Captain of the Chaussées, in other words District Road Superintendent. He accompanied the English to Baku, where the reward of his help was a Bolshevik prison.

Tabriz (4500 ft), 15 October   In Zinjan at last we picked up a lorry. As Christopher was taking a photograph of me sitting in the back, a policeman stepped up and said photographing was forbidden. The driver was an Assyrian from near Lake Urmiya, and by his side sat an Assyrian schoolmistress, who was returning from a missionary conference in Teheran. She regaled us with slices of quince. They were much interested in my acquaintance with Mar Shimun, and advised me to say nothing about it in Tabriz, since there was a persecution of Christians at the moment, and Mrs Cochran's Women's Club in Urmiya had been shut by the police. At the thought of this, they sang 'Lead, Kindly Light' in unison, the school-mistress informing me that she had taught the driver this to prevent his singing the usual drivers' songs. I said I should have preferred the drivers' songs. She added that she had also persuaded him to

remove the blue beads from his radiator cap; they were a superstition of 'these Moslems'. When I told her they were a superstition
generally practised by Christians of the Orthodox Church, she was
dumbfounded. She admitted then that superstitions sometimes
worked: there was a devil named Mehmet, for instance, with a
human wife, through whom he had prophesied the War in her
father-in-law's parlour. She called herself a bible-worker, and wanted
to know if most people in England smoked or did not smoke. Why
doctors did not forbid smoking and drinking, instead of doing so
themselves, she could not understand.

I began to sympathize with the Persian authorities. Missionaries do
noble work. But once they make converts, or find indigenous
Christians, their usefulness is not so great.

Christopher, at this stage, was reading in the back of the lorry, where
his companions were a Teherani, an Isfahani, two muleteers, and
the driver's assistant.

Teherani: 'What's this book?'
Christopher: 'A book of history.'
Teherani: 'What history?'
Christopher: 'The history of Rum and the countries near it, such as
Persia, Egypt, Turkey, and Frankistan.'
Assistant (opening the book): 'Ya Ali! What characters!'
Teherani: 'Can you read it?'
Christopher: 'Of course. It's my language.'
Teherani: 'Read it to us.'
Christopher: 'But you cannot understand the language.
Isfahani: 'No matter. Read a little.'
Muleteers: 'Go on! Go on!'
Christopher: '"It may occasion some surprise that the Roman
pontiff should erect, in the heart of France, the tribunal from whence
he hurled his anathemas against the king; but our surprise will vanish
so soon as we form a just estimate of a king of France in the eleventh
century."'
Teherani: 'What's that about?'
Christopher: 'About the Pope.'
Teherani: 'The Foof? Who's that?'
Christopher: 'The Caliph of Rum.'
Muleteer: 'It's a history of the Caliph of Rum.'

Teherani: 'Shut up! Is it a new book?'

Assistant: 'Is it full of clean thoughts?'

Christopher: 'It is without religion. The man who wrote it did not believe in the prophets.'

Teherani: 'Did he believe in God?'

Christopher: 'Perhaps. But he despised the prophets. He said that Jesus was an ordinary man (*general agreement*) and that Mohammad was an ordinary man (*general depression*) and that Zoroaster was an ordinary man.'

Muleteer (who speaks Turkish and doesn't understand well): 'Was he called Zoroaster?'

Christopher: 'No, Gibbon.'

Chorus: 'Ghiboon! Ghiboon!'

Teherani: 'Is there any religion which says there is no god?'

Christopher: 'I think not. But in Africa they worship idols.'

Teherani: 'Are there many idolaters in England?'

The road led into mountains, where a great gorge brought us to the river of the Golden Swimmer. He was a shepherd, a Leander, who used to swim across to visit his beloved, until at last she built the truly magnificent bridge by which we also crossed. A herd of gazelle frisked along beside us. At length we came out on the Azerbaijan highlands, a dun sweeping country like Spain in winter. We passed through Miana, which is famous for a bug that bites only strangers, and spent the night in a lonely caravanserai where a wolf was tethered in the courtyard. At Tabriz the police asked us for five photographs each (they did not get them) and the following information:

AVIS

Je soussigné { Robert Byron / Christopher Sykes

Sujet { anglais / anglais

et exerçant la profession de { peintre / philosophe

déclare être arrivé en date du { 13me octobre / 13me octobre

accompagné de { un djinn / un livre par Henry James

etc.

*

The features of Tabriz are a view of plush-coloured mountains, approached by lemon-coloured foothills; a drinkable white wine and a disgusting beer; several miles of superb brick-vaulted bazaars; and a new municipal garden containing a bronze statue of Marjoribanks in a cloak. There are two monuments: the wreck of the famous Blue Mosque, veneered in fifteenth-century mosaic; and the Ark, or Citadel, a mountain of small russet bricks laid with consummate art, which looks as if it had once been a mosque, and if so, one of the biggest ever built. Turkish is the only language, except among officials. The merchants were formerly prosperous, but have been ruined by Marjoribanks's belief in a planned economy.

Maragha (4900 ft), 16 October   We drove here this morning in four hours, through country that reminded me of Donegal. Lake Urmiya appeared in the distance, a streak of blue and silver, with mountains beyond. Square pigeon-towers, perforated at the top, gave the villages a fortified appearance. Round about were vineyards, and groves of *sanjuk** trees, which have narrow grey leaves and clusters of small yellow fruit.

Maragha itself is not attractive. Broad straight streets have been cut through the old bazaars, and take away its character. A Persian-speaking infant adorned with eyelashes as long as ospreys conducted us to the necessary officials, and these in their turn showed us a fine polygonal grave tower of the twelfth century, which is known as the grave of the Mother of Hulagu and is built of plum-red brick arranged in patterns and inscriptions. The effect of this cosy old material, transferred as it were from an English kitchen garden to the service of Koranic texts, and inlaid with glistening blue, is surprisingly beautiful. There is a Kufic frieze inside, below which the walls have been lined with nesting-holes for pigeons.

We have conceived the idea of riding from here direct to Miana, thus cutting off two sides of a triangle with Tabriz at its apex. This should take us through unknown country, unknown at least architecturally; it is empty enough on the map. Horses are the difficulty. We agreed to one owner's price; at which he was much taken aback,

* So called by the local Turks; Persian: *sinjid*; a relation of the English service tree.

having lately lost his wife, and having no one to care for his children during the journey. An hour's argument overcame this objection. But then, having seen the horses, we revived it on our own account, to escape from the bargain. The innkeeper is looking for others. We hope to start tomorrow evening. It is the custom in this country to start in the evening.

Tasr Kand (c. *5000 ft*), *17 October*   I have done my best with the orthography of this place, though it is not important, consisting of one house, and that only a farsakh from Maragha. The farsakh (Xenophon's parasang) will be of interest to us now. It has been 'stabilized' at four miles, but in common parlance varies from three to seven.

Our sheepskin coats and sleeping-bags are spread in an upper room. Through the unglazed window peer the tops of poplars and the last gleam of a sky that threatens winter... A match flickers, a lantern lights up the asperities of the mud wall; the window goes black. Abbas the policeman crouches over a brazier, heating a cube of opium in a pair of tongs. He has just given me a puff, which tasted of potato. The muleteer in the corner is named Haji Baba. Christopher is still reading Gibbon. Chicken and onions are simmering in a pot. And I reflect that had we foreseen this journey we might have brought some food, and also insecticide.

The officials in Maragha had heard of the Rasatkhana, which means 'star-house' or observatory; but none had ever seen it. It was built by Hulagu in the thirteenth century, and its observations were Islam's last contribution to astronomy till Ulugh Beg revised the calendar at the beginning of the fifteenth. We set out early, breasted a mountain at full gallop, and found ourselves on a level table, where various mounds were approached from four points of the compass by straight cobbled paths intersecting at right angles. These paths, we supposed, were constructed to assist astronomical calculations; the mounds were the remains of buildings. But if here was our objective, where was the rest of the party, the Mayor, Chief of Police, and Military Commandant, who had preceded us? As our escort galloped hither and thither in search of them, we stood on the edge of the table, overlooking a great stretch of country with Lake Urmiya in the distance, and half expecting hounds to go away from a covert of poplars at the foot of the mountain. Suddenly the missing functionaries were discovered halfway down the precipice at our feet, and literally underneath us; for as we slithered down to them, leading the horses, we saw that the rock had been hollowed away in a semicircle, and that in the middle of this was the entrance to a cave. The latter may originally have been natural, but had certainly been artificially enlarged.

Inside the cave we found two altars, one facing the entrance, southward, and the other on the right, or east. Each was hewn from the living rock, and situated in a kind of raised chancel with a pointed vault. A rough mihrab was carved in the wall behind the altar on the right, pointing away from Mecca. On either side of the back altar were entrances to two tunnels. These gave on to small chambers, whose walls had scoops in them for lamps, and then went on, but were too clogged with earth for us to follow them. We wondered if they had ever communicated with the observatory above, and if so, whether observations were taken by daylight. They say it is possible to see stars from the bottom of a well when the sun is shining.

While I was photographing the interior of the cave, and thinking how uninteresting the results would seem to others, Christopher overheard the Chief of Police whisper to the Military Commandant: 'I wonder why the British Government wants photographs of this cave.' Well he might.

Sitting on their haunches, the horses had been dragged down the cliff to the village at the bottom. We slid after them, to find fruit, tea, and arak awaiting us in the chief house.

As we left the town this evening, I espied another twelfth-century tower just outside the gate, again of old strawberry brick, but square, and mounted on a foundation of cut stone. Three of the sides were divided each into two arched panels, in which the bricks were arranged in tweed patterns. The corners were turned with semicircular columns. On the fourth side, one big panel, framed in a curving inset, surrounded a doorway adorned with Kufic lettering and blue inlay. The interior disclosed a shallow dome upheld by four deep, but very low, squinches. There was no ornament here, and none was needed; the proportions were enough. Such classic, cubic perfection, so lyrical and yet so strong, reveals a new architectural world to the European. This quality, he imagines, is his own particular invention, whatever may be the other beauties of Asiatic building. It is astonishing to find it, not only in Asia, but speaking in an altogether different architectural language.

Saoma (c. *5500 ft*), *18 October*   Abbas and the muleteers were too chloroformed with opium this morning to start punctually. When we complained, they laughed in our faces. In fact their manners are vile; and in a country which sets a premium on manners, there is no need to be good-humoured about it. This evening, therefore, when they began to settle down in our room, I shooed them out, hubble-bubble, samovar, and all. At this Christopher was perturbed, saying it was against custom, and illustrating his point by a story of how once, when he was staying with a Bakhtiari chief and wished to say something in private, he positively appalled his host by suggesting that the servants should be sent out of the room. I answered that I also have customs, and one of them is not to be inconvenienced by the pipe or presence of muleteers in my own employ.

We rode five farsakhs today, sustained by a single bowl of curds and tortured by the wooden saddles. Soon after Tasr Kand, the road crossed a fine old bridge whose three arches, alternating with two little ones above the stone piers, were again of a mellow red brick. Thereafter we ascended into rolling highlands, broad, bare, and sombre in the closing autumn. Parts were ploughed, showing a rich brown earth; but the whole country is cultivable, and could support a larger population than it does. This was the first large village. In the middle of it stands a massive stone slab upheld by a primitive stone ram, on which the villagers make their oil.

We occupy the best room of the headman's house, which is over the stable and smells of it. The walls are newly whitewashed; there is a proper fireplace at one end; and round the walls are niches holding household objects, ewers, basins, and mugs of pewter, some of which contain a pot-pourri of rose-leaves and herbs. There is no furniture but carpets. Along the wainscot lie heaps of bolsters and quilts, covered with old-fashioned chintzes. Before the War these chintzes were specially made in Russia for the Central Asian market: one bolster depicts steamships, early motor-cars, and the first aeroplane, vignetted in circles of flowers on a vermilion background. They look gay and clean. But a flea has just hopped off my hand, and I dread the night, not for myself who am never bitten, but for Christopher to whom fleas are more than a music-hall joke.

A bowl of milk has arrived warm from the cow. We have opened the whisky in its honour.

When speaking Persian, the Azerbaijanis pronounce *k* like *ch*. But when they come to *ch* they pronounce it *ts*.

Kala Julk (c. *5500 ft*), *19 October*   Small clouds are shining in the blue. We rise by gentle slopes to a panorama of dun rolling country, chequered with red and black plough, and sheltering grey, turreted villages in its folds; breaking against the far mountains into hills streaked with pink and lemon; bounded at last by range upon range of jagged lilac. The twin peaks above Tabriz go with us. So do a flight of yellow butterflies. Far below a horseman approaches. 'Peace to you.' 'Peace to you.' Clip, clop, clip, clop, clip, clop... We are alone again.

Yesterday Christopher gave our host a two-toman note to change. This morning Abbas, who took the change, refused to give it up. 'Are you a thief?' asked Christopher. 'Yes I am,' he replied. He then complained bitterly of the insult, said he had 1000 tomans in his pocket, and in the same breath asked how he could live without a present now and then. Our relations with him, already cool enough, were further strained when he tried to steal the money we paid for the loan of a house to lunch in. He raised his whip against the owner, an old man, and would have struck him if I had not ridden them apart and called Abbas the son of a burnt father.

It was thus humiliating to discover, as we were riding by a salt stream through a lonely breathless valley, that Christopher had lost his wallet with our money in it; for we are now entirely dependent on Abbas to beg shelter for us gratis. At the moment he was behind, having said he must visit an outlying village, and we suspected that having found the wallet, he had absconded for good. A few minutes later he rejoined us. We explained our predicament. He triumphed slightly, but has sent back one of the muleteers to look for the wallet.

As a slight compensation, we have been most hospitably received here by the steward of some local magnate, and are now reclining beside a sweet-smelling fire over a game of two-handed bridge. There is comfort in the simmering of the samovar. Pray God the muleteer has been successful – he has just come in. No he hasn't; in fact he hasn't started yet, and now wants Haji Baba to go with him, at the price of a toman each. I have given them two out of my remaining twelve, and here we are in the middle of Azerbaijan with just over a pound to get us back to Teheran.

Later Christopher has found the wallet buttoned in his shirt. It is too late to stop the muleteers, but we have given Abbas two tomans to make up for our suspicions, unspoken though they were.

Ak Bulagh (c. *5500 ft*), *20 October* Christopher was ill when he woke up, from the fleas. Seeing this, the steward brought him a cone of black honey and said that if he ate this for four days, at the same time abstaining from curds and rogand, the rancid butter in which everything is cooked, the fleas would avoid him as they do me. While we breakfasted by the fire off milk and eggs, a boy of some fourteen years old walked in attended by an old man and a train of servants. This, it appeared, was the squire, to whom we owed so much good food and attention, and the old man was his uncle. His name is Mohammad Ali Khan, and our host of tonight describes him as 'the lord of all the villages'.

The muleteers walked twenty miles in the night, to the village where we lunched, and back. They were as active as usual today, perhaps more so, having had no opium.

One farsakh brought us to Saraskand, a village-town dignified by an old brick tea-house. Here we bought some grapes at a shop which also sold Bavarian pencils, steel nibs, and chintz. In the afternoon we came to Dash Bulagh, and rested by a stream to contemplate the little cluster of grey mud houses, the conical towers overspread with drying dung, and the tall white stems of golden-green trees against the bare rose-tinted hills.

Ak Bulagh is higher and very exposed; one stunted, wind-blown tree is all its shelter. The sun has set behind the twin peaks. By

lantern light in our squalid windowless room I have been sponging
Christopher with cold water, as the flea bites have given him fever; in
fact some are so raw that we have put whisky on them, in lieu of any
other disinfectant. Fortunately he is not too ill to repay the headman's courtesies:

'Peace to you.'

'Peace to you.'

'The condition of Your Highness is good, God willing?'

'Thanks be to God, owing to the kindness of Your Excellency, it is
very good.'

'Everything Your Highness commands your loving slave will
endeavour to perform. This house is your house. May I be your
sacrifice.'

'May the shadow of Your Excellency never grow less.'

He is a grave old man, sitting in the ceremonial way, with his legs
under him, his hands hid, and his eyelids dropped, while we sprawl
about the carpets like babies out of arms. Seventeen years ago, he
says, four Russians came here; before and since they have never seen
a Frank. His son Ismail sits beside him, a delicate child, who was
so ill a few years ago that his father went to Meshed to pray for
him.

For medicine Christopher has taken a dose of opium and a bowl of
liquid black honey. It is the best we can do.

Zinjan, 22 October   'Grand Hotel – Town Hall' again.

The long descent to Miana grew increasingly tedious as that place
refused to appear. A shepherd-boy dressed like Darius asked us for a
'papyrus', meaning the Russian word for cigarette. We were often
addressed in Russian at the tea-houses along the road, but it seemed
strange to hear it up in these remote hills. The muleteers and Abbas
smoked their midday pipe in a lonely blockhouse, which was the only
house we passed in twenty miles. When Miana came in sight the
horses quickened, though it was still two hours away. After crossing a
broad river-bed, we entered the town from the west.

We might have dropped from heaven. People rushed from their
thresholds. A crowd besieged us. I took the brunt of the Civil Police.

Christopher called on the Road Police, to which Abbas belongs, and returned with its captain. He was extremely suspicious.

'Did you photograph anything on the road?'

'Yes,' answered Christopher blandly, 'a delicious old stone, a ram in fact, at Saoma. Really, aga, you ought to go and look at it yourself.'

His suspicions were not allayed when Abbas confirmed the truth of this statement.

The muleteers of course had been told to collect more money than was due to them. Christopher gave them one of his Persian visiting cards, and suggested they should either knock their employer down or complain to the British Consul in Tabriz. We hopped into a lorry, reached here at one in the morning, and were given the box-room to sleep in. This morning I killed sixteen bugs, five fleas, and a louse in my sleeping-bag.

Christopher is in a sad state. His legs are swollen up to the knee and covered with water blisters. We have taken seats in a car which leaves here this afternoon, and should reach Teheran by midnight.

Part III

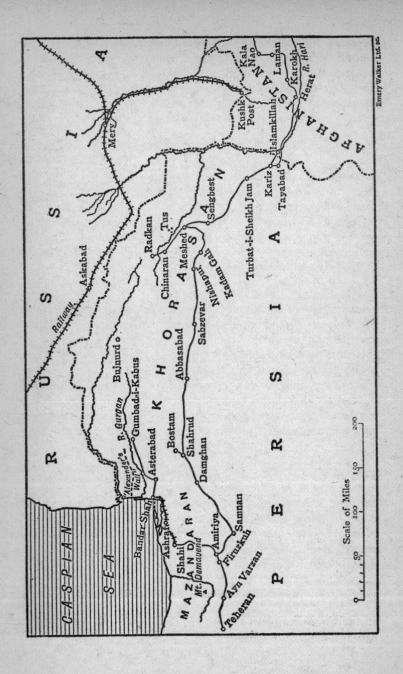

Emery Walker Ltd. sc

Teheran, 25 October   A telegram from Rutter, which has been waiting for me, says the Charcoal-Burners were leaving Beyrut on the 21st. As this was sent off a week before the 21st, there is still no proof that they have even reached Marseilles. Now, I suppose, I ought to wait here till they arrive, or till I hear they never will. But it is a tantalizing waste of time when winter is so close.

We are living in the Coq d'Or, a pension kept by M. and Mme. Pitrau and overrun with their pets. Pitrau used to be chef to the Japanese ambassador; he started his career as kitchen-boy to Lord Derby in Paris. The de Bathes are here too, with Karagozlu, their Turkish sheep-dog.

Christopher has gone to the nursing-home, where his legs are swathed in plaster bandages. These must not be moved for ten days, and even then it may take a month before the sores heal. The fleas of Azerbaijan are a formidable enemy.

I went to the Gulistan, where the Shah gives public audience, a fantasy of eccentric nineteenth-century tiles and cut-glass stalactites. The Peacock Throne is well suited to such an environment; only the jewelled and enamelled relief of a lion below the seat looks old enough to have formed part of the original throne from Delhi. There is also another throne, which the Kajars brought from Shiraz and which is kept in a sort of Durbar hall open to the garden. This takes the form of a platform supported on figures, and is carved from a translucent yellow-grey-green marble or soapstone, with occasional gilding. On the platform, in front of the Shah's seat, is a little pool.

Teheran, 6 November   Still here.

No word from the Charcoal-Burners. But the latest courier from Baghdad brings a rumour that the cars have finally broken down. Meanwhile a cutting from *The Times* says that Colonel Noel has started off from London to India in a Rolls-Royce driven by the same charcoal apparatus. He must have seen the account of the expedition's first departure in *The Times*, and have thought that sufficient voucher for the invention. Good luck to him!

In despair, I nearly set out for Afghanistan on my own two days ago. It was a narrow escape.

Wadsworth, the American chargé d'affaires, introduced me to Farquharson. I beheld an unattractive countenance, prognathous yet weedy, with hair growing to a point on the bridge of the nose. From the mouth issued a whining monotone. Still, I thought, one must make allowances. Now that Christopher is laid up, it will be difficult to find anyone else to travel with.

R. B.: 'I hear you're thinking of going to Afghanistan. Perhaps we could join up, if you really—'
Farquharson: 'Now I must explain to you first of all that I'm here to make a *vurry* hurried trip. I've already spent two days in Teheran. They tell me I ought to see the Peacock Throne, whatever that may be. I don't know that I'm particularly keen on seeing it. Frankly I'm naht interested in seeing things. I'm interested in history. I'm interested in liberty. Even in America liberty is naht what it was. I'd have you understand of course that I am *vurry* pressed for time. My parents were naht anxious for me to come on this trip. My father has recently founded an advertising business in Memphis, and he said he hoped I'd be back home by Christmas. Perhaps I'll stay over till January. It depends how things work out. There's the southern trip, with a day in Isfahan, and another in Shiraz. There's Tabriz. And there's Afghanistan. Frankly, if Afghanistan is pahssible, I should like to go there. My plans aren't fixed. I wasn't sure even, when I left, if I'd come to Persia. People in the States told me it was dangerous. People here say the same about Afghanistan. They may be right. I doubt it. I've travelled considerably. There's no European country, including Iceland and excepting Russia, I haven't visited. I once slept in a ditch in Albania. Of course that wasn't *vurry* difficult, though I talked about it afterwards in Memphis a good deal. So if it is pahssible, I should like to go to Afghanistan. But I could only make a *vurry* hurried trip. We might get through to Kabul, we might not. If we did, I might rent a plane back here. I'm naht anxious to see India for the moment. It's a big place and I'm saving it for another fall. I've already spent two days in Teheran. Those two days have been mainly occupied socially. I've enjoyed them. But that's naht what I came for. I'm here, you understand, to make a *vurry* hurried trip. Now if Afghanistan is pahssible, I should like to start tomorrow. Mr Wadsworth, who also comes from Memphis, gave me a letter to the Afghan Ambassador. When I lost it, he gave me another. I went round this morning, but the Ambassador couldn't

see me. He had some ladies with him. I saw a secretary instead, but he didn't speak English, and my French is only college French, so we didn't get *vurry* far. I may get the visa, I may naht. In any case I should like to start tomorrow morning. You see, I'm here to make a *vurry* hurried trip.'

R. B.: 'I was going to suggest that if you wanted a companion, I might come with you and share expenses. It would suit me, because I can't afford to take a car of my own.'

Farquharson: 'I must admit I'm naht exactly pressed for money. At the same time I work, like everyone else in the States. With you in Europe it's different. But over there we have no leisured class. Everyone works, even if he hasn't gaht to. It would hurt you socially if you didn't. I've set aside four thousand dollars for this trip. But that doesn't mean I'm particularly anxious to throw money away. I expect I can *afford* to go to Afghanistan if I can spare the time. You see I'm here to make a *vurry* hurried trip.'

R. B.: 'If you could tell me exactly how long you do want to spend over the journey, perhaps we could work out a plan.'

Farquharson: 'That all depends.' (Repeats all he has previously said at greater length.)

Eventually I went myself to the Afghan Embassy, to see whether I would assist Farquharson's application for a visa. Meanwhile, we had arranged to meet next day. He came to the Coq d'Or while Christopher and I were lunching with Herzfeld, who had just returned from Europe.

Farquharson (breathlessly, as he lopes across the dining-room): 'I believe my plans have taken a turn for the better. I haven't actually gaht the visa yet. But I think I shall get it. Now there are one or two points I'm *vurry* anxious to discuss with you—'

R. B.: 'May I introduce Professor Herzfeld?'

Farquharson: '. . . I'm vurry glad to meet you, sir. You see I'm here to make a *vurry* hurried trip and I was going to say—'

Christopher: 'Won't you sit down?'

Farquharson: 'I was going to say, first of all, that I'm vurry anxious to start tomorrow morning if pahssible. Of course it may naht be pahssible. But if it is, that's my plan.'

Herzfeld (trying to dissipate the boredom): 'I see you have a tame fox in the courtyard here.'

Christopher: 'There used to be a wild boar as well. But it had to be killed because it would get into the guests' beds when they were asleep. Why they should have minded, Madame Pitrau said, she couldn't imagine; it only wanted its stomach scratching. But they did, and that was the end of it.'

R. B.: 'The fox gets into the beds too, and wets them.'

Farquharson: 'Of course this is vurry amusing, though I'm afraid I don't get the joke. Now there are one or two points I'm *vurry* anxious to discuss with you'.

Herzfeld: 'I keep a porcupine at Persepolis. It is very domesticated. If tea is one minute late it becomes furious, and its spikes, what do you call them, quills, stand up.'

Farquharson: 'There are one or two points I'm *vurry*—'

Herzfeld: 'Also it uses the WC like a human being. Every morning I have to wait for it. We all have to wait for it.'

Farquharsin (wanly): 'That's extremely interesting, though I'm afraid I don't quite get there. Now there are one or two—'

R. B.: 'We'd better go to my room.' (We go.)

Farquharson: 'There are one or two points I'm *vurry* anxious to discuss with you. I want to make it clear that if I do go to Afghanistan, I shall have to make a *vurry* hurried trip. Now I want to speak vurry frankly. You don't know me and I don't know you. I think we'll get on. I hope we will. But we must try and get things clear beforehand. I've written down a few points on a bit of paper which I'll just read out. Number one I've called Personal Relationships. I've travelled a considerable amount. I know therefore that travelling brings out the worst in people. For instance I have a brother in Memphis. He's vurry fond of music. I am naht fond of music. We were together in Paris. After dinner he'd go to a concert. I did naht. I'm fond of my brother, but even so certain difficulties of this class are apt to arise. Now I don't know you and you don't know me. We may have hardships, we may fall sick. In sickness we can't expect to be cheerful. Otherwise I think we should remember this question of Personal Relationships. The second point I've called Political. I'm going to speak *vurry* frankly. I'm pressed for time over here, you understand, and if we go to Afghanistan together, as I hope we will, I want to make it clear that I must have the power on this trip. That's why I've called this second point Political. If I decide I don't want to go anywhere, well then we just shan't be able to go. I shall do my best to meet your wishes. I shall try and be fair. I think I shall be fair. Mr Wadsworth, who also comes from Memphis, knows my family and I think he'll tell you I'm likely to be fair. But I must be the boss politically. The third point is Financial. Since I've taken so much power on this trip, I'm prepared to pay a little more than half the car. But you realize I'm pressed for time, I have to make a *vurry* hurried trip, and it's pahssible I may go right through to India and take a boat from there. Now I understand you're pressed for money, from what you said. I couldn't leave a fellow-traveller stranded in India. So before we start I've gaht to know you've enough money to get back to Persia, and I've gaht to see the notes actually in your hand—'

R. B.: 'What?'

Farquharson: 'I've gaht to see the notes actually in your hand—'

R. B.: 'Goodbye.'

Farquharson: '. . . before leaving, so's I can be quite sure you can shift for yourself in the event of—'

R. B.: 'GET OUT, if you're not deaf.'

Farquharson fled. On the way out, he ran into Herzfeld and Christopher, and wrung their hands warmly. 'I'm vurry glad to have met you. Goodbye. I must be getting along. You see I have to make a *vurry* hurried trip. . .'

He had. I was at his heels. Not that I would have touched him without rubber gloves and a bottle of disinfectant. But he was good to threaten. I had seen him dressing the day before, and had noted a *vurry* poor muscular development.

Teheran, 9 November Still here.

King Nadir Shah has been assassinated in Kabul.

A bazaar rumour reached the Bank in the morning that King Ghazi of Iraq was dead. The Legation heard the truth at one o'clock. Reuter's confirmed it in the evening. The Government of India has hysterics. From Afghanistan itself there is no news whatever. But disturbance or not, such an event will hardly make my journey easier – if I ever manage to start on it.

One of the Bakhtiari chiefs, an old friend of Christopher's, came to dine with us in a private room. He asked for secrecy because intercourse with foreigners is dangerous to one who has inherited the position of tribal khan. All these chiefs, in fact, are kept by Marjoribanks in a sort of unofficial captivity. They can live in Teheran and splash their money about. But they cannot return to their own Bakhtiari country. Marjoribanks is frightened of the tribes and is trying to break their power by settling them in villages under control of the police and depriving them of their leaders. They have been king-makers in the past too often.

Our guest spoke with foreboding of the future. He was resigned to it, he said. Persia had always been like this. The only thing to do was to have patience till the tyrant died.

Teheran, 11 November   Saturday. Still here.

I decided to leave on Tuesday. On Monday I found a Morris car for sale at £30. This seemed a bargain. In fact I actually supposed it would enable me to leave next day.

The sequence, which then began, of getting possession of the car, getting a licence to drive it with, getting a permit to stay in Persia at all, getting a permit to go to Meshed, getting a letter to the Governor of Meshed, and getting other letters to the governors en route, obliterated four days. I was said to be 'recalcitrant de la loi' for having no identity card. To obtain one, I furnished the state archives with the secret of my mother's birthplace, in triplicate. Meanwhile, the owner of the car had left Teheran, confiding his power of attorney to a very old lawyer in a pink tweed frock-coat. A bargain was struck; signatures were officially witnessed; but the police refused to register the transaction because, although the lawyer's power of attorney extended to all his employer's worldly goods, a Morris car was not mentioned in the list of those goods. This decision was reversed, on appeal to a higher police official, who telephoned the fact to his subordinate. But when we returned to the other department, 300 yards away, they knew nothing of it. Neighbouring departments were asked if they had had the message. At last someone remembered that the person who must have answered the telephone had gone out. Heaven favoured us; we met him in the street, and followed him to his desk. This annoyed him. He would do nothing, he said, without a copy of the power of attorney. Till it was ready, perhaps we would be good enough to leave him in peace. The lawyer hobbled off to buy a clean sheet of paper. We, the owner's son, the garage proprietor and myself, sought asylum on the pavement of the main square, squatting round the crabbed old scribe while his spectacles fell off his nose, and his pen harpooned the paper till it looked like a stencil. A sentence was not finished before the police moved us on; another scarcely begun, before they did so again. Like a colony of disturbed toads, we scuttled round and round the square, jabbing down a word here and there, while dusk deepened into night. When the copy was presented, it had again to be copied, in the office. The square had been better than this; for the office electricity had failed, and matches had to be struck in such quantities that our fingers were burned to the quick. I laughed; the others laughed; the police laughed like madmen; but suddenly becoming serious, said the certificate of ownership could not after all be ready for three days. An hour's argument evoked a promise of next morning. Next morning I went in search of it; again they said three days. But now, being alone, I had the advantage, speaking enough Persian to say what I wanted, but not enough to understand a refusal. Once more we trooped off to the officer across the street. Men rushed from room to room. The telephone spluttered. The document was born. And all this, let me add, was only a tithe, a mere sample, of my fate during these last four days.

The date of the car is 1926, and its engine has needed some attention. After testing it yesterday, I proposed to start at six this morning. But by the end of the test, the battery had failed. I shall leave at midday and hope to make Amiriya tonight, where the worst of the passes but one will be over.

The Noel party arrived last night in two Rolls-Royces. They threw the charcoal apparatus away at Dover. The original Charcoal-Burners, they say, spent five nights in the desert between Damascus and Baghdad, and broke two big-ends, which are now being repaired. I still have no certainty of their advent here. It is impossible to wait on chance. The passes may be blocked any day after the fifteenth.

Ayn Varzan (c. 5000 ft), *later 7.30 p.m.*   The back axle has broken, sixty miles from Teheran.

'To Khorasan! To Khorasan!' shouted the policeman at the city gate. I felt a wonderful exhilaration as we chugged through the

Elburz defiles. Up or down, the engine was always in bottom gear; only this could save us from being precipitated, backwards or forwards as the case might be, over the last or next hairpin bend.

Seven chanting peasants pushed the car uphill to a shed in this village. It is a total loss. But I won't go back to Teheran.

Shahrud (4400 ft), 13 November A bus arrived next morning at Ayn Varzan, full of lady pilgrims on their way to Meshed. Their chatter in the yard below woke me up. Five minutes later I was beside the driver, and my luggage underneath the ladies.

From the pass above Amiriya we looked back over a mounting array of peaks, ranges, and buttresses to the white cone of Demavend in the top of the sky; and forward over a plain of boundless distances, where mountains rippled up and sighed away like the wash of a tide, dark here, shining there, while shadows and sunshine followed their masters the clouds across the earth's arena. Trees of autumn yellow embowered the lonely villagers. Elsewhere, desert; the stony black-lustred desert of eastern Persia. At Samnan, while the ladies drank tea in a brick caravanserai, I heard of an old minaret, which I found before the police found me. When they did, I ate sorrow, as the expression is, that I could stay no longer in their beautiful city, and we drove away into the dusk. 'Come with us to Meshed,' said the driver, who was a Negro, offering a price which indicated friendship. Obstinately, I descended at Damghan.

There are two circular grave-towers in that place, which are inscribed and dated as built in the eleventh century, and are constructed of fine but loosely mortared café-au-lait brick. A ruined mosque, known as the Tarikh Khana or 'History House', is even older; its round squat pillars recall an English village church of the Norman period, and must have inherited their unexpected Romanesque form from Sasanian tradition. The whole of Islamic architecture borrowed from this tradition, once Islam had conquered Persia. But it is interesting to see the process beginning thus crudely, before it attains artistic value.

The police, good-natured fellows, began to faint with hunger as I kept them out beyond their lunchtime. Late in the afternoon, a lorry came in from the west, and they bundled me on to it as the only hope of their getting a meal that day. We reached Shahrud at eight, and are to leave at midnight.

That admirable institution, the Persian caravanserai, has refused to be ousted by modern transport. Garages are everywhere, certainly. But they reproduce the old plan. This consists of a quadrangle, as big as an Oxford college, and defended by huge doors. Near the doors, beside the arched entrance, are rooms for cooking, eating, communal sleeping, and the transaction of business. Round the other three sides are rows of smaller rooms, which resemble monastic cells, and accommodation for horses and motors. Comfort varies. Here, in the Garage Massis, I have a spring bed, a carpet, and a stove; and have eaten a tender chicken, followed by some sweet grapes. At Damghan there was no furniture at all, and the food was lumps of tepid rice.

Nishapur (4000 ft), 14 November   One can become a connoisseur of anything. Never in all Persia was there such a lorry as I caught at Damghan: a brand new Reo Speed Waggon, on its maiden voyage, capable of thirty-five miles an hour on the flat, with double wheels, ever-cool radiator, and lights in the driver's cabin. Mahmud and Ismail are making record time from Teheran to the Indian frontier. They ask after my health every five minutes, and want me to go right down to Duzdab with them.

Dawn, like a smile from the gallows, pierced the gusty, drizzling night. I ate a bit of cheese, and the other side of the chicken's breast from Shahrud. Two stunted willows and a tea-house hove out of the murky desert. Mahmud and Ismail went inside, to greet other cronies of the road. I dozed where I sat.

At Abbasabad we huddled over a fire, while the people of the place tried to sell us beads, cigarette holders, and dice, of a soft grey-green stone. They wore scarlet Russian blouses, and are descended from Georgian colonists planted by Shah Abbas. Then on, against the wind and wet, over the grey hummocky wastes. The grey zeppelin clouds drive low and fast. The grey infrequent villages are desolate of people. Clustering round their ruined citadels, those ancient shapes, the beehive dome and ziggurat, are melting in the rain. They have melted thus since the dawn of history; and when summer comes, they will rise again out of new mud bricks till history closes. Streams in purple spate swirl through the walled lanes into the fields, and out into the desert. The track itself becomes a watercourse. In a night, the poplars have lost their leaves, though the planes hold theirs for a day more. Strings of camels sway alongside us – boom goes the bull-camel's bell – boom, and is gone. Shepherds in white tabards tack through the gale after pebble-grazing flocks. Black tents and black fleece hats announce the Turcomans and the verge of Central Asia. So this is the Golden Road. Eight centuries ago, the minaret of Khosrugird watched the traffic as it watches us. Sabzevar is two miles further. The caravanserai produces kabob, curds, pomegranates, and a bottle of local claret.

Soon after dark, the lorry's lights went out. That feckless couple of record-breakers, Mahmud and Ismail, had not a match nor a wick between them. I had both, but the defect was not easily repaired, and instead of reaching Meshed, we have had to put up here.

The home, curse it, of Omar Khayam.

Meshed (3100 ft), 16 November   The distance from Nishapur to Meshed is ninety miles. I supposed I should be here by midday.

But my beautiful Speed Waggon could not go, and it was nine o'clock before I found a seat in a British Bedford pilgrim bus. At Kadam Gah, sixteen miles down the road, the driver obligingly stopped while I walked up to the shrine. This pretty little octagon, surmounted by a bulbous dome, was built in the middle of the seventeenth century, and commemorates a resting-place of the Imam Riza. It sits on a platform beneath a rocky cliff, surrounded by tall umbrella-pines and tinkling streams. The sun struck the tiles, which glittered blue and pink and yellow against the dark foliage and lowering sky. A bearded seyid in a black turban asked for money. Hopping and tapping, the halt and blind converged with terrible rapidity. I fled back to the bus.

That vehicle was carrying twice its proper number of passengers, and their luggage as well. Exhilarated at the prospect of his journey's end the driver tore down-hill at forty miles an hour, lurched across a stream-bed, and had just rebounded against the opposite slope, when to my great surprise the off front wheel ran back towards me, buckled the running-board with a crunch, and escaped into the desert. 'Are you English?' asked the driver in disgust. 'Look at that.' An inch of British steel had broken clean through.

It took an hour and a half to fit another joint. The pilgrims huddled down with their backs to the wind, men beneath their yellow sheepskins, women veiled in black shrouds. Three chickens, tied to each other by the leg, enjoyed a temporary freedom. But their clucking boded little hope. When we started again, the driver was seized with a palsy of caution. He proceeded at five miles an hour, stopping at every caravanserai to refresh his nerves with tea; till at last we reached a small pass and a new view.

Tiers of firelit mountains encircled the horizon. Night, and a surf of clouds, were rolling in from the east. Down in the plain, a blur of smoke, trees, and houses announced Meshed, the holy city of the Shiahs. A gold dome flashed, a blue dome loomed, out of the cold autumnal haze. Century by century, since the Imam Riza was interred beside the Caliph Harun-al-Rashid, this vision has refreshed the desert-weary sight of pilgrims, merchants, armies, kings, and travellers – to become the last hope of several dozen fretful passengers in a damaged motor-bus.

A number of cairns marked the sacred vantage. The male pilgrims descended to pray, turning their backs on Meshed in favour of Mecca. The driver descended to collect his dues, and since the husbands were engaged, perforce approached their wives. A screech of protest, rising to a furious and sustained crescendo, blasted the moment of thanksgiving. On prayed the pious husbands, bashing their foreheads on the cairns, lacerating their stockinged feet, heaving sighs and rolling eyes to heaven, in their resolve to postpone the inevitable reckoning. Round the bus danced the driver and his assistant, repulsed by the hooded harpies in their wire cage. One by one the husbands tried to dodge back to their places unseen. One by one the chauffeurs caught them. Each protested for a separate quarter of an hour. But only three refused to pay in the end, and these, snarling and cursing, were ejected from the company with blows and kicks. Led by a whining pharisee, the most active of the devotees, who had been my neighbour on the front seat of the bus, they started away down the hill at a lolloping trot.

The bus had hardly begun to follow them, before the women at the back set up a threefold clamour. With their fists and household implements they would soon have demolished the thin wooden partition that separated them from the driver and myself. Once more we stopped. Letting fall their veils, the foaming viragos appealed to me to retrieve their three men. By now I had no interest save to reach a hotel before dark. 'Either take the men back,' I told the driver, 'or go on. You'll lose my fare too, if we stay here any longer.' This argument prevailed. He caught up the men, who were still tearing down the road, and invited them to return. They refused. Backing into the gutter, they refused point-blank thus to favour the monster who had defiled the most hallowed moment of their lives. Again the women shrieked and battered. Again the partition cracked. The whole bus began to creak. '*GO ON!*' I yelled, stamping till the floor-boards were entangled in the brake. Jumping out, the driver seized the deserters, belaboured them till they groaned for mercy, and dragged them back to the bus. The pharisee sought his old place in front, by me. But now it was my turn to go mad. I would not have him near me, I said. In reply, he seized my hand, and pressing it to his prickly, saliva-trickling beard, sprayed it with kisses. A shove sent him sprawling, while I leapt out on the other side, declaring to the now befogged, exhausted, and unhappy driver that rather than suffer further contact with the man, I would walk into Meshed on my own feet and keep what I owed him in my pocket. At this, the women turned their abuse to the pharisee. The cringing brute was hoisted into the back. And we set off for the holy city at a pace fit to smash a gun-carriage.

The driver and I looked at one another. We laughed.

Meshed, 17 November The Shrine dominates the town. Turcomans, Kazaks, Afghans, Tajiks, and Hazaras throng its approaches, mingling with the dingy crowd of pseudo-European Persians. The police are frightened of these fanatics; so that access to the Shrine is still denied to infidels, despite the official anti-clerical policy which is opening the mosques elsewhere. 'If you really want to go in,' said the man in the hotel, 'you can borrow my hat. That's all you need.' I looked with distaste on that battered symbol of Marjoribank's rule, parody of a French képi, and concluded that it would hardly pass muster with blue eyes and a fair moustache.

*

Not long ago, Marjoribanks paid a first visit to Sistan. To gratify his appetite for modern street planning, the terrified local authorities built a whole new town, Potemkin-wise, whose walls, though festooned with electricity, enclosed nothing but fields. A lorry preceded him by a day, bearing children's clothes. Next morning, the school assembled dressed like a French kindergarten. The monarch drove up, stopped long enough to sack the schoolmaster because the children's clothes were backward, and drove on; but not before the clothes had been whisked off the children and bundled back into the lorry, to precede him at the next place. Persia is still the country of *Haji Baba*.

The Noel party arrived yesterday. I have taken a seat for Herat in an Afghan lorry painted all over with roses. It aspires to leave the day after tomorrow.

Meshed, 18 November Tus, the home of Firdaussi, existed before Meshed, which grew up round the bones of the Imam Riza. It lies eighteen miles to the north-west, just off the road to Askabad on the Russian frontier.

Mounds and ridges betray the outlines of the old city. An antique bridge of eight arches spans the river. And a massive domed mausoleum, whose brick is the colour of dead rose-leaves, stands up against the blue mountains. No one knows whom this commemorated; though from its resemblance to the mausoleum of Sultan Sanjar at Merv, it seems to have been built in the twelfth century. It alone survives of the splendours of Tus.

However, next year will see the thousandth anniversary of Firdaussi's birth. Foreigners have heard of Firdaussi. They esteem him as only a poet can be esteemed whom no one has ever read. And it is expected, therefore, that their tributes will flatter not his work so much as his nationality. Such at least is the Persian hope. A programme of celebrations is already announced. Governments whose frontiers or other interests march with Persia's, are sending delegations to remind Marjoribanks that while his compatriots were making epics, theirs were wearing woad. Nor, they will observe, is the comparison inappropriate today. His Majesty's new railway, his impartial and open justice, his passion for lounge suits, offer hope to a distracted world. In fact, Shah Riza Pahlevi has left Firdaussi standing.

Tus, long silent between the mountains and the desert, will be the stage of these fragrant utterances. A cenotaph will be unveiled, situated with approximate probability on the site of the poet's grave. This object, which is almost built, proved a pleasant surprise. A square cone, to be covered with white stone, stands on a broad flight of steps. In front of it lies a long pool, framed by lines of trees and announced by a pair of classical pavilions. Given the limitations of Oriental taste when confronted with a Western idea, the design is admirable. The Western part of it, the cenotaph, is as simple as can be; the Persian part, the garden, is beautiful as always; and the two are blended by good proportions. When the ceremonies are over, and only the tinkling goat-bells are heard again, the Firdaussi-lover may find a grateful peace in this unpretentious shrine.

There was a tea-party at the Consulate this afternoon, followed by games. The Chief of Police, who looks like, and possibly is, an executioner, presented a curious spectacle tied by the arm to an American missionary lady in a hunt-the-thimble competition. I met Mr Donaldson, the head of the American mission, who instead of – or perhaps besides – bothering about converts, has just published a book on the Shiah religion.

A telegram from Teheran says the Charcoal-Burners have arrived there and are coming on here as soon as the customs release their guns. There is no sense in waiting for them. We must meet in Mazar-i-Sherif if we meet at all. Even now the road may be closed by snow.

Noel now thinks he will try and get visas for Afghanistan too.

AFGHANISTAN: Herat (3000 ft), 21 November Noel got visas and brought me here; or rather, I brought him. Having driven the whole way from London, he was glad to give the wheel to someone else. He left this afternoon by the southern road to Kandahar.

But for the staff of the Russian Consulate, who lead the life of prisoners, I am the only European in the place, and am on my best behaviour; the public stare demands it. There is company at the hotel in three Parsi Indians, who are riding round the world on bicycles and have come from Mazar-i-Sherif by the new road opened this summer. They met various Russians on the way, who had escaped over the Oxus and were proceeding under escort to Chinese Turkestan by the Wakhan-Pamir road. One of these was a journalist, who gave them a letter describing his sufferings. His boots were already in holes, but he was intending to walk to Pekin.

Herat has its own Secretary for Foreign Affairs, who is known as the Mudir-i-Kharija and says that if I can find transport, I may proceed to Turkestan. I also had audience of the Governor, Abdul Rahmin Khan, a handsome old fellow wearing a tall black astrakhan hat and grey Hindenburg moustaches. He too gives me leave to go where I want, and will furnish me with letters to the authorities en route.

Later I called on the Muntazim-i-Telegraph, who speaks English.
'Where is Amanullah Khan?' he asked suddenly, glancing out of the window to see that no one was about.
'In Rome, I suppose.'
'Is he coming back?'
'You ought to know better than I do.'
'I know nothing.'
'His brother, Inyatullah, is in Teheran now.'
The Muntazim sat up. 'When did he arrive?'
'He lives there.'
'What does he do?'
'Plays golf. He plays so badly that the foreign diplomats avoid him. But as soon as they knew King Nadir Khan had been assassinated, they all telephoned inviting him to play.'
The Muntazim shook his head over this sinister information. 'What is golf?' he asked.

A gentleman from the Municipality called this evening to know if I was comfortable. I admitted I should be more comfortable if the windows of my room had glass in them. The hotel is managed by Seyid Mahmud, an Afridi by the look of him, who used to work in a hotel at Karachi. He showed me his visitors' book, from which I saw that Graf von Bassewitz, the German Consul in Calcutta, stayed here in August on his way back from leave. This is the first I have heard of him since 1929.

*

Herat, 22 November Herat stands in a long cultivated plain stretching east and west, being three miles equidistant from the Hari river on the south and the last spurs of the Paropamisus mountains on the north. There are two towns. The old is a maze of narrow twisting streets enclosed by square ramparts, and bisected diagonally by the tunnel of the main bazaar, which is two miles long; on the north stands the Citadel, an imposing medieval fortress built on a mound, whence it dominates the surrounding plain. Opposite this lies the New Town, which consists of one broad street leading northward from the bazaar entrance, and a similar street intersecting it at right-angles. These streets are lined with open-fronted shops. Above them towers the second storey of the hotel, situated among the coppersmiths, whose clang between dawn and sunset deters the guests from sloth. Further on at the crossroads, is the ticket office for lorries, where passengers assemble daily among bales of merchandise and vats of Russian petrol in wooden crates.

Engrossed by the contrast with Persia, I return the people's stare. The appearance of the ordinary Persian, as dressed by Marjoribanks's sumptuary laws, is a slur on human dignity; impossible, one thinks, for this swarm of seedy mongrels to be really the race that have endeared themselves to countless travellers with their manners, gardens, horsemanship, and love of literature. How the Afghans may endear themselves remains to be seen. Their clothes and their walk are credential enough to begin with. A few, the officials, wear European suits, surmounted by a dashing lambskin hat. The townsmen too sport an occasional waistcoat in the Victorian style, or the high-collared frock-coat of the Indian Mussulman. But these importations, when accompanied by a turban as big as a heap of bedclothes, a cloak of parti-coloured blanket, and loose white peg-top trousers reaching down to gold-embroidered shoes of gondola shape, have an exotic gaiety, like an Indian shawl at the Opera. This is the southern fashion, favoured by the Afghans proper. The Tajiks, or Persian element, prefer the quilted gown of Turkestan. Turcomans wear high black boots, long red coats, and busbies of silky black goats' curls. The most singular costume is that of the neighbouring highlanders, who sail through the streets in surtouts of stiff white serge, dangling false sleeves, almost wings, that stretch to the back of the knee and are pierced in patterns like a stencil. Now and then a calico beehive with a window at the top flits across the scene. This is a woman.

Hawk-eyed and eagle-beaked, the swarthy loose-knit men swing through the dark bazaar with a devil-may-care self-confidence. They carry rifles to go shopping as Londoners carry umbrellas. Such ferocity is partly histrionic. The rifles may not go off. The physique is not so impressive in the close-fitting uniform of the soldiers. Even the glare of the eyes is often due to make-up. But it is a tradition; in a country where the law runs uncertainly, the mere appearance of force is half the battle of ordinary business. It may be an inconvenient tradition, from the point of view of government. But at least it has preserved the people's poise and their belief in themselves. They expect the European to conform to their standards, instead of themselves to his, a fact which came home to me this morning when I tried to buy some arak; there is not a drop of alcohol to be had in the whole town. Here at last is Asia without an inferiority complex. Amanullah, the story goes, boasted to Marjoribanks that he would westernize Afghanistan faster than Marjoribanks could westernize Persia. This was the end of Amanullah, and may like pronouncements long be the end of his successors.

On approaching Herat, the road from Persia keeps close under the mountains till it meets the road from Kushk, when it turns downhill towards the town. We arrived in a dark but starlit night. This kind of night is always mysterious; in an unknown country, after a sight of the wild frontier guards, it produced an excitement such as I have seldom felt. Suddenly the road entered a grove of giant chimneys, whose black outlines regrouped themselves against the stars as we passed. For a second, I was dumbfounded – expecting anything on earth, but not a factory; until, dwarfed by these vast trunks, appeared the silhouette of a broken dome, curiously ribbed, like a melon. There is only one dome in the world like that, I thought, that anyone knows of: the Tomb of Tamerlane at Samarcand. The chimneys therefore must be minarets. I went to bed like a child on Christmas Eve, scarcely able to wait for the morning.

Morning comes. Stepping out on to a roof adjoining the hotel, I see seven sky-blue pillars rise out of the bare fields against the delicate heather-coloured mountains. Down each the dawn casts a highlight of pale gold. In their midst shines a blue melon-dome with the top bitten off. Their beauty is more than scenic, depending on light or landscape. On closer view, every tile, every flower, every petal of mosaic contributes its genius to the whole. Even in ruin, such architecture tells of a golden age. Has history forgotten it?

Not quite. The miniatures of Herat in the fifteenth century are famous, both for themselves and as the source of Persian and Mogul painting afterwards. But the life and the men that produced them, and these buildings as well, hold no great place in the world's memory.

The reason is that Herat lies in Afghanistan; while Samarcand, the capital of Timur, but not of the Timurids, has a railway to it. Afghanistan, till literally the other day, has been inaccessible. Samarcand, for the last fifty years, has attracted scholars, painters, and photographers. Thus the setting of the Timurid Renascence is conceived as Samarcand and Transoxiana, while its proper capital, Herat, remains but a name and a ghost. Now the position is reversed. The Russians have closed Turkestan. The Afghans have opened their country. And the opportunity arrives to redress the balance. Strolling up the road towards the minarets, I feel as one might feel who has lighted on the lost books of Livy or an unknown Botticelli. It is impossible, I suppose, to communicate such a feeling. The Timurids are too remote for most people to romance over them. But such is the reward of my journey to me.

All the same, these Oriental Medici were an extraordinary race. With the exception of Shah Rukh, Timur's son, and of Babur who conquered India, they sacrificed public security to private ambitions; each remained, in politics, what Timur himself had been, a freebooter in search of a kingdom. Timur, in founding an empire by this impulse, had delivered Oxiana from the nomads and brought the Turks of Central Asia within the orbit of Persian civilization. His descendants, by the same impulse, undid this work and destroyed themselves. They recognized no law of succession. They murdered their cousins, and boast among them one parricide. One after another they drank themselves to death. Yet if pleasure was the object of their lives, these princes believed the arts to be the highest form of pleasure, and their subjects followed their example; so that to be a gentleman was to be, if not an artist oneself, at least a devotee of the arts. When the famous minister Ali Shir Nevai records of Shah Rukh, that though he did not write poetry, he often quoted it, there is an accent of surprise on the first part of the statement. Their taste was inventive. They sent to China for new ideas in painting. Not content with classical Persian, they wrote in Turki as well, a more forcible medium of expression, such as Dante, not content with Latin, found in Italian. Among the gifts of the age was an instinct for biographical detail. Though its chronology is insupportable, a tedious record of intrigue and civil war, the actors are flesh and blood. Their characters correspond with our own acquaintance. We know very often, from portraits, how they looked, dressed, and sat. And the monuments they built have a similar impress. There is a personal idiosyncrasy about them which tells of that rare phenomenon in Mohammadan history, an age of humanism.

Judged by European standards, it was humanism within limits. The Timurid Renascence, like ours, took place in the fifteenth century, owed its course to the patronage of princes, and preceded the emergence of nationalist states. But in one respect the two movements differed. While the European was largely a reaction against faith in favour of reason, the Timurid coincided with a new consolidation of the power of faith. The Turks of Central Asia had already lost contact with Chinese materialism; and it was Timur who led them to the acceptance of Islam, not merely as a religion, for that was already accomplished, but as a basis of social institutions. Turks, in any case, are not much given to intellectual speculation. Timur's descendants, in diverting the flow of Persian culture to their own enjoyment, were concerned with the pleasures of this world, not of the next. The purpose of life they left to the saints and theologians, whom they endowed in life and commemorated in death. But the practice of it, inside the Mohammadan framework, they conducted according to their own common sense, without prejudice or sentiment except in favour of a rational intelligence.

The quality of mind thus fostered is preserved in the Memoirs of Babur, which were written in Turki at the beginning of the sixteenth century and have been twice translated into English. They show a man as concerned with day-to-day amenities, conversation, clothes, faces, parties, music, houses, and gardens, as with the loss of a princedom in Oxiana and the acquisition of an empire in India; as interested in the natural world as the political, and so remarking such facts as the distance swum by Indian frogs; and as honest about himself as others, so that in this picture of himself – so real that even in translation one can almost hear him speak – he has left a picture of his whole line. Born in the sixth generation after Timur, it was not until the end of his life that he conquered India and became the first Mogul. Even that was only second best, after he had spent thirty years trying to re-establish himself in Oxiana. But as a man of taste he did what he could to make life possible in so odious a country, and his comments on it show the standards he aspired to. He thought the Indians ugly, their conversation a bore, their fruit tasteless, and their animals ill-bred; 'in handicraft and work there is no form or symmetry, method or quality... for their buildings they study neither elegance nor climate, appearance nor regularity'. He de-nounces their habits as Macaulay denounced their learning, or as Gibbon denounced the Byzantines, by the light of a classical tradition. And since that tradition, after the Uzbeg conquest of Oxiana and Herat, was extinguished elsewhere, he set about implanting it anew. He and his successors changed the face of India. They gave it a lingua franca, a new school of painting and a new architecture. They revived again that theory of Indian unity which was to become the basis of British rule. Their last emperor died in exile at Rangoon in 1862, to make way for Queen Victoria. And the posterity of Timur survives to this day, in poverty and pride, among the laby-rinths of Delhi.

To return to my hotel in the coppersmiths' bazaar, where Babur, in Mrs Beveridge's translation, occupies the table and I am in my flea-bag on the floor. Herat lies midway between the two halves of Timur's empire, Persia and Oxiana; and of the two roads that join them, it commands the easier, the one that I shall take; for the other, via Merv, is desert and waterless. Geographically, therefore, it was more suited to be capital than Samarcand; and on Timur's death, in 1405, Shah Rukh made it so. Politically, culturally, and commercially it became the metropolis of middle Asia. Embassies came to it from Cairo, Constantinople, and Pekin; Bretschneider in *Mediaeval Researches from Eastern Asiatic Sources* gives the Chinese descriptions of it. After the twenty years' confusion that followed Shah Rukh's death in 1447, it was taken by Hussein Baikara, a descendant of Timur's son Omar Sheikh. And he gave it peace for another forty years. This was the summer of the Renas-cence, when Mirkhond and Khondemir were writing their histories, Jami was singing, Bihzad painting, and Ali Shir Nevai was the champion of literary Turki. It was the Herat of this epoch, when the Uzbegs were on the march and Samarcand had already fallen, that Babur saw as a young man. 'The whole habitable world,' he recalls afterwards, 'had not such a town as Herat had become under Sultan Hussein Mirza... Khorasan, and Herat above all, was filled with learned and matchless men. Whatever work a man took up, he aimed and aspired to bring it to perfection.'

Babur was here for three weeks in the autumn of 1506. He may have had the same sort of weather: crisp, sunny days growing shorter and colder. Every day he rode out sight-seeing. This morning I followed him and looked at the buildings he looked at. There is not much left. Seven minarets and a broken mausoleum are all my portrait of the age. But their history supplies the rest, and for this I must turn to later writers, soldiers and archaeologists. Two in particular have guided my curiosity here.

There was a long interval before they came; for the light of the Timurid Renascence went out in 1507, when Herat fell to the Uzbegs. Babur, seeing that it would, had removed himself, and vents his annoyance by recording how Shaibani, their leader, was so puffed up of his own culture that he presumed to correct Bihzad's drawing. Three years later it was taken by Shah Ismail and joined to his new Persia. The shadows deepen. A last flicker of the old splendour greets the arrival of Humayun, Babur's son, on his way from India to visit Shah Tahmasp at Isfahan in 1544. Three hundred years later, the curtains lifts on the fragments of Nadir Shah's empire and the military travellers of the nineteenth century.

Several British officers visited Herat in the early part of that century. One of them, Eldred Pottinger, organized the town's defences against a Persian army in 1838 and has become the hero of a novel by Maud Diver; not a bad one either, if you like the Flora Annie Steel school of fiction. Another was Burnes, later assassinated in Kabul, whose Indian secretary, Mohun Lal, published a notice of the monuments in the *Journal of the Bengal Asiatic Society* for 1834. There was also Ferrier, a French soldier of fortune, who in 1845 made two attempts to reach Kabul in disguise and was eventually turned back. He too sits on my table, though the weight of the book has hardly been worth the confusion. Then, in the middle of the century came two scholars, the Hungarian Vambéry and the Russian Khanikov. The authenticity of Vambéry's journey to Bokhara has often been doubted; certainly his description of Herat contains nothing he could not have gleaned from such officers as Conolly and Abbott. Khanikov is almost equally disappointing. Though he was in Herat a whole winter, his account in the *Journal Asiatique* of 1860 contains only a few inscriptions and a plan.

In 1885 the military come to the rescue after all. Russian troops were massing on the north-west frontier of Afghanistan, and the Government of India could not stop them because neither it nor the Afghans knew where the frontier was. A joint commission was arranged between the two powers to settle it, whose historians, on the English side, were two brothers, A. C. and C. E. Yate. Travelling through what was then almost unknown country, they reported on everything with soldierly precision, and the latter devotes a chapter to the antiquities of Herat as if they were a new field gun – though he was by no means insensible to their beauty. He is the first of my two main guides, and I have transferred him from the table to my lap.

The second is also a soldier, if the word can be applied to a man who tries to make a war single-handed. In the autumn of 1914 a small body of Germans assembled in Constantinople on their way to make trouble for the British in Asia. Some stayed in Persia, among whom was Christopher's hero Wassmuss. Some went on to Afghanistan, and how well the latter succeeded was proved by Amanullah's attack on India in 1919, a year too late. Among these was Herr Oskar von Niedermayer. In 1924 his photographs of the country were published as a picture book. To this Professor Ernst Diez contributed a preface, in which, by collating Niedermayer's photographs with historical and travellers' references, he identifies and dates most of the buildings here. Diez is an old acquaintance; I started out from Teheran with his *Churasanische Baudenkmäler*, a gigantic quarto whose weight probably broke the Morris's axle. Niedermayer I did not know. By good luck I found his book in the Consulate at Meshed, when I called to leave the other Diez behind, lest it should expose Noel's Rolls to a like fate.

Enough of this for the moment. The local doctor has called.

A friendly Punjabi, in the Afghan medical service. He came for news and to practise his English. I told him of my interview with the Governor, remarking that it was pleasant to escape from Persian suspicions into this freer atmosphere.

'You make large mistake, sir, when you think there are no suspicions here. It is all suspicions. I tell you, sir, Persia cannt compare with Afghanistan in this respect. At the present time, twenty foreigners reside in this town, Indians and Russians. About one hundred and twenty agents are employed to watch them. You suppose they do not watch you? Downstairs they watch you now. I see them. They see me. They watch me all the time. They will report immediately that I have ascended to your room. Also the Russians watch you, I expect. Undoubtedly they are curious for your movements here. They are in everything here. I tell you for certain they control the post office. In the beginning of this year I wrote a letter to a relative in England, in which by chance I referred to the Russian railway at Kushk and the distance from here. Yes, it is only eighty miles away. The next time I visited the Russian Consulate, professionally of course, they said to me straight out: "Why do you give away this kind of informations? You have no business." They were not pretending to hide that they had read my letter. So I have not written any letters since then at all.

'It is bad time to be here, sir, in Afghanistan. There will be trouble now King Nadir Shah is murdered. In one month there will be trouble. Or perhaps in the spring, when the tribes can move better in the mountains. But I think in one month. Do what you want here, sir, quickly. See what you want. Then clear out, double time. I go on leave now. When I can arrange lorry, I and my family go. We go to Kandahar, and then to my home in Lahore. This is a bad country, sir. I hope I will not return ever.'

Herat, 23 November Keeping my two guides in my head, I walked up the northern of the four New Town roads in the direction of a gigantic mound, about 600 yards long, which appears to be artificial and must resemble, from all accounts, the mounds in the neighbourhood of Balkh. Hence one can climb up on to another wall, an outwork of the town's defences, and survey the lie of the Musalla. This is the popular name for the whole of the seven minarets and the mausoleum. But actually they were part of separate buildings built at different times, some in the reign of Shah Rukh, one in that of Hussein Baikara.

*

All the minarets are between 100 and 130 feet high. They lean at various angles; their tops are broken, their bases twisted and eaten away. The furthest distance between them, stretching from west-south-west to east-north-east is about a quarter of a mile. The two on the west are fatter than the others, but like the four on the east have one balcony each. The middle one, which stands by itself, has two balconies. The mausoleum lies between the two on the west, but to the north of them. It is only half their height, but from a distance seems less.

This array of blue towers rising haphazard from a patchwork of brown fields and yellow orchards has a most unnatural look. The monarchs of Islam in early days had a habit of putting up isolated minarets, singly or in pairs: witness the Kutb at Delhi and the base of its fellow. But this did not extend till the fifteenth century, and never to such a number as seven. However, it can be seen from the insides of these minarets, where the tilework stops short some forty feet from the ground, that they were originally joined by walls or arches and must have formed part of a series of mosques or colleges. What has happened to these buildings? Things on this scale may fall down, but they leave some ruin. They don't vanish of their own accord without trace or clue, as these have done.

It is a miserable story. Even Yate, who saw it happen, betrays an unsoldierly sigh. Ferrier thought these buildings, ruined as they then were, the finest in Asia. The other travellers concur in their extraordinary beauty, the radiance of their mosaic and the magnificence of their gilt inscriptions. Conolly, if I remember right, speaks of thirty minarets. In fact, allowing for the difference between English prose and Persian, his description is not unlike Khondemir's of the buildings in their prime.

In the seventies and eighties Herat was incessantly on English lips. It even crops up in Queen Victoria's letters. If the Russians took it, as they were expected to do, the low-lying Kandahar road would be theirs for a railway to the Indian border. In 1885 the Panjdeh incident occurred. Though St Petersburg had already agreed to the joint Boundary Commission, Russian troops attacked the Afghans south-east of Merv and drove them back. An advance on Herat was expected any day, and the Emir Abdurrahman sent orders that the town was to be placed in a state of defence. The Russians would approach from the north. All buildings, therefore, that might give them cover on this side of the town must be demolished. For years officers of the Indian Army had been advising on such measures. I suspect this particular order was on British inspiration; though proof must wait till the archives of Delhi and the War Office give up their dead. In any case the most glorious productions of Mohammadan architecture in the fifteen century, having survived the barbarism of four centuries, were now razed to the ground under the eyes, and with the approval, of the English Commissioners. Nine minarets and the mausoleum escaped.

Even this epitaph of an epitaph is insecure. Two minarets have already disappeared since Niedermayer was here. They fell during an earthquake in 1931, which also destroyed a second domed mausoleum photographed by him. I saw the site of it yesterday, near the fork of the roads to Kushk and the Persian frontier: a mound of rubble. Unless repairs are done and foundations strengthened, the other monuments will soon be rubble too.

However, there is enough left, and enough information, to show how the buildings stood up to 1885.

The minarets that fell down the year before last were a pair to the two fat ones on the west. Together, the four marked the corners of a mosque. This was the real Musalla. According to an inscription on one of the minarets, which Niedermayer photographed and which must have perished in the earthquake, it was built, at her private expense, by Gohar Shad Begum, the wife of Shah Rukh, son of Timur, between the years 1417 and 1437. The architect, in all probability, was Kavamad-Din of Shiraz, who served Shah Rukh in that capacity during the greater part of his reign, and is mentioned by the historian Daulat Shah as one of the four great lights of his court.

Diez, who knows the subject as well as anyone, and is not the slave of his journey's emotions like me, says these minarets are adorned with such 'fabulous richness and subtle taste' ('märchenhafter Pracht und subtilem Geschmack') that no others in Islam can equal them. He speaks from photographs only. But no photograph, nor any description, can convey their colour of grape-blue with an azure bloom, or the intricate convolutions that make it so deep and luminous. On the bases, whose eight sides are supported by white marble panels carved with a baroque Kufic, yellow, white, olive green and rusty red mingled with the two blues in a maze of flowers, arabesques and texts as fine as the pattern on a teacup. The shafts above are covered with small diamond-shaped lozenges filled with flowers, but still mainly grape-blue. Each of these is bordered with white faience in relief, so that the upper part of each minaret seems to be wrapped in a glittering net.

In point of decoration minarets are generally the least elaborate parts of a building. If the mosaic on the rest of the Musalla surpassed or even equalled what survives today, there was never such a mosque before or since.

Yet I don't know. Gohar Shad built another mosque, inside the shrine at Meshed. This mosque is still intact. I must see it somehow if I come back this way.

Looked at in detail, the decoration of the mausoleum is inferior to that of the two minarets. The drum of the dome is encircled with tall panels filled with hexagons of lilac mosaic combined with triangles of raised stucco. The dome itself is turquoise, and the ribs, like those of Timur's mausoleum at Samarcand, are scattered with black and white diamonds. Each rib is three-quarters in the round and as fat as a 64-foot organ-pipe. The walls below are bare, but for a few glazed bricks and a peculiar three-windowed bay that reminds one of a villa in Clapham. But the quality of these separate elements, if sometimes coarse, is transcended by the goodness of their proportions and the solidity of the whole idea. Few architectural devices can equal a ribbed dome for blind, monumental ostentation.

This too seems to have been the work of Gohar Shad. Babur speaks of her three buildings: her mosque, which is the Musalla; her Madrassa or college; and her mausoleum. And Khondemir states several times that the mausoleum was inside the college. She was certainly buried in the mausoleum; Yate noted the inscription on her tombstone. He also noted those on five others, all of Timurid princes. Twenty-five years earlier Khandikov had noted nine altogether. Now there are only three, of a matt black stone, shaped like oblong boxes and carved with flower designs. One is smaller than the others.

Next, on the east of the mausoleum, stands the solitary minaret with two balconies. The origin of this baffles me. Its ornament of blue lozenges, jewelled with flowers but separated by plain brickwork, is not to be compared with that of the Musalla minarets. Perhaps it was part of Gohar Shad's college. A college would naturally be more sober than a mosque. Babur speaks as if college, mosque, and mausoleum were all close together.

I feel some curiosity about Gohar Shad, not on account of her piety in endowing religious foundations, but as a woman of artistic instinct. Either she had that instinct, or she knew how to employ people who had it. This shows character. And besides this, she was rich. Taste, character, and riches mean power, and powerful women, apart from charmers, are not common in Mohammadan history.

Four minarets remain, near the bridge over a winding canal. They too are girt with a white network; though their blue is brighter than that of the Musalla minarets, so that from close at hand it seems as if one saw the sky through a net of shining hair and as if it had been planted, suddenly, with flowers. These mark the corners of the College of Hussein Baikara, who ruled Herat from 1469 to 1506. His grandfather's tombstone, of the same type as those in the mausoleum but known as the Stone of the Seven Pens from its more profuse carving, lies close by and is still revered as a popular shrine.

The lyrical and less stately beauty of these minarets reflects the reign that produced it. Unlike Gohar Shad, Hussein Baikara is more than a name. His body at least is familiar. Bihzad drew it. Babur described it, and his amusements as well. He had slant eyes, a white beard, and a slender waist. He dressed in red and green. Ordinarily he wore a small lambskin cap. But on feast-days he would 'sometimes set up a threefold turban, wound broad and badly, and stick a heron's plume in it and so go to prayers'. This was the least he could do; for towards the end of his life he was so crippled with rheumatism that he could not perform the prayers properly. Like small people, he enjoyed flying pigeons, and matching fighting cocks and fighting rams. He was also a poet, but published his verses anonymously. To meet he was cheerful and pleasant, but immoderate in temper and loud-spoken. In love, orthodox and unorthodox, he was insatiable. He had innumerable concubines and children who destroyed the peace of the state and his old age. As a result 'what happened with his sons, the soldiers and the town was that everyone pursued vice and pleasure to excess'.

Babur was not a puritan. But the parties in Herat obliged him to get drunk. And in explaining how this happened, for the first time in his life, he reveals the effect of such an atmosphere on a young man's equilibrium. Nevertheless, looking back to Herat when he himself had become great, he still writes with deference, as one has seen a great age, and having learned how to live, has seen it vanish – like Talleyrand. The humanism of that age was the model of his life. His achievement in history was to replant it, and leave descendants to cherish it, amid the drab heats and uncouth multitudes of Hindostan.

The Mudir-i-Kharija tells me a lorry is leaving for Andkoi in four days' time. This will mean finding another from there to Mazar-i-Sherif. He adds that the road from Turkestan to Kabul is excellent, and that the post-lorries are still running.

The Imperial Bank of Persia in Meshed gave me rupee drafts on its branch in Bombay to use in Afghanistan. This morning I went to change one with the Shirkat Asharmi, the newly established State Trading Company. No one in the office could read the draft or even its figures. But they took my word for its being worth 100 rupees, and after discovering, apparently by telepathy, the current rate of exchange in Kandahar, counted out 672 silver coins each the size of a shilling. These I took away in two sacks, plodding through the bazaar crowds like a millionaire in a cartoon.

Herat 24 November   Local suspicion came out into the open today.

I have mentioned the Citadel of Ikhtiar-ad-Din on the north of the walls. It was built originally by the Kart Maliks of the fourteenth century, presumably when they threw off their allegiance to the Mongols. The revival of Persian nationalism denoted by this act was short-lived. At the end of the century another wave poured out of Central Asia; the armies of Timur destroyed both the Karts and their castle. Later, Shah Rukh found he needed a castle. In 1415 he put 7000 men to the work of rebuilding the old one, and the political history of Herat has revolved round it ever since. It is now the seat of the Commander-in-Chief and garrison.

The north face consists of a massive rampart nearly a quarter of a mile long and bulging at intervals into semicircular towers, of which the westernmost has a pattern of blue bricks set in its mud surface: an unusual combination of materials suggesting that this tower, if any, may date from Shah Rukh's restoration. When I had examined it, I walked back to the furthest corner of the walled parade-ground that separates the citadel from the New Town, to take a photograph. This led me near to an artillery park of about twenty guns, which might have been mistaken, at a distance, for a dump of dismantled perambulators. I then went back to the hotel to fetch some chalks with which to copy a Kufic inscription at the bottom of the tower. Simultaneously, the old fellow appointed by the Mudir-i-Kharija to look after me went off to his lunch.

When he came back, I said we must return to the citadel for the inscription. He replied that the parade-ground was shut.

'Shut, do you say? We were there an hour ago.'

'Yes, we were, but now it is shut.'

'All right, we will go tomorrow instead.'

'It will be shut tomorrow too.'

'In that case I shall go at once.'

And I set off at a fast pace, while the old fellow lumbered after me protesting. As I expected, the gate of the parade ground was still wide open. But on a whisper from my attendant, the sentry fetched me out. I argued that the Governor himself had told me I could visit the citadel. Never mind, said the old fellow, these were the Mudir Sahib's orders.

Back in the hotel I found the doctor. He was on his way to the citadel, to attend the Commander-in-Chief. Half an hour later he returned with an officer, who said the Commander-in-Chief saw no objection to my copying the inscription. He would accompany me.

I now kept my eyes off the artillery park in order not to embarrass him. But my fancy lusted after it. I held the secret of a formidable armament, capable of withstanding, or worse, expediting, an advance of the Soviet army on India. I saw myself earning the VC and probably a seat in the Cabinet, by reporting its existence.

It was interesting to discover, from personal experience, how spies find their vocation.

There is a cab rank outside the parade ground. As we came out, two young horses reared forward, dragging no gossamer chariot but a thundering blue landau blazoned with the royal arms of Persia and quilted inside with sky-blue satin. Seated in this equipage, the old fellow and I drove out to the shrine of Gazar Gah, which stands on the first slopes of the mountains to the north-east of the town.

Everyone goes to Gazar Gah. Babur went. Humayun went. Shah Abbas improved the water supply. It is still the Heratis' favourite resort, and their greatest pride in face of visitors. There are three enclosures. The first contains a grove of umbrella-pines and a decagonal pavilion of two storeys for picnics. The second is surrounded by irregular buildings; in the middle is a pool shaded by mulberries and rose bushes. The third is oblong in shape and filled entirely with graves, among which is that of the Emir Dost Mohammad. At the further end rises a tall arch in a wall eighty feet high, an ivan properly called, whose interior mosaic shows Chinese influence. In front of this, beneath an old ilex tree, lies the tomb of the saint. Its headstone, of white marble, is inscribed with his history, to which legends have been added.

Khoja Abdullah Ansari died in the year 1088 at the age of eighty-four, because some boys threw stones at him while he was at penance. One sympathizes with those boys: even among saints he was a prodigious bore. He spoke in the cradle; he began to preach at fourteen; during his life he held intercourse with 1000 sheikhs, learnt 100,000 verses by heart (some say 1,200,000) and composed as many more. He doted on cats. Shah Rukh conceived a particular devotion for him, and rebuilt the shrine in its present form in 1428. This was the period of the Chinese embassies, which may account for the patterns in the ivan. Later in the century some of the lesser Timurids, for whom there was no room in the mausoleum, were buried here. Khanikov noted five of their tombs, including that of Mohammad-al-Muzaffar, brother of Hussein Baikara, whose inscription, rejecting funerary platitudes, informs posterity that he was murdered by his cousin Mohammad, son of Baisanghor. In the cells that line the side arcades I found one royal tomb of black stone, even better carved, on three different planes, than the Stone of the Seven Pens. I could not identify the others.

In the south-east corner of the middle court stands a domed pavilion, which is painted inside with gold flowers on a lapis ground. Attached to this painting Ferrier observed the signature of Giraldi, an Italian painter employed by Shah Abbas. This again I could not find.

*

On the way home the landau stopped at Takh-i-Safar, 'the Travel-ler's Throne', a terraced garden all in ruins, whose natural melan-choly was increased by the close of an autumn afternoon and the first whistle of the night wind. From the empty tank at the top a line of pools and watercourses descends from terrace to terrace. This pleasaunce of Hussein Baikara was built by forced labour; for when his subjects overstepped even his broad limits of the morally permissible, they had to help with the Sultan's garden instead of going to prison. Up till the last century there was a pavilion here, and the water was still running; Mohun Lal mentions a great foun-tain, 'which with its watery arrows fights with the top of the build-ing'. What a phrase! But Mohun Lal, though he apologizes for his English to the editor of the *Bengal Journal*, sometimes wrote very well. It would be hard to improve his description of Yar Moham-mad, the then ruler of Herat: 'He is a gloomy and decrepit prince; he excites the pity of mankind.'

A Hungarian has arrived here. He has just spent a month in hospital at Kandahar, and his stomach is still so deranged that he cannot eat. In fact he is starving to death. I gave him some soup and ovaltine which cheered him up and made him talk in bad French.

'Five years, monsieur, I have been travelling. I shall travel five years more. Then perhaps I shall write something.'

'You like travelling?'

'Who could like travelling in Asia, monsieur? I had a good education. What would my parents say if they saw me in such a place as this? It is not like Europe. Beyrut is like Europe. Beyrut I could support. But this country, these people ... the things I have seen! I cannot tell you of them. I cannot. Aaaaah!' And overcome by the recollection of them, he buried his head in his hands.

'Come, monsieur,' I said, giving him a gentle pat, 'confide in me these terrible experiences. You will feel better for it.'

'I am not the type, monsieur, who thinks himself superior to the rest of humanity. Indeed I am no better than others. Perhaps I am worse. But these people, these Afghans, they are not human. They are dogs, brutes. They are lower than the animals.'

'But why do you say that?'

'You don't see why, monsieur? Have you eyes? Look at those men over there. Are they not eating with their hands? With their *hands*! It is frightful. I tell you, monsieur, in one village I saw a madman, and he was naked ... naked.'

He was silent for a little. Then he asked me in a solemn voice: 'You know Stambul, monsieur?'

'Yes.'

'I lived in Stambul a year, and I tell you, monsieur, it is a hell from which there is no way out.'

'Really. But you, since you are here, did you find a way out?'

'Thank God, monsieur, I did.'

Herat, 25 November   I ought to have left today.

It rained in the night and was still raining this morning. Nevertheless I packed, and sat in my room till twelve, when general opinion decided the lorry would not start. Having unpacked, I went to the Masjid-i-Juma.

Masjid-i-Juma means Friday Mosque. Every town has one. It corresponds to a parish church or metropolitan cathedral according to the size of the place, and is generally the oldest, and often the biggest building there. As in a European town, whose abbey or cathedral still proclaims the Middle Ages, while the rest has changed with the times, so in Herat this morose old mosque inside the walls growls a hoary accompaniment to the Timurid pageant of the suburbs. The glories of that pageant grew up overnight; they commemorate extraordinary individuals; they flowered and they fell. The Friday Mosque was old and ruined before the Timurids were heard of. It is less ruined now they are not heard of. For seven centuries the people of Herat have prayed in it. They still do so, and its history is their history.

I emerged from the gloomy labyrinths of the old town into a flagged court 100 yards long by 65 broad. Four ivans, vaulted open-fronted halls, break the four arcaded sides. The main ivan, on the west, is attended by two massive towers with blue cupolas. But for these, and a leaning umbrella-pine in one corner, there is no colour; only whitewash, bad brick, and broken bits of mosaic. A square pool reflects a mullah and his pupils, who pass all dressed in white. Silence and sunshine give peace to the worn pavement. It was peace I wanted. Curse the lorry and my doubts about the journey. I forgot them.

The mosque was founded in 1200 by Ghiyas-ad-Din, son of Sam, of the Ghorid dynasty, who made Herat his capital after the break-up of the Ghaznavide Empire, and is commemorated in the bottom inscription of the Kutb Minar at Delhi. The arcades are his, intersecting corridors of pointed arches ten deep or more; also, I imagine, a Kufic legend in fancy brick over an arch in the north-east corner, which gives a clue to the original ornament. Near this stands Ghiyas-ad-Din's mausoleum, a square annexe to the mosque, whose dome has entirely collapsed. There are graves among the rubble, but no stones or inscriptions.

This remained the royal mausoleum till the coming of the Timurids. Rulers of the Kart dynasty were buried here, and in the fourteenth century they replastered the walls, incising the surface with squiggles to look like ye olde bryckeworke. They also put up an inscription round the inside of the main ivan, using a curious brambly Kufic which they seem to have borrowed from Ghazni in another fit of conscious antiquarianism.

Behind the main ivan, as might be expected, there used to stand a sanctuary chamber which became unsafe and was pulled down by Ali Shir Nevai in 1498. After the princes themselves, Ali Shir was the pattern of the Timurid Renascence, alike in his manners and his actions. He had stood by Hussein Baikara in his early days, and rose to fortune with him. But having neither wife nor children to stimulate ambition, he resigned power for the arts. 'No such patron,' says Babur, 'or protector of men of parts and accomplishments is known, nor has one such been heard of as appearing.' He rescued Hussein Baikara from Shi'ism; yet that he was of a rational mind is illustrated by his contempt for astrology and superstition. His fortune was devoted to public works. In Khorasan alone he built 370 mosques, colleges, caravanserais, hospitals, reading-halls, and bridges. He collected a vast library, which he placed at the disposal of the historian Mirkhond. 'In music also,' Babur adds, 'he composed some good things, some excellent airs and preludes.' The people of Herat held him in such esteem that commercial inventions were named after him, including a new saddle and handkerchief, as biscuits were named after Garibaldi. Among scholars he is remembered for his championship of the Turki language as a literary medium, and his defence of it against Persian ridicule. He died in 1501. Babur, five years later, stayed in his house.

Towards the end of his life, seeing the old Friday Mosque in ruins, and conscious of its historical importance, he got permission of the Sultan to restore it. The work was carried out in feverish haste, while he himself superintended it, with his robe tucked up and trowel in hand. On top of the arcades a screen-wall was added, pierced by arches corresponding with those below; and the surface of the two, as it faced the court, was unified by a coating of mosaic. Such at least was the plan. It was never completed, and survives intact only in the south-west corner. A new sanctuary was also built, and was embellished, according to Khondemir, with Chinese designs. This has entirely disappeared.

One other relic of the Timurids is preserved in the mosque: a bronze cauldron some four feet in diameter, covered with arabesques and inscriptions in relief. A similar cauldron was cast by order of Timur for the Mosque of Hazrat Yassavi in Turkestan City, where it still is.* The one at Herat, which is kept in a hutch on the steps of the main ivan, finds mention in the descriptions of the Chinese embassies.

On Friday 21 February 1427, Shah Rukh suffered an attempt on his life in this mosque, and his escape was the salvation of the Empire for another twenty years. The same day of the week and the same spot have just witnessed the frustration of another plot to upset the existing government.

Two days ago officials of the Russian Consulate spread a rumour in the bazaar that the new king had been assassinated as well as the old, their purpose being to foment a disturbance in Amanullah's favour. In this they reckoned without the Governor, who detests Amanullah, and having suppressed a mutiny in his interest a year ago, is respected by the troops accordingly. The Russians no doubt thought that if they cast their bait on a Thursday afternoon, on Friday the people would have leisure to swallow it. As it turned out, they swallowed the Governor's instead. Addressing himself to the congregation in the Friday Mosque, Abdul Rahim Khan denied the rumour and assured them that in any case order would be main-

* It was removed to Leningrad for the Persian Exhibition in 1935, and will probably remain there.

tained. The last announcement depressed them. They cared nothing for the king, but were looking forward to a riot in which they could prosecute their quarrels and loot the Shiah merchants. This delightful dream is now postponed till the spring.

This afternoon a horde of turbaned infants dashed into my room, one carrying a hammer, another a nail, another a chisel, and put some glass in the windows. I wish they had come earlier. The lorry must surely go tomorrow if it keeps fine.

A message arrived from the Hungarian to say he was ill. Last night he had been as white as a ghost. Now I found him flushed with fever and being sick. His only protection from the floor was a small mat, and his only covering a threadbare rug. I dosed him as best I could, gave him a blanket and said he must see the doctor. After half an hour's argument in the kitchen, the doctor was sent for. The answer came back that he was asleep. I then went to see him myself, forced my way into his house with some trepidation lest his women should be without their veils, and persuaded him to come. He diagnosed the fever as malaria and said the patient must go to the hospital; in answer to which the patient called him an Indian fool and said he would not go to hospital. After three hours a man came to take him to the hospital. At the same moment orders arrived from the Mudir-i-Kharija that he must not go to the hospital until the doctor had written a formal note requesting his admission. I sent my old fellow to fetch this note. Then a Turk walked in to say that since the Mudir-i-Kharija had already left his office, no order of admission could be issued till tomorrow. I gave it up.

The Parsis say the Hungarian is absolutely without money, and that the Afghan authorities have to nourish and transport him at their own expense. He certainly bites the hand that feeds him. Apparently the British Legation in Kabul refused him a visa for India; quite rightly in the Parsis' opinion, who, though they are no great loyalists, disapprove of 'poor whites'. I have left him with a tin of soup-cubes and some cream cheese to help him on his journey back to Meshed.

Not knowing the Persian for hot-water bottle, I made the kitchen laugh tonight by asking for my khanum.

*

Herat. 26 November dawned cloudless and warm, an ideal day for the time of year. At nine o'clock I met the lorry driver, who said we should be starting at eleven. At eleven the lorry was loading petrol vats, and the driver's assistant told me to be ready at one. At one I had my luggage brought down, to learn that we should not start today. The other passengers all went back to their villages yesterday, owing to the rain, and have not reappeared.

As I shall probably be here for the rest of my life (which won't last long at this rate), I have had my room cleaned out. I must describe it, and indeed the whole hotel. Downstairs three large rooms with glass fronts give on to the street. The first is the kitchen, indicated by a pool of blood and a decapitated cock's head on the pavement. The second and third are filled with marble-topped tables, and hung with European scenes painted on glass by an Indian familiar with the early numbers of the *Illustrated London News*. Here too are Seyid Mahmud's desk, a cabinet gramophone on legs from Bombay, and a pile of Indian records. Adjoining the kitchen, an outside staircase leads up to a long corridor lit by skylights, which has rooms on either side. My room is at the back, where it avoids part of the coppersmiths' din: a square box, with a ceiling of bare poles and laths, white walls, and a sky-blue dado. The floor is paved with tiles, whose interstices secrete a cloud of dust and straw; half of it is covered with a carpet, and half the rest with my bedding and waterproof sheets. Two Windsor chairs and a table draped in white American cloth are the furniture. On the table stands a vase of blue and white spirals adorned with a pink glass rose – the kind you win at hoop-la – in which Seyid Mahmud has placed a tight round posy of yellow chrysanthemums enclosing a ring of chocolate-red ones enclosing a centre of yellow button daisies. A pewter basin and a graceful ewer enable me to wash on the bare part of the floor. My bedding consists of a green flea-bag, yellow sheepskin coat, and an Afghan quilt of scarlet chintz. Beside it, my lamp, Boswell, clock, cigarettes, and a plate of grapes are conveniently disposed on a dispatch-case. The khanum waits to be filled. I have had a nail put in for my ties, another for my hat, and a third for my looking-glass. If the door and the window were not opposite one another, if the door would shut and the window had its full complement of panes, I should be comfortable enough. But the draught is like a storm at sea. All the refuse goes out of the window into the garden of the Municipality.

I caught my breath just now as I stepped into the moonlit corridor. Four rifles menaced my stomach, aimed by four ghostly figures cloaked in white, who were squatting in the room opposite. I could see the glitter of their eyes in the dark beneath their dim white turbans. Four others had their backs to me and their rifles pointing out of the window. No doubt it was just a pleasant evening party. But the Muntazim-i-Telegraph had been croaking again this morning about the coming upheaval, and I wondered for a moment if Amanullah had actually arrived.

One monument here is even older than the Friday Mosque. Writing in the tenth century Mukadasi describes the Bridge of Malan, saying it was built by a Magian. For a thousand years it has carried the traffic to and from India over the Hari river. Today it still has 26 arches – there were 28 in Khondemir's time – and room for two lorries abreast. The arches are of different shapes, and since one or two generally collapse every year in the spring floods, the bridge must have been rebuilt many times over. But the piers probably rest on the old foundations.

The town is worth seeing from the south. As we drove back from the river in the blue landau, its grim grey battlements commanded plain and villages as though cannon were still in the future. There are three walls. The topmost is eighty feet high, and defended by a line of towers. The other two are pierced by a network of loopholes. Below them lies a broad reed-grown moat. Constantinople has the same system on the land side, except that there it is of stone, and here of mud.

On the road along the moat we met three gentlemen taking the air behind a high-stepping pony. They were seated on top of one another in a tiny brown governess cart, which bristled with enough weapons for a baronial hall.

Karokh (4400 ft), 28 November Instead of packing this morning, I settled down to read. The ruse succeeded: at one o'clock the lorry left. I nearly missed it.

A wide macadam road runs due east up the valley of the Hari river, on its way over the mountains to Bamian – though it has yet to arrive there. Thirteen miles down this, at the village of Pala Piri, we turned up a narrow track to the north. 'Ra Turkestan, Ra Turkestan,' cried the passengers in chorus. The road to Turkestan! It sounded too good to be true.

The next twenty miles involved repeated crossings of a river in a ravine, whose gradients, or rather the absence of them, showed that a motor can be as good as a mule if driven with enterprise. At half-past three we stopped for the night. A shrine stood near the road, screened by a grove of umbrella-pines, whose sweet smell has reminded me of the Pinetum at Ravenna. How vivid those memories of Italy remain! I might have been a dentist, or a public man, but for that first sight of a larger world. The inner court is planted with the same trees; *horhju* they are called. At the top of the avenue stands a demure arch, whose tin cupolas flashed us welcome from a distance. This marks the tomb of a Sheikh-al-Islam who was killed – beheaded they say – while fighting the Persians in 1807. His son Abul Kasim erected the shrine, and planted the trees, to his memory.

A range of buildings separates the two courts, in which we were allotted an upstairs room. The other passengers, who are soldiers, at once took advantage of this to exchange their uniforms for turbans, long coats and loose trousers. Disturbed by the rain of puttees and tunics, I ensconced my bedding on a balcony, and was unrolling it when a procession of portly middle-aged gentlemen entered the court below. Taking off their gowns and turbans, they stopped before a cleft tree, and each in turn tried to squeeze himself through it. Those that succeeded, I was told, might expect salvation hereafter. They were in a minority.

'Do you happen to have any arak with you?' whispered the gatekeeper when they had gone.

He led me up the avenue to the tomb. As I stood on the roof of the arch, watching the cranes wheel overhead and a ruddy glow suffuse the horizon of snow-covered mountains, another procession, portlier still, began to approach. At its head strode a lordly figure in black top-boots and a green quilted gown, beneath whose vast turban a white beard projected horizontally over a chest as big as a pouter pigeon's. 'The Hazrat Sahib,' vouchsafed the gate-keeper, 'comes to greet Your Excellency the Frankish traveller.'

'What big fish you have in the pond down there,' I opened politely.

'Those!' answered the Hazrat Sahib with contempt. 'You should see the ones in the madrassa.'

The people stood up and bowed as we walked in procession to the village school. Beneath a verandah hung with texts from the Koran sat a mullah in a ring of little boys, who were repeating their lessons to him. Willow trees and other groups were dotted round a square pond. The Hazrat Sahib called for bread and threw it on the water. A flock of ducks made a dash for it, but a shoal of leviathan carp rose to the surface and beat them off. The ducks went hungry.

The trunks of the pines throw long shadows across the moonlit avenue. A breeze stirs the flame inside the hurricane lantern. Nur Mohammad, a soldier who had attached himself to me, is asleep in a corner of the balcony. His head is on his rifle which is pointing at my nose. We have just had a feast; the Hazrat Sahib returned after dinner, preceded by a pewter tray of nuts and pomegranates. Tea followed him, in bowls instead of glasses, which made me feel nearer to China.

'What Government do you belong to?' asked the Hazrat Sahib.

'The Government of Inglistan.'

'Inglistan? What is that?'

'It is the same as Hindostan.'

'Is Inglistan part of Hindostan?'

'Yes.'

A caravan is coming up the road. Boom, boom, the bull-camel's bell fills the night. The treble bells grow louder in spite of Nur Mohammad's snores. My pen is making signs of its own. It is time to sleep.

Kala Nao (2900 ft), 30 November We arrived here at half-past nine this morning and have stopped to rest.

The road from Karokh proceeded over an undulating grass country, cleft by the river in its canyon. A tribe of Kazaks passed by, pudding-faced people riding horses, donkeys, and oxen. At a lonely caravanserai two lorries on their way down from Andkhoi gave us news of the road; it was not reassuring. At length the river, now reduced to a stream, led us into one of those endless twisting valleys where the spurs on either side project alternately, in the manner of two cogwheels. After twenty miles, we climbed out of this on the north. When we reached the snow-line, the lorry stopped, while the wheels went round like egg-whisks.

We were well prepared. Bunches of chains, three spades, a pick, and stout ropes to prevent the lorry falling over the edge, were quickly in action. The next mile took four hours. Some dug; some hung on to the ropes; some cast down branches of a peppermint-smelling herb as though before the Saviour's ass. The day was almost gone when a zigzag spurt and cheers brought us to the narrow saddle of the Sauzak pass.

Fifty miles away through the failing light stood the ramparts of the promised land: the Band-i-Turkestan, a flat-topped mountain wall reaching out towards the Hindu Kush. Plumes of golden cloud floated up the storm-stored sky. Sheaves and pinnacles of bare red rock kept guard over the pass itself. The moisture of its northern face was announced by juniper trees, solitary battered sentinels, converging into woods on the hummocks far below.

That moisture was the undoing of us. Beneath the snow, and after we had left it behind, the road was as greasy as vaseline, as steep as a scenic railway, and often not a yard wider than the lorry's wheel-base. In vain we tore down branches, clung to the ropes and piled up rocks at the hairpin corners. Indifferent to brake or steering-wheel, the lorry went its own way, lurching crabwise down the boulders, dangling its tyres over space, cannoning from cliff to cliff, while we stumbled after it through the dusk and the freezing slush. A shepherd hailed us from underneath. Beside him, in the moonlight, lay another lorry with its wheels in the air. By now our lights were failing. When at last we reached the open slopes, the driver could not drive, and we could not walk, any further.

Choosing a narrow defile, which compressed the wind to fury, the soldiers lit a fire. We had nothing to cook, and still worse, no water. I had been thirsty since the morning, and now drank a supply of white mud, melted snow, and oil, which was kept in a petrol tin for the radiator. The moon shone bright, the road was hard, the wind blew my blankets off; tramping up and down, the soldiers kept watch and sang to reassure themselves. I was bemoaning these obstacles to sleep when I woke up in daylight, having slept for ten hours.

The village we had hoped to reach that night was only a quarter of an hour away. Here we found two more lorries from Andkhoi. Their passengers were Jews, whom I recognized, by their oval faces, delicate features and conical fur-brimmed hats, as cousins of the Bokhara community. They too had slept in the open. But their trouble was worse than that, an exodus of some sort; several of the women beckoned me aside and started to mutter in Russian. When I said I did not understand this language, they were incredulous, pointing to my fair hair as a proof that I must be Russian. Our account of the pass reduced them to pitiable agitation. Mothers clasped their children; the old men rocked and moaned, combing their beards with grimy nails. Further on, we met another couple of lorries carrying more Jews at breakneck speed.

Kala Nao or 'New Castle' is a small market town of about 2000 inhabitants. At the end of its one broad street I found the Governor sitting in a ruined garden, while his horse, a grey stallion of nearly fifteen hands, pawed the derelict flower-beds. On seeing my letter from the Mudir-i-Kharija in Herat, he assigned me a room over-looking the street, where Nur Mohammad continues to attend me. 'Don't you bother about the price of chickens,' he says, 'you are a guest here.' This is courteous and friendly, but has prevented my buying two chickens, one of which I need for the journey tomorrow.

This afternoon Nur Mohammad and I walked a mile and a half back along the road we had come by to look at some caves in the hillside. Just below them, I was attacked by vertigo and had to go down again before I was marooned. Nur Mohammad completed the exploration, and assures me they contain neither paintings nor carvings.

The Governor's Secretary, wrapped in a purple fur-lined cloak and holding an electric torch, has just called, and has written a long sentence in this diary, for the privilege, as he put it, of using my beautiful fountain pen.

Kala Nao, 1 December   Another day of rest, but not so grateful.

A storm got up in the night, which blew with such force that the two doors on opposite sides of the room flew open with a crash, and I was almost swept off the floor. Thus woken, I found I was ill. There are no 'usual offices' in this establishment; the court at the back serves instead, for men and beasts alike. As I reached the outside staircase, I slipped. The lantern went out; my only garment, a mackintosh, flew over my head; and I found myself lying naked in a bed of snow and excrement, which clove to my body in the frost. For a moment I was too dazed to move. Something had broken: I had to feel if it was my skull or the bottom step. When I found it was the step, I chuckled aloud.

It is now snowing hard, and we cannot start.

The Governor's Secretary sent a messenger this morning to tell me, after a lot of circumlocution, that he would like my pen as a present. This I resisted. Later he came to ask for it in person. Seeing I ought to give him something, I sat him down and did his portrait in colours. He drew my attention to the fur-lined cloak, which I reproduced with exquisite care. This contented him.

All the Jews have come back; the four lorry-loads amount to over sixty people. In addition a party of Turcomans have arrived, whose women wear tall red head-dresses hung with cornelian-studded plaques of silver gilt. Owing to this influx, food is short. There is no fuel. And as I can only light the room by opening the doors, I have to keep warm by putting on all my clothes and staying in bed. The shops sell Russian cigarettes and Swan ink, neither of which is much comfort. But I have bought some home-knitted socks that would resist the North Pole.

Kala Nao, 2 December The people here now say that even if we do reach Turkestan, the road down to Kabul will be snow-bound. I might have seen this from the heights on the map. By horse the journey takes a month, and needs, I imagine, more money and equipment than I possess. I am also worried by the prospect of not being able to telegraph home for Christmas. Meanwhile the snow continues, and they have sent to Herat for horses, to fetch the Jews. Perhaps I ought to go back with them.

Even Nur Mohammad is depressed. He prays incessantly, and if I happen to be in the way, prostrates himself on top of me.

Kala Nao, 3 December   Diarrhoea has turned to dysentery. I must go back.

It may be cowardice. I prefer to call it common sense. In any case the difference is lost in the disappointment. However, I have discovered the journey can be done, which no one knew before.

The weather has cleared, which makes my resolve the more difficult. Lest it should break down, I took a stiff dose of whisky and waited on the Governor early. I found him in conclave, squatting by a brazier at the end of a long room. He felt my pulse, and said that I was not ill, while even if I was, he must telephone to Herat before he could give me a pass. For the moment the telephone was broken and anyhow there were no horses. This evening a message arrived to say that the telephone has been mended, that the pass is waiting, and that horses will be paraded for my inspection at eight o'clock tomorrow morning.

The lorry is leaving at 4 a.m. I might still go with it if I did not feel so weak.

Laman (4600 ft), 4 December   The village below the pass.

The horses were punctual. One could not put its near foreleg to the ground, and the other two resembled the mount of Death in the Apocalypse. My protests roused the Governor before he was dressed, and in order to spare himself any further breach of manners on my part, he offered me three government horses and a guide for £5. The money was well spent. In spite of my disorder, which delayed us every twenty minutes, we have done a double stage in half a day, and shall try to make Karokh tomorrow, though it is said to take thirteen hours.

Neither an Afghan saddle nor the pangs of starvation could spoil the beauty of our ride among the glistening silver hills. Where the ravines join the valley, Kazaks had taken up their winter quarters inside mud walls, which serve them year after year. Each encampment made a silhouette of low black domes against the white landscape. Generally a pack of snarling dogs came rushing down the slopes to greet us, among which the salukis were rugged as carefully as entrants for the Waterloo Cup. But at one camp two men stopped us. 'Where is your kibitka?' they asked.

'My what?'

'Your kibitka?'

'I don't understand.'

With expressions of contempt and irritation, they pointed to their own felt-and-wattle huts: 'Your kibitka – you must have a kibitka. Where is it?'

'In Inglistan.'

'Where is that?'

'In Hindostan.'

'Is that in Russia?'

'Yes.'

The people of this village are strangely disobliging. Eggs? Paraffin? Hay? They had nothing of the sort. I said I would pay. But seeing me accompanied by a government servant, they would not believe it. His authority evoked what we wanted in the end, and also a house for us to sleep in, which consists of four walls and a roof with a hole in it. Unfortunately, the smoke from the bonfire in the middle of the floor does not escape by this hole. But it is nice to be warm for a change. We are a party of seven.

My guide suspects the villagers of evil intentions towards us. I am not quite easy myself. There is a rent in the wall above me, which was stopped with a bit of rag. Suddenly, to my astonishment, the rag disappeared and a hand took its place, which came groping after my possessions. I told the guide, who seized his rifle and rushed outside. But there were no shots.

We have blocked the hole with a stone. Sleep I must. My mind is full of plans to do this journey in the summer. Perhaps Christopher will be able to come then.

Karokh, 6 December, 2.30 a.m. I rode nearly sixty miles today and have just got into bed with a cup of soup. The first cock is crowing.

*

Herat, 8 December What a day it was! God save me from any more adventures on a drained stomach.

Dawn had scarcely broken when we rode out of Laman to ascend the pass. The ghostly shapes of the junipers bobbed up and vanished in the grey mist. Snow muffled the horses' steps. At last the sun revealed the pinnacles above the pass, redder still against a blue sky and a white world. I looked goodbye to the Band-i-Turkestan, wondering if the lorry was already there, and deploring my irresolution. On the descent, the horses began to trot. In vain I tried to make mine pace; either it could not, or I had not the knack. If I rose in the stirrups, the wooden saddle tore my legs, despite its tasselled scarlet cloth. If I sat tight, easternwise, and jogged, the disturbance to my intestines was almost past bearing. I tried one, and then the other; I tried sitting forward on the pommel and back on the cantle; I tried sitting sideways; I considered turning round and facing the tail. But pain or no pain, I intended to reach Karokh that night, and so did the guide, since the people of Laman had prophesied that we should not. All the afternoon, after stopping to graze the horses, we plodded down that endless valley. Round the corner of each spur I expected to see the grass uplands; round each waited only another spur; and Karokh, I knew, was a long way from the opening of the valley. As the sun fell, I exchanged my horse for the guide's, which was saddled with a soft pack. At last we were out. Across the river in its canyon, the dank yellow uplands stretched away to ink-blue mountains streaked with snow and capped with leaden clouds. A white-cloaked shepherd with his flock, and the smoke of a distant village, gave human measure to their vast inhospitality. Down the canyon and up again. Down again and up. The guide was worried and urged me to canter.

The last glimmer of light had gone as we splashed through the river for the third time; neither moon nor stars replaced it. While lighting the lantern, we heard footsteps. The guide stiffened, but when they proved to be those of a single person, he spurred forward, brandishing his rifle and threatening to shoot the man for being out after dark. Eventually we came to a village. It was not Karokh, but Karokh Sar, and from here, the guide said, he knew a short cut. The path narrowed. We turned this way and that. We tried to retrace our steps. At last we were following a mere rabbit-run.

'Is this really the way to Karokh?' I asked for the tenth time.

'Yes, it is. I have told you again and again it is. You don't understand Persian.'

'How do you know it is?'

'I do know it is.'

'That is no answer. It is you who don't know Persian.'

'Oh, I don't know Persian, don't I? I don't know anything. I certainly don't know where this path goes.'

'Does it go to Karokh or does it not? Answer me, please.'

'I don't know. I don't know Persian. I don't know anything. You say Karokh, Karokh, Karokh. I don't know where Karokh is.'

And all of a sudden, sinking down upon the herbage, he put his head in his hands and groaned.

We were lost. It was a tiresome predicament in a country where personal safety ceases with the curfew. But it dispelled my pains like magic. I wondered for a minute if the guide had brought me to this pass for some purpose of his own. His moans contradicted the idea; he might be a robber, I thought unjustly, but not an actor. He would not even help me unload the luggage. Finally I shook him out of his despair and he consented to hobble the horses. Then he sank on to his tuft again, refused the food I offered him, and tried to refuse the blanket till I tied it round his shoulders. It was very cold; we were again in a thick damp cloud. I spread my own bedding, dined off some egg, sausage, cheese, and whisky, read a little Boswell, and fell fast asleep among the aromatic herbs with my money-bags between my feet and my big hunting knife unclasped in my fist.

At one o'clock I was woken by the moon, and saw that we had stopped on the very edge of the canyon. Far below, the river wound away like a silver snake. In front of us, about two miles off, appeared a dark patch which I recognized as the pine trees of Karokh.

It was a lucky glimpse. We had no sooner found the horses than the clouds closed in again. But the guide had taken his bearings, and an hour later we were knocking at a big caravanserai, which he said was more comfortable than the shrine. So it proved. I went to bed by myself in a spacious carpeted room, where I was roused, late next morning, by three bearded sages who had come to say their prayers and were not deterred from doing so by my inquisitive glances.

*

We reached Herat at four o'clock. Seyid Mahmud and his whole staff greeted me like a prodigal son. One spread carpets. Another brought water to wash with. The nails for my ties, looking-glass, and hat were replaced without my asking. There was a new pot of the jam I had liked so much, and tomorrow Seyid Mahmud promised a batch of sponge cakes.

Yes, the Indians had gone, and also the Hungarian. Some other Franks had come in the meantime, friends of mine he believed. Ah, here they were.

In the door stood the Charcoal-Burners.

'Hullo,' I said from my corner.
'YOU? er – Hullo.'
'I'm sorry I've finished the whisky.'
'Not at all.'
'On account of my health.'
'We heard you were ill.'
'Do you find it cold in Afghanistan?'
'The rain has inconvenienced us.'
'But you like the buildings, I hope.'
'Oh, charming.'

It was not the reunion we had imagined. Being ten days too late for Turkestan, they must now go south to Kandahar. They expect me to go with them.

A partridge for dinner brightened things up.

Herat, 11 December They have gone by themselves. Turkestan was my objective, not a charcoal demonstration. It still is. I shall go back to Persia and wait for the spring.

PERSIA: Meshed, 17 December A vile journey, which has knocked me up. Hence the interval.

Still, we were lucky in the weather. The road had just dried and the going was good. A party of pilgrims on their way to Nejef occupied the back of the lorry. Beside me in front sat a sanctimonious young seyid dressed in a black turban and brown camel's-hair cloak, who had come from Irak to see the cities of Islam and was now on his way to India, via Duzdab and Quetta. After sleeping at Islamkillah, the frontier post, we bumped across the twelve-mile strip of no-man's-land that separates the two countries, accompanied by flocks of marsh birds and their gloomy plaints. At Kariz, while the Persian customs delayed us, a German accosted me. He had just escaped from Russia, where he had been naturalized, and had walked this far on his way to India, only to be turned back by the Afghan authorities. His wife was ill in the village; they were penniless and desperate. I was fumbling for some money to give him, when he vanished in a fit of pride.

A pustule had developed on my thigh, which was now of such a size that the whole leg was swollen from the ankle to the groin; I could hardly walk. To drown the pain, I ordered some arak, at which the seyid protested a theatrical horror. Pussyfooting in Persia was no business of his, I thought. Whisking out the cork, I thrust the mouth of the bottle into his beard. He fled like a raped nun; but in the lorry there was no escape. Whenever the bottle appeared, he swooned on to the steering-wheel as though overcome by the fumes, calling on God and the driver to avenge the impiety. The driver laughed. God took no action till Turbat-i-Sheikh Jam, where we arrived at midnight.

Here, as I was unloading my luggage in the caravanserai, some soldiers stole my saddle-bags. Thinking their door was locked, I launched myself against it with all the strength of my sound leg. But it wasn't, and the vigour of my entry sent four of them sprawling, including one whose behind, as he bent over the loot, unexpectedly met my knee. The rest were furious, and chased me, still hopping like a locust, to the kitchen, where the crowd laughed them to shame. I then asked where I could sleep, and was shown ceremoniously to the edge of a mat near the stove already occupied by five others. Taking a teapot of hot water, I sought a ruin across the court, where I poulticed my leg in peace; three separate draughts froze the bandage to my flesh. 'Is it comfortable here?' asked the seyid, creeping up behind me with a white bundle in his arms. I exorcised him with the arak bottle.

No pilgrim was ever so glad as I to see the domes of Meshed. Mrs

Hamber, at the Consulate, had asked me to stay if I came back; I had no strength to pretend hesitation. My leg was cupped at the American hospital. Next morning, waking up to find clean sheets against my chin and breakfast on a tray, I wondered at a forgotten world.

Meshed, 21 December Energy and good spirits are returning – mainly thanks to *Anna Karenina*, which I had not read before. My leg is so reduced that I can dress it myself. This saves me the intimacies of the hospital. Yesterday, while I was in the room, one man had seven teeth removed without anaesthetic, while another was being examined for cancer in the testicles.

People who abuse missionaries have not seen their medical work. The whole health of Khorasan depends on them. For this, not for their conversions, the authorities hate and hamper them; there is nothing to be jealous of in a religion which has no more appeal here than a Mohammadan mission would have in Rome. The Persians have a talent for cutting off their nose to spite their face. They stopped the Junkers air service because it exhibited foreign superiority. They make roads, but their customs duties prohibit the import of motors. They want a tourist traffic, but forbid photographing because somebody once published a picture of an Iranian beggar, while conformity with their police regulations is a profession in itself, as I have discovered in the last day or two. Indeed Marjoribanks-land ablaze with Progress offers a depressing contrast with Afghanistan. I am reminded of the hare and the tortoise.

Meshed, 24 December—Mrs Hamber has gone to India. Hamber has most kindly asked me to keep him company for Christmas.

Every morning I take a two-horse cab to the shrine of Khoja Rabi, where I sit and draw, at peace with the world, as long as the short winter days allow. It was built in 1621 by Shah Abbas, and stands in a garden outside the town. The gay tiles, turquoise, lapis, violet, and yellow, have a singular melancholy among the bare trees and empty beds a-flutter with dead leaves. It suits my mood.

*

Other monuments here are the Masjid-i-Shah, a ruined mosque in the bazaar dating from 1451, which has two minarets spangled with blue and purple in the same fashion as the two-balconied minaret at Herat; and the Musalla, a ruined arch of later date, which is faced with intricate but unbeautiful mosaic. There is also the great Shrine of the Imam Riza.

This congeries of mosques, mausoleums, booths, bazaars, and labyrinths is the hub of the town. The sacred area has recently been insulated by a broad circular street, whence the other main streets radiate in all directions, so that every vista is completed by domes and minarets. On my first arrival at dusk, a huge sea-blue dome hovered in the misty sky; a gold dome shone dully beside it; between the ghostly minarets hung a string of fairy lights.

Two funerals transferred the capital of Khorasan from Tus to Meshed. In 809 the Caliph Harun-al-Rashid was disturbed by a rebellion in Transoxiana. His son Mamun marched ahead to Merv; the Caliph, in following, was taken ill at Tus, died, and was buried in a holy place twenty miles off, which is now Meshed. Mamun stayed at Merv, and in 816 he summoned thither the eighth Imam of the Shiahs, Ali-ar-Riza of Medina, whom he proclaimed heir to the Caliphate. But two years later the Imam also died at Tus, while accompanying Mamun on a visit to his father's grave. In orthodox doctrine, he died of a surfeit of grapes. But the Shiahs believe Mamun poisoned him. In any case he was buried next to Harun-al-Rashid, and his tomb became, after that of Ali at Nejef, the holiest place in the Shiah world.

So the Shrine grew up, and the city round it. Pilgrims, when they adore the Imam's tomb, still spit on that of Harun-al-Rashid. To us that name suggests all the splendours of Asia. To the Shiahs it recalls no more than the father of a murderer of a saint.

Attended by an unhappy police officer, I spent the morning on various roofs examining the Shrine through field-glasses from the other side of the circular street. There are three main courts, each with four ivans (no other word will describe those huge open-fronted halls with pointed vaults and high façades, which are the special feature of Persian mosque architecture). Two of the courts point north and south, and are situated end to end, though not on the same axis; the tilework in these, from a distance, looks like chintz and must date from the seventeenth or eighteenth centuries. Between them rises a helm-shaped dome plated in gold, which marks the tomb of the Imam and was erected by Shah Abbas in 1607; Chardin, in 1672, saw plates being made at Isfahan to repair it after an earthquake. Beside it stands a gold minaret, and there is another such minaret to the east of the southern court.

The third court points west, at right angles to the north and south courts. This is the mosque which Gohar Shad built between 1405 and 1418. Above the sanctuary chamber at the end, which is flanked by two enormous minarets, rises the sea-blue dome, bulbous in shape, inscribed on the bulge with bold black Kufic, and festooned from the apex with thin yellow tendrils.

The mosaic of the whole court appears to be still intact. Even from a quarter of a mile away I could see the difference in quality of its colour from that of the other courts. Here is the clue to the vanished glories of Herat. I must and will penetrate this mosque before I leave Persia. But not now; I haven't the initiative. It must wait till the spring, by which time perhaps I shall have found out more about Gohar Shad.

Meshed, Christmas Day   Hamber and I had lunch with Mr and Mrs Hart, also in the Consulate, and their little son Keith. I ate too much pudding, felt sick as one always does on Christmas afternoon, and was in form again for dinner. To this Hamber entertained the whole American mission, the Harts, and a German girl from Bolivia, governess to a family here, who was mondaine in a Teutonic cocktail-sniggering sort of way. Games followed. I won a fountain pen, the men's prize for trimming a lady's hat.

Teheran, 9 January   It was a sad moment when I exchanged Hamber's kind home for the brutal world again.

On the way back I stopped at Shahrud. It was early in the morning, and being now Ramadan, which means that no one gets up till mid-day, I took a horse without permission and rode off to Bostam, a sleepy little place on the way over the mountains to Asterabad. The fourteenth-century Shrine of Bayazid had so pastoral an exterior, with its towers like Kentish oast-houses, that the richness of the cut stucco mihrab inside it was a surprise. Indeed this technique is always a surprise; its effect is out of all proportion to its plain material. Here it is not exuberant as at Hamadan, depending more on line than relief. But it has the same virtues of splendour without ostentation and intricacy without incoherence. Near the mosque stands a grave-tower, built at the beginning of the century, whose round shell is encased by small sharp-edged buttresses. The brick-work has a fine texture, which results from the ends of the bricks, as they alternate with the sides, being stamped in a small design.

I was arrested on returning to Shahrud, but the Chief of Police was amiable enough when I produced my documents. I explained that much as I sympathized with the habit of turning night into day during Ramadan, it could not profit me to adopt it, in my search for monuments. He assented – rather shamefacedly. Probably some ridiculous edict has been circulated that Ramadan is backward.

To ears throbbing with the noise of a lorry on low gear, Teheran seemed a city of velvet-footed ghouls. I was laced into an evening suit at the Anglo-Persian mess and taken to the New Year's Eve ball. Expecting only that casual politeness which seeks to prevent the returned traveller's reminiscences, I was touched at people's interest in my excursion. Suddenly I saw Busk, the new secretary at the Legation, and showed my astonishment that he was taller than myself; for at school, since when we had not met, he had been one of the shortest boys.

'But I wasn't a *notorious* dwarf, was I?' he asked plaintively.

Part IV

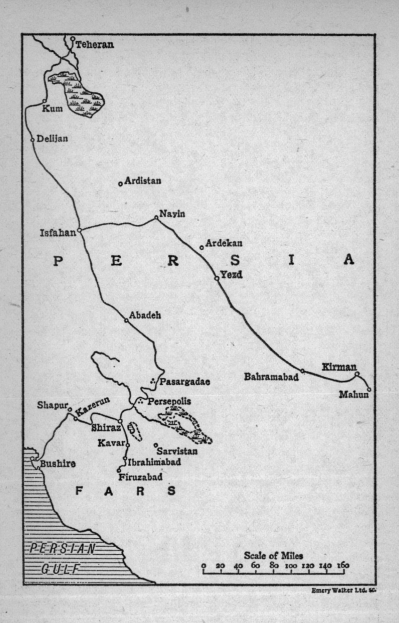

Teheran

Kum

Delijan

Ardistan

Nayin

Isfahan

Ardekan

Yezd

P E R S I A

Abadeh

Pasargadae

Shapur   Kazerun   Persepolis   Kirman

Bahramabad

Mahun

Shiraz

Kavar

Sarvistan

Bushire   Ibrahimabad

Firuzabad

F A R S

PERSIAN

GULF

Scale of Miles

0   20   40   60   80   100 120 140 160

Emery Walker Ltd. sc.

Teheran, 15 January   Damn this place.

Soon after I left in November, Marjoribanks thought himself threatened with a coup d'état. He had gone to Asterabad to see his new railway and attend the Turcoman races. With him was Sardar Assad, the Minister of War and chief of the Bakhtiari Khans. The first public indication of a plot was Sardar Assad's unexpected return to Teheran by lorry: an unusual mode of travel for the richest and most prominent member of the tribal aristocracy. He and his brothers, including Sardar Bahadur and Emir-i-Jang whom we met at tea with Mirza Yantz, are now in prison; troops and aeroplanes have been sent to the Bakhtiari country south of Isfahan. Meanwhile, suspicion has fallen on the Kavam-al-Mulk, a Kashgai magnate from Shiraz, who has hitherto enjoyed the dangerous honour of being Marjoribanks's chief confidant. He at present is confined to his house, and Miss Palmer-Smith, his daughters' companion, is in an ecstasy of apprehension about poison in the food.

No one know if there really was a plot. But everyone now thinks there will be. There are rumours that Marjoribanks has cancer in the stomach, that the Crown Prince will be murdered on his return from school in Switzerland, that the tribes will revolt in the spring. I don't believe any of them; dictatorships always breed these rumours. What annoys me is the anti-foreign feeling that has come to a head. The disgrace of the Bakhtiaris is partly ascribed to their friendship with the English; visitors anxious to see the more civilized side of Persian life, always travelled through their country. In consequence, all Persians, except those officially instructed to associate with foreigners, shudder away as though one were a mad dog.

This feeling has been strengthened by an article de Bathe wrote in *The Times* on his return to England, in which he described Marjoribanks' assault on the Turcoman jockey under the eyes of the Diplomatic Corps. The Persian press reported that in England the King dare not leave his palace without a guard of 3000 men, while the Prince of Wales keeps 100 dogs that climb on to his bed by a special ladder and sleep there. Intimidated by these outbursts, the London Foreign Office persuaded *The Times* to make amends in a leading article, which compared the state of modern Persia to that of Tudor England, and the achievement of Marjoribanks to that of Henry VIII. This only added vinegar to the Persian wound, since the Tudors are considered backward. Its interference has cost the

Foreign Office several hundred pounds in telegrams, and has confirmed the Persians in their twin obsessions – painstakingly established by our previous Minister – that petulance on their part strikes terror in London, and that the English Foreign Office controls the English press. In this hell of English good intentions, the Persians find inexhaustible response to the tremors of affronted dignity. Thank God my letters of recommendation are American.

Teheran, 17 January Another kink in the Persian mind is a mortal jealousy lest the Afghans should steal a march on them in the matter of westernization. On hearing I have been to Afghanistan, the educated Persian draws a deep breath, as though to restrain himself, expresses a polite interest in Afghan welfare, and enquires with feline suavity whether I found any railways, hospitals, or schools in the country. Hospitals and schools of course, I answer; all Islam has them; as for railways, surely steam is old-fashioned in a motoring age. When I told Mirza Yantz that the Afghans discussed their political problems frankly, instead of in whispers as here, he answered: 'Naturally; they are less cultured than we Persians.'

The Afghans return the dislike, but in different kind. Contempt, not jealousy, is all they feel.

I called on Shir Ahmad, the Afghan ambassador, yesterday, to tell him about my journey. Wrapped in a dressing-gown of iridescent velvet, stroking his egg-cosy beard, he looked more tigerish than ever.

R.B.: 'If Your Excellency gives me permission, I shall go back to Afghanistan in the spring.'
Shir Ahmad (*p*): 'You will go back? (*Roaring ff*) OF COURSE you will go back.'
R. B.: 'And Sykes hopes to accompany me.'
Sir Ahman (*m*): 'Hope? He need not hope. (*Roaring ff*) OF COURSE he will accompany you. (*pp*) I will give him visa.'
R. B.: 'I liked the Afghans because they speak loud and speak the truth. They are not full of intrigues.'
Shir Ahman (*leering p*): 'Ha, ha, you are wrong. They have many intrigues, (*m*) many, (*cr*) many. You are not clever. (*p*) You have not seen them.'
R. B. (*crestfallen*): 'At all events, Your Excellency, your people were

hospitable to me. If I write anything about Afghanistan, I shall show it to you first.'

Shir Ahmad (*ff*): 'WHY?'

R. B.: 'In case it should offend you.'

Shir Ahmad (*m*): 'There is no need. (*cr*) No need. (*f*) I will not see it. I do not wish. If you write kindly, we are pleased that friend praise us. If you write not-kindly, we are pleased that friend give advice. You shall write what you think. (*p*) You are honest man.'

R. B.: 'Your Excellency is too good.'

Shir Ahmad (*mf*): 'I am good, ha, ha. All Afghans good peoples. They have good lives. (*pp*) No wines, (*f*) no other men's wives. (*mf*) They believe God, and religion. All Afghans good peoples, all fiddles.'

R. B.: 'Fiddles?'

Shir Ahmad (*mp*): 'Fiddles, no? Is it French? Faithfuls, yes?'

R. B.: 'Very different from the Persians.'

Shir Ahmad (*mf*): 'Not different. (*cr*) Not different. Persians also fiddles. (*pp*) I will tell you story:

'(*m*) You know, Persians they are Shiahs, Afghans they are Sunnis. Persians love Ali. Afghans think Ali (*ff*) poof! (*m*) In Mohurram-time, Persians remember death of Ali and make feast. Last year they ask me to go feast at Baladiya, how you say, at Municipality. I go. (*cr*) I go. (*m*) I stand by Mayor. Round him stand all mullahs. There is big crowd. (*cr*) Very big crowd. (*m*) All crowd, all, yes, young mens, old mens, (*ff*) even officers from Persian army, (*pp*) weep and weep and (*f*) smack chest, so, for remember death of Ali. (*mp*) All fiddles. All love religion. I am Sunni. I do not like see such things, men weep, officers weep. (*Roaring. ff*) I DO NOT LIKE. (*mp*) Mullahs say to me, "Your Excellency will make speech?" (*ff*) "WHY NOT?" I say, (*pp*) "I will make speech." (*mp*) First I ask them question:

(*pp*) "Was Ali a Persian?" I ask.

(*m*) Mullahs they think I am stupid man. They say, (*f*) "Your Excellency is educated man. Your Excellency knows Ali was an Arab-man."

(*mp*) I ask them second question: (*pp*) "Was Ali Aryan-man?"

(*m*) Mullahs they think I am more stupid man. They say, (*f*) "Your Excellency knows that Arab-men are not Aryan-men."

(*mp*) I ask them third question: (*pp*) "Persians and Arab-men, are they same race?"

(*m*) Mullahs they think I am most stupid man. They are right. (*cr*) They are right. They say, (*f*) "Your Excellency is educated man. Your Excellency knows that Persians are Aryan-men and that Arabs are not Aryan-men."

(*m*) I am fool. All mullahs, all crowd, think me fool. I ask them: (*pp*) "Ali was he not relation of Persians?"

(*m*) Mullahs say, (*f*) "He was not relation."

(*mf*) "Thank you," I tell them, (*ff*) "THANK YOU."

(*m*) Then I ask if some peoples in crowd have passed Mohurram-time in Arabistan. When they tell me yes, I ask: (*pp*) "Arab-men do they weep for remember Ali?"

(*m*) They tell me no.

(*f*) "So," I say, "Arab-men are relation of Ali, but do not weep for remember him. Persians weep, but they are not relation of Ali."

(*m*) Mullahs they tell me I speak truth.

(*ff*) "It is strange," I say. "It is very strange. I do not understand why Persians weep. (*Roaring*) In Afghanistan, if boy of six years weep, WE CALL HIM WOMAN."

(*m*) Mullahs they very sorry, they have much shames. They tell me: "Your Excellency did not pass Mohurram-time in Persia twenty years ago. Then we weep more than today. In future, after ten years, we shall have Progress. We shall not weep and smack chest any more. Your Excellency shall see."

(*mp*) Next week after that Mohurram-time, Shah he invite me to palace. I go. (*cr*) I go. (*m*) Shah he say to me: "Your Excellency is friend of Persia."

I tell him: (*pp*) "Your Majestee is too kind. I do not deserve. Of course Your Majestee speaks truth. Of course I am friend of Persia. But Your Majestee shall permit me ask how Your Majestee sees I am friend."

(*mf*) "Your Excellency," say Shah, (*cr*) "Your Excellency has forbid Persians weeping in Mohurram-time. I also forbid. (*Roaring ff*) Next year they shall NOT weep. I have given orders."

(*pp*) Now Mohurram-time comes again. We shall see. (*cr*) We shall see.'

Teheran, 18 January Madame Nasr-al-Mulk gave a reception yesterday in the Karagozlu mansion. The Karagozlus are another tribal family, from Hamadan, but have so far escaped royal displeasure. Indeed Madame Nasr-al-Mulk is said to be the one person living who occasionally speaks her mind to Marjoribanks. I can believe it. She spoke her mind to me when she thought I was going to spill some lemonade over a brocade chair.

It lasted from five to eight. There were about 300 people and a jazz band. The rumour went round that Sardar Assad has 'died' in prison.

A Russian architect named Markov has opened a rest-home here for newly escaped Russian refugees. In a small house near the Meshed Gate we found about fifty people exhaling that same old Russian smell – what does it come from? They all looked healthy enough, but for two wretched little girls; old clothes and toys for the children had been collected from various sources. One was a priest from Samarra, who spent three years getting jobs nearer and nearer the frontier before he could sneak across it. He had a fine old icon with him, but those which the other families had so laboriously saved were hideous and worthless.

The purpose of the home is to receive the refugees as they arrive, give them a rest and good food after the journey, and fit them out with boots and clothes before they are distributed to Isfahan, Kirman, and other places in the middle of the country. Apart from Turcomans, of whom 25,000 crossed the border last year alone, people are escaping from Russia to Persia at the rate of 1000 a year. Most of them are not anti-Bolshevik; they simply flee from starvation. If their accounts are true of the heaps of empty tortoise-shells that surround the workmen's houses in some places, tortoises being their staple food, it is no wonder that foreigners are discouraged from visiting Russian Central Asia.

To discover if this discouragement amounts to denial, I have been hobnobbing with M. Datiev, the Russian consul. He is not so austere as some comrades, dresses in loud tweeds like Bloomsbury in the country, and wears a hat instead of a cap. The first time I went to see him, he regaled me with a cherry tart, the second time with crème de menthe.

Teheran, 22 January Christopher has bought a car, and we intended to leave for Isfahan yesterday. But the road is blocked by snow. The bag and its messenger are lost between here and Hamadan.

To increase the tedium, there has been a performance of *Othello* in Armenian. The chief part was taken by Papatzian, a Moscow star, who certainly upheld the Muscovite reputation for finished acting. The rest were local amateurs, and knowing no other models of our bygone costumes, had dressed themselves after the Europeans in the frescoes at Isfahan.

On top of this, Blücher the German Minister gave a party in a cinema to see the Nazi propaganda film *Deutschland Erwacht*. Hitler, Goebbels, and the rest of them roared away. Tea and cakes in the interval. Datiev in his hat, his ambassador in a cap. I felt sorry for Blücher and thankful I was not a German.

Teheran, 25 January   Still here. Still snow. The bag and its messenger still lost.

Walking into the local stationer's to buy some drawing paper, I found the Papal Nuncio at the counter, and could think of nothing to say outside my own train of thought.

'Bonjour, monseigneur.'
'Bonjour, monsieur.'
Silence.
'Vous êtes artiste, monseigneur?'
'Quoi?'
'Vous êtes peintre? Vous achetez des crayons, des couleurs?'
Horror ravaged his saintly countenance.
'Certainement non. J'achète des cartes d'invitation.'

Shir Ahmad and Tommy Jacks, the resident director of the Anglo-Persian Oil Company, came to dinner at the club. It was a good dinner: caviare, beetroot, bortsch, grilled salmon, roast partridge with mushrooms, potato chips and salad, hot meringue pudding with an ice in the middle, and mulled claret.

Shir Ahmad (*mf*): 'Madame Jacks where she is? (*dim*) She is pretty lady.'
Jacks: 'She could not come.'

Shir Ahmad (*roaring ff*): 'WHY NOT? (*Purring furiously mf*) I am very angree, (*cr*) very angree.'

We played bridge afterwards, but could not finish a rubber, as Shir Ahmad continually left the table to illustrate his stories by acting. The history of the Afghan royal family took half an hour, in which it transpired that Shir Ahmad's cousinship to both Amanullah and the present king was due to its founder's having had 120 children. After the next hand, he proceeded to Amanullah's tour of Europe. Attended by various noble Italians they were in a box at the Roman opera.

'(*m*) Italian lady she sit beside me. She is (*eyes blazing ff*) big lady, yah! great? no, fat. (*mf*) She more fat than Madame Egypt [the Egyptian Ministress] and her breast is (*cr*) too big. (*mf*) It fall out of box, so. Much diamonds and gold on it. (*pp*) I am frightened. I see if it shall be in my face (*f*) I suffocate.'

The scene moved to the State Banquet at Buckingham Palace.

'(*m*) Prince of Wales he talk to me. (*p*) I tell him, "Your Royal Highness (*ff*) you are fool! (*roaring*) You are FOOL!" (*m*) Prince of Wales he say, (*p*) 'Why am I fool?' (*m*) I tell him, "Sir, because you steeple-jump. It is dangerous, (*cr*) dangerous. (*p*) English peoples not pleased if Your Royal Highness die." (*m*) King he hear. He tell Queen, "Mary, His Excellency call our son fool." He very angree, (*cr*) very angree. (*mf*) Queen she ask me why her son fool. I say because he steeple-jump. Queen say to me, (*dim*) "Your Excellency, Your Excellency, you are right, (*cr*) you are right." (*m*) Queen thank me. King thank me.'

Teheran, 29 January   Still here.

Yesterday morning we got up at three and were out of the town by six, intending to make Isfahan in one day. After ten miles the road became an ice floe; a drift had thawed and frozen again. I accelerated. We crashed on twenty yards, nearly overturned, and came to a lugubrious full-stop. At this moment the sun rose, a twinkle of fire lit the snowy plain, the white range of the Elburz was suffused with blue and gold, and a breath of warmth endeared the icy wind. Cheered by the beauty of the scene, we returned to the capital.

*

To relieve the claustrophobia, we spent the day in the mountains aboue Darbend, where Marjoribanks has a palace. Christopher got into conversation with one of the royal gardeners. It appears that Marjoribanks likes flowers.

Teheran, 6 February Still here.

Christopher left on the third. I was taken ill the night before, from that same Afghan infection, and had to go to the nursing-home instead of Isfahan, where I have been poulticed, lanced, cupped, and purged 100 times a day. The nursing-home is English, and a credit to the colony; but its management is such a source of contention between the Legation and the Anglo-Persian Oil Company that it may not survive.

The doctor says I can leave the day after tomorrow.

Kum (3200 ft), 8 February I have left.

Mr and Mrs Hoyland are transporting me. He has been consul at Kirmanshah; and being now transferred to Shiraz they are moving house with two cars and a black spaniel. It rained for twenty-four hours before we started, and we have made bad time; a boat would have been faster than a car today.

The Shrine here, though rebuilt in the early nineteenth century, makes a good group with its tall gold dome and four blue minarets.

Delijan (5000 ft), 9 February Stuck again.

We were expecting to be in Isfahan for tea, when a turn of the road disclosed two lorries and a Ford embedded in a torrent fifty yards wide. There was nothing to do but come back to this village, where we have hired the chief house. It has two wind-towers, giving on to secret chambers that can be opened in summer to induce the proper draught, and a large room adorned with patterns of looking-glass in the plaster, beneath which hang cabinet photographs of gentlemen in Norfolk jackets taken at Bombay in the eighties. As Mrs Hoyland led her spaniel over the threshold, a cross-eyed witch burst into protest, less the unclean animal should defile the place where a certain holy man once slept. She was silenced by the brothers who own the house and wanted our rent.

In the afternoon, I drew the courtyard: one pollarded tree-stump, an empty pond, and a line of washing all dripping with rain, give a new idea of a Persian garden. At the end stood a vaulted summer-house, but just as I put pencil to it, the whole thing collapsed in a heap. Since then there have been other crashes in the distance. As building material, the mud of Delijan is unsuited to bad weather.

I sit in my own little room beside a blazing wood fire, while Aga Mahmud, the eldest of the brothers, reads to me about Hazrat Hassan from the Shiah scriptures. From time to time he pauses, to whisper that the house is his, and that the rent must be paid to him alone.

Delijan, 10 February   We drove to the river. It is higher than ever. But the sun is out and we have hope.

The bombardment of falling architecture continued all night. There is hardly a roof intact in the whole village.

Isfahan (5200 ft), 11 February   We arrived this afternoon. I ought to have been here, but for weather and illness, exactly three weeks ago.

It rained in the night again at Delijan. We dressed in despair, and were eating a leisurely breakfast when news came that the river had subsided *but was rising again fast.* In five minutes we were tearing down the road for dear life, with a peasant carrying a spade on the step of each car. Hoyland took the torrent in a dashing zigzag and landed safe on the other side. Mrs Hoyland and I stuck, till twenty men pushed us out.

There was time to drive round Isfahan before dark. Passing the Chihil Sutun, long familiar from pictures of its pool-reflected pines and huge verandah, I entered the Maidan. Blind whitewashed arcades, in two tiers, enclose a space a quarter of a mile long by 150 yards wide. At the near end, by me, stands the ruin of the Bazaar Gate; at the far, facing it, the blue portal of the Masjid-i-Shah, with dome, ivan, and minarets clumped obliquely behind it in the direction of Mecca; in front of each, a pair of marble goal-posts for polo. On the right rises that brick boot-box the Ali Gapu; opposite, the flowered saucer dome of the Mosque of Sheikh Lutfullah, skewed sideways over a blue recess. Symmetry; but not too much. The beauty lies in the contrast between a formal space and a romantic diversity of buildings. To spoil this effect, and to show that Bakhtiari gentlemen are no longer allowed to play polo or exercise their horses here, progress has constructed a sheet of ornamental water in the middle. This is surrounded by a Gothic iron railing and incipient petunia-beds.

The Maidan and its monuments date from the seventeenth century. The Friday Mosque, in the heart of the town, is older; it was built in the eleventh. Here, as in the same mosque at Herat, the whole history of the town is pictured in a single building and its restorations; the charm of Safavid colour, like that of Timurid, recedes before its venerable grandeur. Much of it is clumsy, some ugly. But the great egg-dome of plain brick, erected by Malek Shah the Seljuk, has few equals for that blind expression of content which is the virtue of Mohammadan domes.

Dusk was falling when I reached the College of the Mother of the Shah which was built by Sultan Hussein the Safavid in 1710. Through the entrance a narrow sunk pool led to a black arch and doubled it unrippled, creating, as it were, an architectural playing-card. The old white-stemmed poplars had just been pollarded; twigs and branches were scattered over the paving. I emerged into the Char Bagh, Shah Abbas's avenue, and drove beneath the double line of trees to the bridge of Ali Verdi Khan, which carries the road to Shiraz, and the royal vista, across the river to a slope a mile long. The bridge encloses the road by arched walls, on the outside of which runs a miniature arcade for foot passengers. This was crowded with people, and all the town was hurrying to join them; there was never such a flood in living memory. The lights came out. A little breeze stirred, and for the first time in four months I felt a wind that had no chill in it. I smelt the spring, and the rising sap. One of those rare moments of absolute peace, when the body is loose, the mind asks no questions, and the world is a triumph, was mine. So much it meant to have escaped from Teheran.

Isfahan, 13 February There is a lot of missionary effort here, of the muscular, wicked-to-smoke-or-drink type. Men in spectacles, tweed coats, and flannel trousers go striding down the Char Bagh accompanied by small boys and bearing the unmistakable imprint of the British schoolmaster; their behinds stick out as if their spines were too righteous to bend. Behind it all lurks an Anglican bishop, who has lately become an apostle of the Oxford Group Movement. Buchmanism in Isfahan! This is a cruel revenge for the Bahais in Chicago.

A more humane exponent of English ethics was Archdeacon Garland, who lived here thirty years. During that time, he used to say, he made one convert. She was an old woman, who was ostracized for her apostasy, so that on her deathbed the Archdeacon was the only friend she could send for. She had one last request, she told him.

'What is it?' asked the Archdeacon, anxious to ease his protégée's last moments.

'Please summon a mullah.'

He did so, and repeated the story afterwards.

The pleasure of a walk in the rain this afternoon was completed by the clutch of a corpse. It was passing on a stretcher, the road was a bog, and we collided; the hands and feet, escaping from a check tablecloth, beckoned convulsively.

There is an Armenian cathedral at Julfa across the river, which resembles a Mohammadan shrine of the seventeenth century. Inside, the walls are covered with oil paintings in the Italian tradition of that date. Attached to it is a museum, but the treasures are of historic rather than artistic interest.

Abadeh (6100 ft), 14 February Persia can be very pleasant when the officials give rein to their natural good nature.

*

The Hoylands and I arrived here early; seeing a good horse in the street, I asked the Chief of Police if he could mount me for an hour. Two foaming steeds were immediately at the rest-house gate. And we set off across the fields at a racing gallop, full in the face of the setting sun, so that I could see neither ditches nor banks as the horse took them in its stride. Our objective was a lonely garden. For some minutes Habibullah the policeman sat silent, entranced by the sound and twinkle of a stream. 'You should come here in summer,' he said sentimentally. And then, as though ashamed of his emotion, talked of the shooting: gazelle and moufflon.

Since the brown horse I rode was his, I gave him ten crowns. Later in the evening he brought the money back, by order of the Chief of Police. If I wanted to do him a good turn, I could recommend him to the Chief of Police at Shiraz.

Abadeh is a favoured village. The main street is neatly gravelled; the inhabitants are prosperous – they make the best shoes in Persia. It is very dry. Even now, when everywhere else is flooded, they have had no rain.

The red wine of Julfa tastes of a Burgundy grown in Greece. We have drunk a bottle apiece today.

Shiraz (5000 ft), 17 February The South, the blessed South! It gives me the same exhilaration as a first morning by the Mediterranean. The sky shines without a cloud. The black spires of cypresses cut across the eggshell-coloured hills and the snow-capped purple of distant mountains. Turquoise leek-shaped domes on tall stems rise from a sea of flat mud roofs. Tangerines hang from the trees in the hotel garden. I am writing in bed, the windows are open, and the soft spring air breathes paradise into last night's frousty cubicle.

We stopped a few minutes at Persepolis on the way from Abadeh, running up the great ballroom staircase on to the platform. I have always been curious about the stone used there. The columns are of white marble, which has weathered to cream, brown, and black; it has a pinkish glow, but is chalkier and less translucent than that of Pentelicon, lacking that impress of absorbed sunshine which is the beauty of the Parthenon. The reliefs are carved in dull grey stone, quite opaque and very fine in texture, which exposure has turned to mottled black.

There was no time to see the new staircase, but we left cards on Herzfeld to prepare him for a longer visit.

Arrival at the Consulate was a crucial moment for the Hoylands, who have to make it their home for the next three years. As we sat at tea, Christopher came in, much pleased with his discoveries anent the villainy of Wassmuss, that mysterious agent to the Persian tribes in the War, who, if the Germans had won it, would now occupy the place of Colonel Lawrence. We are going to Firuzabad together, where the topography of a battle between British soldiers and the tribes thus disaffected will occupy him, and the Palace of Ardeshir me.

There are still relics of the British occupation here. The cabs bear advertisements for Tennant's beer. The manager of the hotel offered us potato-cheeps for dinner. Nature, before the War, planted a singular mountain in the vicinity, which completes the prospect of the main street with a Lysippus-portrait of Lord Balfour lying on his back. This is now called the Kuh-i-Barfi, which means mountain of snow. It might seem a rational name if there was ever any snow on it. But there isn't. The real name is Kuh-i-Balfour, of which Barfi is a Persian corruption.

When I went to the English Mission to have an injection, Dr Mess, a lady doctor, offered me a cigarette and took one herself. The South again!

The monuments of Shiraz are curious rather than important; though the facing of the court in the Friday Mosque, itself in ruins, seems to cover masonry of great antiquity. A sort of stone tabernacle stands in the middle of the court, flanked by four fat round pillars built of cut stone. The tops of these, which now support nothing, are encircled with texts cut out of stone but surrounded by a blue background. This is the only example I have seen of stone and faience used together. It is not a happy combination, as one can tell from Sarre's reproductions of Konia.

The court of the college is also ruined, a state which improves its eighteenth-century tilework of pink and yellow flowers. The chief ornament is a spreading fig tree beside an octagonal pool. A pretty octagonal vestibule gives access to it, covered by a saucer-dome on shallow bat's-wing squinches. These are embellished with a rich cold mosaic of the seventeenth century.

Outside the town stands a tall square building, once domed, which is known as the Khatun and is said to be the mausoleum of the daughter of a Muzaffarid king, though it looks later. The front has collapsed, but the sides and back, of plain brick, are relieved by double rows of arched panels, each with mosaic spandrels. The brick is rosy buff, like the hills.

Beyond this lie the gardens of Hafiz and Saadi, each containing the poet's tomb, and many others equally delicious for their cypresses, pines, and orange trees a-flutter with white pigeons and orchestras of sparrows. On the bare earth outside, lambskins were drying or being packed in bundles; so early is the lambing season in the South.

This evening I went to see Bergner, a member of Herzfeld's staff, and consult him about photographing at Persepolis. On his advice I wrote Herzfeld a note, formally asking permission, but carefully disclaiming any wish to steal his new discoveries. Bergner was staying near the Allah-ho-Akbar Gate, and yesterday being Friday, the whole of Shiraz was on this road, some promenading to see their friends and the town below them, some returning from picnics, and many on horseback. The horses here are an endless pleasure, being mainly of Arab blood, though not so fine-boned as the desert Arabs, and escaping that weedy mongrel look which comes from cross-breeding with the Turcoman strains of the north. They are well turned out, often with initialled saddle-cloths. Even the asses have a fashionable air, large white beasts loaded with cushions, fringes, and tassels; so that horsemen and assmen trot side by side on equal terms in the gay parade. Asses are for the middle-aged, and the youngest horses for the youngest boys, who sit them with extraordinary firm-ness. Persians regain their dignity on horseback; even the Pahlevi hat cannot spoil it then. They sit well down in the saddle and they stay there, as if they had grown out of the horse's back. Yet according to Christopher, who played polo with them when he was attaché, they have no grip and ride entirely by balance.

Wine is another boon of the Persian South. Its fame has spread, and etymologists dispute as to whether sherry derives its name from Xerez or Shiraz. So far we have discovered three varieties here: a very dry golden wine, which I prefer to any sherry, though its taste is not so storied; a dry red claret, nondescript at first but acceptable with meals; and a sweeter vin rosé, which induces a delicious well-being. If the vineyards had names, and the makers corks, enabling different wines to be distinguished and stored, Shiraz might produce real vintages. But Persians, broad as their views on religion are, drink mainly for the sin of it and care little for the taste. While if foreigners introduce these improvements, they will inevitably try to imitate their own brands, as the Germans have done at Tabriz. Second-rate hock is drinkable, but not interesting; I prefer a worse wine with a taste of its own. Meanwhile, Mr and Mrs Hoyland, who have lived much in the Mediterranean, are planning a systematic research of the vineyards in the coming autumn.

Shiraz, 18 February   The charm of Shiraz has evaporated.

Christopher and I called on the Chief of Police to complete the ordinary formalities, and to ask permission to go to Firuzabad, which is not generally granted owing to the lawlessness of the Kashgais; indeed Herzfelt and Aurel Stein seem to be the only people who have looked at the monuments there since Dieulafoy in the eighties.

'You,' said the Chief, looking hard at me, 'can go. But you must go alone.'

'I don't understand. Do you mean that I can go and Mr Sykes can't?'

'Exactly.'

This was mortifying enough. But worse followed. As we sought to drive out of the town for a breath of mountain air, the police at the Allah-ho-Akbar Gate stopped the car, and only allowed us to proceed on foot.

Later, I called on the Governor, a man of wide interests. Translation, he said, was an art, as he had learnt from rendering Plato and Oscar Wilde into Persian. When I told him of our encounters with the police, he telephoned to the Chief, who said there had been no mistake.

On hearing this, Christopher went again to the police-station and asked for an explanation. Thus cornered, the chief revealed that he had had orders from Teheran to prevent Christopher from leaving the town. No, he could not go to Firuzabad; nor on to Bushire; nor out shooting; nor even, in future, for a country walk.

Of all the foreigners I have met in this country, diplomats, business men, and archaeologists of many nationalities and varying terms of residence, Christopher is the only one who likes its inhabitants, sympathizes with their nationalist growing-pains, and consistently upholds their virtues, sometimes to the point of unreason. The Persian authorities, in their present fit of xenophobia, should have picked on him last instead of first. Poor old Marjoribanks is so sensitive to European comment that revenge is easy. But the satisfaction of driving a senile megalomaniac into a tantrum is not much compensation for the destruction of one's immediate pleasure in the country.

Kavar (c. *5200 ft*), *20 February* The start of a journey in Persia resembles an algebraical equation: it may or may not come out. I gave all yesterday to it, and we got off at six this morning; but have spent the rest of the day here awaiting cavalry and horses.

There are two kinds of police: the Nasmiya, which controls the towns; and the Amniya, which controls the roads and such of the hinterland as admits the law. On the advice of the Chief of the Nasmiya, I called on the Chief of the Amniya, since his men must be responsible for my journey to Firuzabad. He was a fat, jocular fellow, and was anxious to help me.

The Governor had already telephoned to him, explaining my purpose and identity. His first act, therefore, was to telephone to the Governor inquiring my purpose and identity. Having received a satisfactory answer, he bethought himself, and the Governor concurred, that the matter would be simplified if the Governor were to set forth my purpose and identity in a letter.

Before going to fetch the letter, I asked him if I ought to have an escort, since there were rumours of thieves on the road. Quite unnecessary, he replied, quite unnecessary. Hurrying in a cab to the Ark, I rattled off the polite formulas, complimented the Governor on his orange trees, and asked if the letter was ready.

'Don't you think,' he said pensively, 'that you ought to have an escort for the journey?'

'Really, Your Excellency must advise me on that point. The Reis-i-Amniya says it is unnecessary.'

'I will telephone to him . . .'

'Certainly,' answered the Reis-i-Amniya over the wire, 'certainly he must have an escort. He can't possibly go without.' But there was a difficulty. The local Finance Minister had just started on a tour of land assessment (to include, among others, the property of the Kavam-al-Mulk) and had taken 100 mounted guards with him; thus there were no horses left, and any escort with me would have to go on foot.

'In that case,' I said, 'let me hire horses for them.'

The Governor and the Reis-i-Amniya thought this an excellent solution.

Meanwhile, the secretary in the next room was writing the Governor's letter to the Reis-i-Amniya. When the Governor had approved it, a fair copy was made. This he signed and sealed and handed to me. I jumped into the cab, and was back at the Amniya within two hours of leaving it.

'Do you think, perhaps,' asked the Reis-i-Amniya blandly, 'that you ought to have an escort to take you to Firuzabad?'

'Really, Your Eminence must advise me on that point.'

'In my opinion, you ought. Will one man be enough?'

'Certainly. I am not a millionaire to hire horses for a troop.'

'Of course not; who is? Five men will be enough, I imagine. Naturally, they will all be mounted on Government horses; we have plenty to spare. And it may facilitate matters if you take an officer with you in the car as far as Kavar. He will arrange your own horses there. I will tell him to call on you at the hotel at five o'clock, to arrange things.'

'Your Eminence is too kind. Could he come at eight instead of five, as I am going out to tea?'

'Just as you wish. I will tell him to come at seven.'

We left in a Ford, the party consisting of my new servant Ali Asgar, the Sultan, which means Captain, the chauffeur, his assistant, and myself, together with luggage, food, and wine. I am travelling en prince for once, to save time; without a servant, one spends half every day packing and unpacking.

As we approached the tribal country, the Sultan stopped to inspect the Amniya block-houses, bare workmanlike places whose parapets were pierced by loopholes. It was interesting to see the machinery of tribal subjection, and watch the Amniya at work. They are a fine corps, the best of Marjoribanks's innovations.

Block-houses and motor-track ended at Kavar, a village belonging to Haji Abdul Karim Shirazi, who has just built himself a new house. This makes me unusually comfortable, though the mud on the walls is still wet. The pool in the courtyard is kept clear by a stream, which spurts from a stone gargoyle.

Outside the village, he has an old garden of about twelve acres. The gardener let me in by a wicket in a thatched wall, and I spent the afternoon wandering about the straight grass paths that divide Persian gardens into squares and oblongs. Each path is an avenue of poplars or planes, and is accompanied by irrigation runnels; inside these, each square contains fruit trees or bare plough. Squares sound formal; but really, plantation or wilderness is the proper word to describe a Persian garden. Winter and spring had met on this afternoon. A strong warm wind carried a sound of chopping with it and a rustle of dead plane-leaves; through those leaves perked the green crooks of young ferns. Here and there the rose-leaves had budded too early, and were blackened with frost. The bare apple branches bore tangles of dead mistletoe; another such tangle in the fork of a massive chestnut some hundreds of years old, was the nest of a *palamdar* – according to the gardener; did he mean magpie or squirrel? its dome was of one or the other. The first butterflies were out: a dusty white, of a kind I did not know, newly hatched and flying in a puzzled sort of way as if the world was still too brown for it; and a painted lady, newly awakened, and surveying the garden it knew in September with familiar swoops from point to point. There were some flowers for them. A peach (or plum) was in blossom, and I caught my breath at the dazzle of its red buds, white transparent petals and black stalks defined by the shimmering blue sky. From over the wall peered the endless mountains, mauve and lion-coloured, deathly barren. The bleating of lambs and kids drew me to the gate again. A little girl was guarding them beside the village graveyard, where stood three giant weeping conifers of the cypress family. 'Those are called *Karj*,' said the Sultan, 'but why say they are big? You have not seen the ones at Burujird in Luristan.' A grey owl flew out of the first, from a hole it was inspecting. On a marshy pond dotted with the yellow bullet-heads of water lilies, the moorhens were already nesting.

*

I am lying in bed over a bottle of vin rosé. Ali Asgar, who was cook to a British regiment in the War, is 'baking' a partridge in a pot. The cavalry have collected and horses been paraded. They say it is a two days' ride to Firuzabad, but I hope to do it in one.

Firuzabad (4400 ft), 22 February   I did, with an effort; though it was hard on the rest of the party. Opinion at Kavar gave the distance as nine farsakhs, thirty-six miles. I rode eleven hours, excluding one stop for lunch, and as the good going and the bad were about equal, I can hardly have averaged less than four miles an hour. It must have been more than forty miles.

After the usual mishaps, a broken girth, luggage thrown to the ground by a bucking horse, we left at seven. A sounder of pig crossed the path, running in file according to size. The ground was too stony for us to head them off, though one of the escort tried; but a gallop along the path brought us level with them, and the man shouted, 'Do you want one?' The fact that I didn't, combined with some dim inhibition implanted by the English game-laws, made me hesitate. They veered away, and I lost my chance of seeing a Persian shoot from the saddle at full gallop.

The mountainside was covered with bushes and wild fruit trees in pink blossom. Beneath one lay a dead wolf. After a hard climb, ending in a glissade of shale which was difficult for the horses, we reached the top of the Muk Pass; thence we followed a stream whose banks were dotted with deep blue grape-hyacinths. This brought us to the Zanjiran gorge, a narrow gate between two overhanging cliffs and a famous place for robbers. The path disappeared. There was only room for the stream, which was blocked to an unusual depth by a confusion of crags, tree-trunks, and brambles, so that the horses could hardly force a passage. Directly the water escaped from the gorge, it was collected into irrigation channels branching this way and that at different levels.

A hot scrubby plain intervened, separated from another like it by a step of 100 feet, from whose brink we saw villages in the distance. A black cleft in the opposite mountains was our object: the Tang-Ab or Water Pass. At Ismailabad I sat under a tree on a patch of emerald grass strewn with ox bones, and ate a bowl of curds.

It was a tumbledown place, and the headman was frightened out of his wits; for the police are seldom seen in these parts. 'You should have gone to Ibrahimabad over there,' he said apologetically. When I asked him to fetch my horse, he misunderstood and thought I wanted a new one, which he produced. This was too great a convenience to forgo. I gave him five crowns, which he was loath to accept, till I employed the unfailing formula: 'For your children.'

The cliffs of the Water Pass are stratified diagonally, as though the mountain had been cloven by an axe and would fit together again if pushed; I have seen nothing like it, or the gorge that followed, since those of Aghia Rumeli on the south coast of Crete. As we approached it, a river, which had come along the base of the hills from the east, suddenly turned at right angles into the gate, and seemed to be flowing rapidly uphill, an illusion which persisted during the whole four miles of the gorge. This extraordinary formation varies in width from half a mile to 100 yards; its cliffs are from 500 to 800 feet high. The path crosses and recrosses the river in its serpentine course. About the middle, I saw the first signs of antiquity: a Sasanian castle perched on a salient of the east cliff, and connected by a long wall with a lesser stronghold. These two buildings are known as the Kala-i-Dukhtar and Kala-i-Pisa. *Kala* means castle, and *Dukhtar* maiden, being the same as our word daughter. But I had forgotten this for the moment, and when I asked Ali Asgar what it was, he suddenly answered in English: 'Dukhtar, Sahib? Dukhtar – baby missis.'

Fantastic strata led up this eastern cliff, composed of huge rectangular blocks thirty feet long and twenty broad; I thought at first they were artificial roads, such as the Incas built to Cuzco. By now the light was going. Ali Asgar and the luggage were miles behind. He had three of the escort with him, but the two with me grew more and more worried.

'What is the matter?' I asked.

'Robbers.'

'But the great Riza Shah-in-Shah has destroyed all the robbers in Persia.'

'Oh, has he? Last month they shot four horses under me, and wounded me in the head. They would murder Your Excellency for a crown.'

We emerged at last by the south gate on the east bank of the river. There was just light enough to distinguish, half a mile away on the other, the vaulted phantom of Ardeshir's great palace, which my men called the Artish-Khana or House of Fire. And later, among the open fields, there was starlight enough to silhouette a minaret of enormous thickness. The men had no idea where the town was, but a village, where they wanted to stop, directed them in order to get rid of us. In half an hour we found ourselves among silent streets and moonwashed walls. A passing wraith showed us to the Governor's house.

I walked upstairs.

There was no furniture in the room. In the middle of the floor stood a tall brass lamp, casting a cold white blaze over the red carpets and bare white walls. It stood between two pewter bowls, one filled with branches of pink fruit blossom, the other with a posy of big yellow jonquils wrapped round a bunch of violets. By the jonquils sat the Governor, with his legs crossed and his hands folded in his sleeves; by the blossom his young son, whose oval face, black eyes and curving lashes were the ideal beauty of the Persian miniaturist. They had nothing to occupy them, neither book nor pen nor food nor drink. Father and son were lost in the sight and the smell of spring.

The irruption of the barbarian, dusty, unshaved, and lurching tired, was a trial of manners to which they rose, not without astonishment, but with a bustle and goodwill that must have hurt their mood of poetic contemplation. While I lowered myself to the floor, creaking and sprawling like a dog in a doll's-house, and feasted my nose in the jonquils, fire was kindled, the samovar relit, and thick red wine poured out; with his own hands the Governor chopped and skewered the meat to make me a kabob, and roasted it over the charcoal embers; then he was dismembering tangerines and sugaring them, for my pudding. In the end he went so far as to offer me his own bed. I explained that mine was coming, and begged the room below to put it in.

There are no police in this small tribal market town, neither Amniya nor Nasmiya; the Governor's safety depends on a few soldiers. People dress as they will, the men wearing striped gowns, loose cummerbunds stuck with weapons, and black bun-shaped hats without brims. The Pahlevi hat is a rare exception. This at last is that other Persia which so many travellers fell in love with, and having found it I would willingly stay here a week if I could. But if Christopher and I are to reach Afghanistan in time to forestall that much prophesied 'trouble in the spring', we ought to leave Teheran by 15 April, and I can't dawdle. Not that there is really much likelihood of trouble. But the mere rumour of it would be enough to close the country to foreigners for a month or two.

It was thus with an energy quite opposed to my inclinations that I set out to see the ruins this morning. The Governor offered me a horse, knowing mine must be tired. I thanked him, explaining that the mere mention of a saddle made me groan, and began to walk. Firuzabad is actually further south than Bushire. It was very hot. From outside the town I saw palms waving over the flat roofs. I had covered the two and a half miles to Gur, the city that Ardeshir founded about AD 220, and was regretting my refusal of a mount, when the clatter of horses in pursuit made me turn. First rode the Governor on a rearing brown stallion, followed by his son on a bucking grey; next the mayor and some other gentlemen; then a posse of armed soldiers, one mounted on a strawberry roan. In the middle of the cavalcade pranced a huge white ass, carrying a mountain of carpets but no rider. 'This,' said the Governor, 'is for you. Our guests do not walk.'

The 'minaret' of the night before proved to be a solid square shaft eighty to a hundred feet high, and twenty broad, built of coarse Sasanian masonry and having no entrance or trace of one. The sides gave evidence of an ascending ramp, which must have engaged the shaft in a four-sided spiral. I remember now that Herzfeld in his *Reisebericht* suggests that the ramp was enclosed in its turn, the whole thus forming a tower with an interior ascent of which only the core remains. Dieulafoy, more picturesque, believes the column served as a fire-altar and pictures the priests filing up its ramp in full view of the populace below, as though it were an Aztec teocalli. But neither theory explains what purpose, other than megalomania, can have prompted the erection of 40,000 cubic feet of solid stone in this form. Even the pyramids were slightly hollow.

The tower has no name, but is said to mark the site of a stone fallen from heaven. All round it, within a radius of half a mile, the ground shows the contours of Ardeshir's capital. Many of the foundations, or of the walls that fell on them, seem to be only a foot or two below the earth, and there is one platform still above it. This is built of rectangular blocks, neatly cut and fitted in the Achemenian way, and very different from the higgledy-piggledy masonry of the tower, where stones of any shape are embedded in a sea of mortar. I should like to dig here; it must be the richest site in Persia still untouched. Sasanian fragments are seldom beautiful. But they document an obscure passage of history at the junction of the ancient and modern worlds.

The others mounted their horses and I the ass, which beat the Governor's stallion by a nose at every corner, flapping its ears and hopping its ditches as if it could outpace any horse living. We stopped at a garden on the way back, to recline beneath a grove of old orange trees, and drink curds with nutmeg. Outside the town, three ragged children salaamed the Governor from the back of a camel. Reining back the stallion on his hindlegs, as though the scene were another Field of the Cloth of Gold, he gave them in return the polite formulas: 'Peace to you. Your Excellencies' health is good by the grace of God?' It was a great joke, we all laughed, and so did the children. But it was also a true benevolence, that warmed my heart towards Haji Seyid Mansur Abtahi Shirazi, the Governor of Firuzabad.

Ibrahimabad (c. *4400 ft*), *23 February* That charming man had intended to come with me to the gorge, but was engaged, today being Friday, in entertaining the Municipality to a picnic in the garden of Nasrabad. He had not believed I would leave so soon, and had expected me at the picnic too. Indeed he was almost offended by my going. But I could assure him, with truth for once, that his grief was nothing to mine.

Today has been the perfect day, the one day which, even if there is no other like it, makes the whole journey from England worth while.

The start was unpropitious. Last night, as my horse from Ismail-abad was being shod in the bazaar, it broke its halter and fled. The escort promised me one of theirs instead, but were late in getting up, thinking they now had the advantage on me. Outside the town, we found the missing horse, which delayed us still further. It was nibbling the road with that air of hopeless indecision characteristic of lost horses, vacantly looking up now and then as if in search of some kind person to take it home. Having wasted half an hour trying to effect this kindness, during which our own horses were goaded into a lather while the truant remained as cool, as vacant, and as helplessly innocent as before, we drove the brute into the gorge. One of the escort stayed on guard at our end, so that if it did escape by the other it could only arrive at its native place.

The Palace of Ardeshir assumed enormous dimensions as we crossed the river and could distinguish the smallness of two Kashgai tents encamped on a lawn below it. These tents were black and oblong, and were stretched over low stone walls. Dogs, children, lambs, and chickens tottered about the grass, enlarging still further the uncouth skeleton above them. Two women wearing full pleated skirts were pounding corn on a cloth by means of pestles attached to long staves.

There was not time to measure the palace properly. But I soon saw that Dieulafoy's elevation was wrong. This is interesting, considering the importance of the building in the history of architecture and the fact that Dieulafoy's has so far been the only information available to writers on the subject.

The entrance was originally on the south, through a big barrel-vaulted ivan. Today what appears to be the main façade faces east, looking across the river towards the mouth of the gorge. Behind it, at either end, are two courts, the southern covering about half an acre, the northern rather less. These are divided from one another by a series of three domed chambers, which stretch right across the palace from side to side one behind the other. Only half the east chamber is still standing, with half its dome above it; so that the line of the façade appears at first sight to be interrupted by an open vestibule thirty feet across and fifty high. But one soon sees that really there is no façade at all – though I use the term for convenience – and that the whole of the east wall, having stood on the brink of the green slope now supporting the Kashgais, has gradually collapsed and taken the front of the first chamber with it.

The two inner chambers are also about thirty feet square, and their domes, resting directly on simple corner squinches, have the same diameter. The apex of each dome is pierced by a broad hole, round which the outside masonry projects upwards. At present these holes afford the only light there is; if they were originally enclosed, the chambers beneath must have been artificially lit, and each dome must have been surmounted by a sort of rough cupola, thus discovering a precedent for those extraordinary nipples on the Romanesque domes of Perigueux. The dome of the middle chamber is some fifteen feet higher than the other two. Higher still is the elliptical cupola which separates it from the front dome, and which roofs the passage between the middle chamber and the outer ruined one. This passage is divided into two storeys; but a light well in the floor of the upper enables the hole in the cupola to illuminate the lower. A similar passage separates the middle and hinder chambers. This is roofed by a massive barrel-vault and is entirely unlighted.

Dieulafoy makes all three domes the same height, and omits the cupolas of the passages altogether.

It would need a long time to make sense from the maze of internal walls and heaps of fallen masonry that occupy the two courts. One can see, however, that a barrel-vaulted room, or succession of rooms, ran beside the dome-chambers on the north. The vault is gone, but two of the transverse walls whose semicircular tops supported it still stand. These walls are pierced at the bottom by shallow archways like those of a bridge, whose curve, being less than that of the vault above, is rendered doubly hideous by a pier at the apex necessary to support the weight of the wall.

Most of the walls are about five feet thick. The stones are uncut and the mortar fills the gaps. Stucco adorned the three chambers, whose refinements are of two styles. One we call Romanesque: the squinches rest on a dog-tooth cornice; doorways with rounded tops are framed in concentric mouldings; and a similar niche in the south court has these mouldings also dog-toothed. The other is bastard Egyptian, copied from Persepolis: arched doorways are surmounted by horizontal canopies which are scalloped, as they spread forwards and outwards, with a radiating feather design. This convention is unattractive enough in its own country and original stone. As a third-hand reminiscence, in cheaper material, it foreshadows the taste of the London County Council in the early twentieth century.

However, only archaeologists see beauty in Sasanian architecture. The interest here is historical. This palace, founded at the beginning of the third century AD, is a landmark in the development of building. Its revelation of the squinch, a simple arch across the angle of two walls, coincides with the appearance of the pendentive, a kite-shaped vault supported by an angle pier, in Syria; and from these two inventions derive two primary architectural styles, in the wake of two religions: medieval Persian, branching into Mesopotamia, the Levant, and India; and Byzantine-Romanesque, spreading to the confines of northern Europe. Previously, there was no means of placing a dome on four square walls, or on a building of any shape whose inside area much exceeded that of the dome itself. Henceforth, as squinches and pendentives became enlarged, and as the former were multiplied into zones of stalactites and bats'-wings, a dome became possible to buildings of all shapes and sizes. The Christian expansion of this possibility reached its height in St Sophia at Constantinople, and began a second life with Brunelleschi's dome at Florence. The Mohammadan is waiting to be mapped, by anyone who can keep his temper among the jealousies of modern archaeology. But one thing is certain. Without these two principles, of which one has its prototype here, architecture as we know it would be different, and many objects most familiar to the world's eye, such as St Peter's, the Capitol, and the Taj Mahal, would not exist.

I wish I could go to Sarvistan. It is nearer Shiraz than this, and has another Sasanian palace, in which a row of arches that spring from the wall are supported by round pillars. Here perhaps is the germ of that other great feature of Mohammadan architecture, the arcade. Pillars certainly played their part in Sasanian architecture, as the excavations at Damghan have shown, and in view of the Sasanian aptitude for vaulting, it is probable that they were used in most cases to support arches.

Fired by this train of revelation, I clambered down from the roof to find the Kashgais had made tea for us. An old tribesman obligingly produced an awl and thread to mend the cross-piece of my saddle-bags. One of the younger men, having said he knew the path up to the Kala-i-Dukhtar, had gone ahead to await us in the gorge. He hailed us from above as we rode by. The climb was easier than it looked, but nasty enough.

Seen from behind, the castle stands on a promontory, and is thus defended on three sides by precipices that fall almost sheer from its outer walls. The last stage of the climb was up a saddle connecting the promontory with the main cliff. This leads to the back of the building, which faces north, a mighty rampart lacking door or window and curved as though it contained a stadium. Tall thin buttresses support it at close intervals, and are joined at the top by rounded arches.

Creeping gingerly round the edge of the wall, for there was a high wind, I attained the central chamber.

The castle is built in three terraces. From the gorge below a gaping black arch can be seen, which gives entrance to a basement on the east side. This I could not reach as the spiral ramp communicating with it was blocked and I had no wish to climb down the outside. There are two such ramps, contained in square turrets which led originally from the bottom of the building, past the east corners of the chamber I stood in, to a third level above.

In general form this chamber resembles those in the Palace of Ardeshir, being square and supporting a dome on squinches. The stucco is dotted with bullet-holes, but is otherwise extremely well preserved, though it has no ornament. Each wall is pierced by a broad round-topped arch, which, in the case of the south, east, and west walls, is open to the air. That in the north wall has been blocked up, and the masonry stucco'd over. But its outline is plain enough.

This wall is on that side of the chamber which faces away from the gorge and is enclosed by the curved rampart at the back. And now arose a mystery. Between the chamber and the rampart lies a large area to which there seems to have been no entrance other than the arch now blocked or some hidden passage cut through the rock below. I could see no trace of such a passage from the back. There may be one from the basement. But I think not. For I saw then that others had noticed this mystery too, and had burrowed deep into the wall on either side of the arch in their attempts to penetrate the sealed area. They would hardly have wasted so much effort for no reason. The longer of the tunnels stretched twenty feet into solid masonry and came to a dead end.

The opposite arch on the south side gives on to a grass platform between high walls, which extend to the brink of the gorge sixty feet away. These walls, as can be seen from the semicircular top of the wall at the inner end, supported a barrel-vault some forty feet in diameter. The other end was always open. Thus the Kala-i-Dukhtar at Firuzabad provides another Sasanian prototype for Persia's next most important contribution to Mohammadan architecture after the dome on squinches: the ivan or open-fronted hall. This form, more than any other, changed the character of the early mosques. At first it was employed on one side only, to announce the sanctuary and the direction of Mecca. Later it was used to break the monotony of the other sides as well. It grew taller and taller. Its flat screen-like front became a field for all kinds of ornament and writing. It sprouted minarets at the side, arcades and cupolas at the top. Its vagaries have changed the face of every town in Islam, and it was pleasing, I thought, to find myself hanging on to an old nut-tree and eating an orange in the place where the idea began.

Suddenly the Kashgai guide said: 'Do you want to see the hammam?'

I did want to know what he meant; Turkish baths aren't generally situated on the tops of desolate mountains. My guards picked up their rifles, and we followed the man down a devious little path along the cliff's edge. After a few moments the guards ran away, shouting 'Nargiz! Nargiz!' Presuming they had seen some animal I continued with the guide, from whom, if from anyone, they were supposed to be guarding me, and who at length lowered himself over the cliff, beckoning me to follow. We found ourselves at the mouth of a tunnel festooned with ferns and emitting a rank smell, as though it were the lair of a beast: a notion which was supported by some heaps of bones and feathers.

Forty feet up this tunnel brought us to the threshold of a cavern. It was now almost pitch dark. A hot vapour and a sound of bubbling assailed us. Suddenly our feet exchanged the solid rock for a crust of quaking mud.

'You had better go first,' I said.

'I think,' said the Kashgai, 'that you had better go first.'

We decided to light a bonfire.

Even this did not reveal the end of the cavern or the whereabouts of the bubbling. Taking a brand, I was just stepping out on to the mud, when the smoke disturbed a cloud of bats. There was only one exit for them, and I was blocking it. With the breath of their wings on my neck, I fled down the tunnel into daylight, where I stood watching the verminous little creatures suspend themselves among the ferns. They were of the short-eared kind, in size between a sparrow and a thrush, and their small pink faces gazed malevolently down into mine.

A sound of laughing and two pairs of legs showed the guards had found us. Dropping down on to the ledge, they were carrying, instead of the expected pelt, armfuls of those same big jonquils, twice the size of ours, which I had seen at the Governor's. This was the meaning of *nargiz** – narcissus!

* The same name is found in Aramaic and Armenian, and is recorded by the Chinese as *nai-ki*; see *Sino-Iranica*, by Berthold Lanfer (Chicago, 1919), p. 427.

Looking over the edge to see if there had once been a way up from below, I found traces of an artificial path built out of the side of the cliff. Mortar and stonework were both Sasanian. In those days, therefore, the cavern may have been used as a Turkish bath; it is difficult to see what other reason there could have been for making a path to it. The records of Sasanian royalty are particularly impersonal. But I now begin to imagine it in slippers, so to speak, during week-ends at the Kala-i-Dukhtar, when the rheumatic members of the party took the waters of a morning and the dowagers had face-massage in that mud. After all, if Mlle Tabouis can write a life of Nebuchadnezzar which is almost too heavy to lift, I might make two such volumes on Ardeshir out of today's material.

When we reached the bottom, I jumped into the river. It was deep enough to swim, not too cold, and most grateful after a hot morning. But the escort thought it fatal, and uprooting several trees, lit a bonfire to bring me to life when I came out. Including the Kashgai, we were now six; but the splendour of Ali Asgar's travelling arrangements enabled me to lunch them all out of my saddle-bags, reserving a bottle of wine for myself. A pied kingfisher was flitting up and down the river, black and white and rather larger than ours, but unmistakably its cousin, having the same large head, stumpy tail, and lightning flight. On the bank grew one or two mauve leafless irises, or lilies, three inches high.

There are two Sasanian rock-carvings in the gorge, of which Flandin and Coste give drawings, though no photographs have been published of them. The more interesting depicts a tilt between Ardeshir and his enemy Ardarun V, the last of the Arsacid dynasty, which he displaced. This is near the Firuzabad end; unfortunately I had missed it, and there was no time to go back so far. I did ride back to see the other, which the Kashgai had pointed out from the top of the cliff. This depicts the usual god, Hormuzd, and king, also Ardeshir in this case, grasping a ring; the king wears a balloon on his head, said by some authorities to be a bag for the hair, is followed by several attendants, and assumes an attitude of defence (meant by the artist to be deference) as practised in modern boxing. Small and alone among the huge cliffs, carved on a face of morose purplish rock where river, trees, and kingfisher were the only life, the row of ancient figures was reminder less of the Sasanids' triumph than of the dark age they triumphed over. Neither they nor the gorge have changed, save that passers-by are not so common and find less convenience; for there used to be a bridge near the relief, and the river is still parted by a fallen pier, built of cut stone, whose mortar has withstood the spate of thirteen centuries. Forcing my horse through the reeds, till its belly touched the water, I looked hurriedly and in vain for the inscription Herzfeld saw here, which records that the bridge was built by Aprsam, Ardeshir's minister.

The escort were beside themselves at the prospect of being benighted in the gorge again. A mad gallop, careless of rocks or trees, brought us in sight of the Water Pass before the light failed and the frogs began to croak. From there a moon guided us over the fields to this peculiar village of Ibrahimabad, whose streets are contained, like the Underground, in a maze of tunnels with houses built above them.

Ali Asgar was waiting on a rooftop by an open door. Tea-things were set out on a tray; books and wine on a shelf. 'What would Your Excellency like for dinner?'

Goat, horse-dung, paraffin, and Flit have been vanquished by the smell of the jonquils.

Shiraz, 25 February Christopher is still here, but has now got permission to go on to Bushire, on condition he leaves Persia forthwith. This is the end of our Afghan hopes unless the decision is reversed; but as a diplomatic row is brewing, that may happen. Sir Reginald Hoare is not the type to suffer insults gladly when they take the form of a covert attack on his Legation, Christopher being a former attaché and his own cousin. The authorities have not had the sense, from their own point of view, to placate him by producing a reason; Ayrum, the Chief of Police in Teheran, simply repeats that the order of expulsion has come from the General Staff, in other words from Marjoribanks himself. Perhaps the lion disguised as a worm will turn at last.

I saw Krefter for a minute, who told me the Governor of Shiraz is wrong in asserting that Herzfeld has no right to refuse people permission to photograph the old remains at Persepolis; that right having been expressly confirmed by the Minister of Public Instruction. I must ask the Governor again, in case this is bluff. As a result of this conversation I dreamt that Persepolis had become a centre of art-weaving and the columns been draped with tweed curtains of Jacobean pattern, to which the Professor now gave his whole attention and pointed that of visitors.

Kazerun (2900 ft), 27 February   I see yesterday was my birthday.

There is a drop of about 5000 feet from the top of the Pir-i-Zan pass to this place, mostly perpendicular, and tackled by a narrow shelf-road which is among the benefits conferred on Persia by the War. West of the pass a new colour begins, the steely grey of the Persian Gulf. At this time of year, when the emerald grass is sprouting, the grey villages, irregular fields, winding lanes, and broken-down stone walls of the Kazerun valley remind one of Ireland. Even the palms are not wholly out of place in such a comparison.

The neighbouring ruins of Shapur, although close to the main road, offer as virgin, if not so interesting, an archaeological field as those of Firuzabad. The place was named after its founder, Shapur I, whose relations with the gods, numerous victories, and capture of the Roman Emperor Valerian are depicted on the walls of a miniature gorge. As documents, these reliefs give a detailed picture of Sasanian fashions in harness, hats, trousers, shoes, and weapons. As monuments, they are an interesting survival of that uncouth impulse which prompted the early monarchies of Egypt, Mesopotamia, and Iran to hew themselves immortality out of the living rock. As works of art, they have borrowed from Rome, possibly through Roman prisoners, and mask their barbarous ostentation under a veneer of Mediterranean stateliness and opulence. Those who admire force without art, and form without mind, find them lovely.

The statue of Shapur, in full round and three times life-size, improves on the reliefs only by its situation, which is at the mouth of a cave three miles up the valley behind the gorge. A climb of 600 feet leads up to it. The last fifteen were perpendicular, and I stuck, while the valley swam below me. But before I could resist, the villagers had bundled me up like a sack, as they did our lunch and wine. The statue must have been twenty feet high, and have stretched from floor to ceiling just inside the entrance. At present a crowned head with a Velasquez beard and the curls of a Spanish Infanta lies at the bottom of a cavity, above which inclines a torso sprigged with muslin tassels and broken off at the thighs. Mr Hyde carved his name on it in 1821. We were just in time to stop Jamshyd Taroporevala, our Indian chauffeur, from adding his. Two feet in square-toed shoes still occupy the pedestal.

The back of the cave descends into a series of enormous pits, whence ramify cathedrals of impenetrable obscurity. We had a lantern, but its range was helpless against such distances, and it served only to warn us there was too much water to explore them.

After walking back to the gorge, Christopher and I had a swim in the river that runs through it. We remembered our last bathe together at Beyrut. This morning I said goodbye to him. He has gone to Bushire and we meet again for Afghanistan or lunch at the Ritz.

Persepolis (5500 ft), the same evening   I stopped in Shiraz on the way here, to get a letter from the Governor to Dr Mostafavi, who is watching the excavations for the Persian Government. On the way out of the town I met Krefter driving in to a dance at the Bank. He gave me another letter:

PERSEPOLIS SHIRAZ
Oriental Institute Persian Expedition

DEAR MR BYRON,

Excuse my late answer, I simply forgot. The situation is this: as there is no law protecting copyright, etc. in Persia, the only way of preventing everybody to come, to take photos and to sell and publish them, is not to allow photographing. For, as soon as a foreigner is seen taking photos, there appear articles in the press (already 3 times) complaining, that everyone is allowed to photograph the National Monuments of Persia except the Persians. I have had the most unpleasant correspondence with the Government on this account.

Hence, we have made the arrangement, that people interested in the publication of photos might get them from the Oriental Institute, Univ. of Chicago, and publish them acknowledging the provenance. I am sorry I cannot make an exception. – I do not count as photograph, if somebody takes a picture, with a small camera, with groups of people, of themselves on it, for a souvenir. But *not* to be published.

Yours very sincerely

ERNST HERZFELD

Krefter added: 'You'll find the Professor alone. He'll be glad of company.'

Will he? For the moment I'm sleeping in a stable attached to a tea-house, beside a heap of fresh dung.

Persepolis, 1 March The tea-house is a mile and a half up the road from Persepolis. Being in the direction of Naksh-i-Rustam, I decided to go there first, and was just starting, when the people said I could not walk as the streams were too full. At this moment a passing horseman stopped for breakfast. 'You,' I said, 'need a car for the road'; and I need a horse for the fields. Shall we exchange?' He agreed with pleasure.

The carvings on the cliff at Naksh-i-Rustam range over twenty centuries, from Elamite to Achemenian to Sasanian. Below them stand two fire-altars of uncertain date and an Achemenian tomb-house. Only the last is beautiful. The rest are negative art or repellent. But while the mountains last, the rock-maniacs who commanded these things must be remembered – and they knew it. They were indifferent to the *gratitude* of posterity. No perishable aestheticism or legal benevolence for them! All they ask is attention, and they get it, like a child or Hitler, by brute insistence. In this one sentence of gigantic ideographs, they have recorded a crucial moment in the history of human ideas, when the divine right of kings emerged from prehistory to the modern world.

The accent is struck by the four tombs of the Achemenid kings, regular landmarks hacked out of the cliff in the form of crosses. Each is carved with a tedious uniformity of low reliefs. These begin at the top with the usual pact between god and king – the god at this period being a human scarab – continue with a couple of couches in the Tutankhamen style, one above the other, which enclose lines of tributaries, and then expand into the arms of the cross with a false façade of pillars in half-round supporting bull's-head capitals. The face of the rock between the pillars is covered with cuneiform writing. With the help of a goat-hair rope let down by two men who were living in it, I climbed up to one tomb, the second from the west it was, as the cliff faces south. The inside was arranged in three niches, each divided into three bins; one or two of the latter had conical lids which have been prised open. The whole chamber must have been sealed by a stone door revolving on stone pins at the top and bottom, whose sockets are still visible.

The panels at Naksh-i-Rustam, below the tombs, have been often described and identified. The cliff faces south. From east to west I noted the following, without reference to their historical meaning:

Between the angle of the cliff and the second tomb –

1 A blank ready for carving but bearing only a small modern inscription.

2 A Sasanian group. The king, wearing muslin cowboy trousers, squared-toed shoes fluttering long ribbons, and a hair-balloon, confronts an allegorical figure whose municipal crown, piled with sausage curls, might have been designed by Bernard Partridge. This creature, whose sex is disputed, upholds the ring denoting a pact between the king and itself. Between them stands a child, and behind the king a man in a Phrygian cap. The whole extends below the existing ground level which has been excavated to show it.

Below the second tomb –

3 A Sasanian king in a hair-balloon tilting with an enemy. This is much damaged.

4 Beneath the above, the heads and shoulders of two other warriors tilting. Here the ground has not been excavated and most of the relief is hidden.

Between the second and third tombs –

5 A composition three times life-size of Shapur on horseback receiving homage from the kneeling Emperor Valerian. The horse has borrowed a Roman pose, but has no strength. Like all Sasanian reliefs it is unmuscular: a stuffed dummy. One of the heads on the east side has an Achemenian look. Is it possible there was an earlier relief here, which the Sasanids destroyed to make way for their own advertisements?

Below the fourth tomb –

6 A Sasanian king tilting with a losing enemy. His hair-balloon is smaller than the others, lemon-shaped, and attached to the head by a stalk. This carving has more spirit. Its debt to Rome is less and it approaches those equestrian figures on silver plates which display the real genius of the period.

Beyond the fourth tomb –

7 A Sasanian king and his court in a pulpit or gallery. This curious composition is carved on the front of a three-sided bulge in the rock. The king stands in the middle of the group, where a gap in the balustrade allows his full length to be seen. Three half-length figures attend him on either side, and two more on the west facet of the bulge. These figures have an Achemenian look too, though the king's head is typically Sasanian. Again I wonder if there was an Achemenian relief here before, or if this look is the result of conscious antiquarianism.

8 Whatever the Achemenians did on this particular surface, the Sasanians were preceded by somebody, who seems to have lived about the middle of the second millennium BC, and may therefore be called Elamite. On the east side of the bulge can be seen a primitive, bird-like figure in very flat relief, whose angular outline reminds one of a Mexican hieroglyph. On the west side, below the two half-length figures, appears a single head in the same style. Both heads are in profile, but have eyes in full, a convention familiar from Egypt.*

9 Almost touching the pulpit group on the west stand a couple of affronted horsemen, each leaning forward to grasp the symbolic ring. Here, the Sasanian king wears his balloon on top of a Phrygian cap, while the god has a municipal crown. The horses trample on their riders' enemies and present a fine exhibition of Sasanian saddlery. An enormous tassel, suspended by cords from the saddle, dangles between the hind legs of each.

The cliff turns to the north after this relief, and is gradually absorbed in a gentler slope. The two fire-altars are round the corner. They are four feet six inches high, and could be mistaken, if painted brown, for a pair of neo-Greek wine-coolers.

The Achemenian tomb-house stands by itself, opposite the fourth tomb. It is known as the tomb of Zoroaster, a name long ridiculed by archaeologists until Herzfelt discovered that there might be some reason for it.

* Gerald Reitlinger in his *Tower of Skulls*, p. 99, notes another sculpture of this type on the main face of the bulge beside the Sasanian king's feet, where a 'king in a kind of tight-fitting dressing gown sits on a throne formed of a folded snake.

This is real architecture; or perhaps one should say, since its function has no relation to its form, that it represents a real architectural tradition of which we are otherwise ignorant. It is a copy of a house. Where was that house? In Persia? It gives no hint of that expensive, cross-bred sophistication about to blossom at Persepolis. If it stood in a Mediterranean country, it would be hailed as the original source of domestic architecture in quattrocento Italy and Georgian England. Unlike the Greek temple, which developed out of a wooden form concerned with the stress of weights, this tomb-house derives from a form of brick or mud conveying an idea of content; its beauty is in the spacing of ornament on a flat wall. It is surprising to find this principle, on which all good domestic building since the Renascence has depended, fully stated in Persia about the middle of the sixth century BC. It is equally surprising to remember how little attention, from this point of view, visitors to Naksh-i-Rustam have so far given it.

The building stands about seventeen feet square, and twenty-seven high above the present ground-level; though originally, as revealed by an unenterprising trench dug round the north side only, it must have been some ten feet higher. The walls are four and a half feet thick, and are constructed of large white marble blocks as well fitted as those in the Golden Gate at Constantinople. Each angle is reinforced by shallow buttresses, between which, but not outside them, runs a miniature cornice. The flat roof is composed of two enormous monoliths laid side by side.

The east, south, and west sides are each adorned with three pairs of windows, framed in a darker stone flush with the marble, and containing blind panels; these panels are enclosed by secondary, inside frames along the sides and top only. The lower windows are taller than they are broad; the middle windows square; and the upper windows copies of the lower ones, but in miniature, and touching the cornice: an arrangement which recalls Vitruvius and Palladio. Vertically, the distances between the pairs are equal. But horizontally, the distance between each window is more than twice the distance between it and the inside of the corner buttresses. Apart from windows, the walls are decorated with a pattern of small shallow niches, oblong and upright, which cut across the joints of the stonework as if they were clamps – though clamps with the light and shade reversed, in the manner of a photographic negative.

The north side, facing the cliff, has no pairs of windows, but only a single low aperture more than halfway up the building, whose threshold, and the floor inside it, cut across the level of the middle side-windows. This entrance is surmounted by a horned architrave, on which sits a small blind window without any frame. One can climb up to it, as attempts have been made to cut through the masonry below into a supposed lower chamber.

In the afternoon I went to Persepolis, and gave my letter from the Governor of Fars to Dr Mostafavi.

Herzfeld joined us. He was very entertaining as he showed me round the excavations, and let loose Bul-bul, his wild sow, who made off with a stone belonging to her enemy, a grumpy old airedale. The result was a grotesque pursuit through the ruins, in which the sow's trotters slithered about stairways and pavements like Charlie Chaplin's feet, to an orchestra of growls and grunts and roars from the Professor. Eventually we sat down to tea in the house Krefter has built for the diggers. I say house; it is a palace, reconstructed of wood on the site, and in the style, of its Achemenian predecessor, whose stone door and window frames are incorporated in it. The money was supplied by Mrs Moore and the University of Chicago, and the outcome is a luxurious cross between the King David Hotel in Jerusalem and the Pergamum Museum in Berlin. This is as it should be, for it will have to serve the purposes of both when the excavations are finished.

R. B.: 'Perhaps you misunderstood my letter.'
Herzfeld: 'I perfectly understood it. You cannot photograph anything here at all. If the Persians saw you, they would make trouble.'
R. B.: 'I think you must be mistaken. The Governor of Fars said he wanted me to take pictures here.'
Herzfeld: 'It is inconceivable the difficulties I have had on this point. When I first came here, I sent my pictures to be developed in Shiraz. The photographer made copies of the plates and sold the prints as his own. Then that terrible fellow X— came when I was away and took 100 pictures of my discoveries. The first I knew of it was when they appeared in the newspapers as his discoveries. Now Mr Myron Smith has been asking permission. He has influence with my supporters in America, and in order to get rrrrid of him I have presented my whole collection of photographs to the University of

Chicago. I have had to write as many as twelve letters on the subject of this man.'

R. B.: 'I quite see that if other people sell pictures of your discoveries, they are stealing money from the excavation fund. But listen to my point of view. I'm not an archaeologist. I've no concern with your discoveries. All I'm interested in here is the architectural forms, not because they are old, but because they are a part of architectural history. The doors for instance. Doors only exist in relation to the human figure; you can judge these doors and Renascence doors and Corbusier's doors all by the one same standard. To make that kind of comparison I simply want a few reference pictures of things people have been looking at for 2000 years and have already sketched and photographed hundreds of times. And I want to take these pictures myself, because I know exactly what details I want to illustrate. If you don't trust me to leave your discoveries alone, you can send someone round with me; that's reasonable, isn't it? You may think you have the legal right to prevent my taking any photographs at all. But you must admit it would be morally indefensible. It would be as if the Parthenon had suddenly become a private villa and the rest of the world been excluded from it.'

Herzfeld (bridling): 'Not at all. In Europe there have always been these rules. When I was a young man, making excavations, we were never allowed to photograph anything.'

R. B.: 'But that is no reason why you should follow a bad example now you are older.'

Herzfeld (puffing furiously at his cigarette): 'I think it is perfectly rrrright!'

This attitude of German authoritarianism seemed unbecoming in a man about to be turned out of his own country by the Nazis. Fortunately, I was prevented from saying so by the entrance of Krefter, at which I got up to go.

'Where is your car?' asked Herzfeld more affably. 'We have a garage at the back. I will tell them to bring your luggage in.'

'It's very kind of you, but I'm staying at the tea-house up the road.'

'That is not comfortable. Why don't you stay here?'

They looked quite haggard when I refused, not at the loss of my company, but at my escaping the shackles of their hospitality.

'Well,' said Herzfeld cheerfully, 'perhaps we shall see you tomorrow.'

'Yes, indeed,' I beamed. 'Goodbye, and thank you for your kind offer. I only wish I could accept it.'

That was true. No one in his senses enjoys forsaking comfort and good company for a dung-heap.

Persepolis, 2 March, midday   I delivered this letter early:

DEAR DR HERZFELD,
Since both the Governor of Fars and Dr Mostafavi have stated categorically that you have no right to prevent my photographing the portions of arches and columns which have always been above ground, the only means of stopping my photographing them are either
  (1) to show me the wording of your concession proving that you have the right, or
  (2) force.
Please choose your means.

While I was photographing, a small round figure twinkled across the platform. 'I have never,' it said, 'met with a way of acting as illoyal as yours,' pirouetted, and twinkled away again.

Illoyal to whom, I wondered.

It was a question of principle. I got my pictures, and did a service to travellers in calling Herzfeld's bluff. But it was a pity to lose conversation.

There are still things to be said about Persepolis.

In its prime, when the walls were mud and the roofs wood, it may have looked rather shoddy – rather as it would look, in fact, if reconstructed at Hollywood. Today, at least it is not shoddy. Only the stone has survived, but for a few of Alexander's ashes which they dig up now and then. And stone worked with such opulence and precision has great splendour, whatever one may think of the forms employed on it. This is increased by the contrast between the stones used, the hard opaque grey and the more lucent white. Isolated ornaments have also been discovered in a jet-black marble without vein or blemish.

Is that all?

*

Patience! In the old days you arrived by horse. You rode up the steps on to the platform. You made a camp there, while the columns and winged beasts kept their solitude beneath the stars, and not a sound or movement disturbed the empty moonlit plain. You thought of Darius and Xerxes and Alexander. You were alone with the ancient world. You saw Asia as the Greeks saw it, and you felt their magic breath stretching out towards China itself. Such emotions left no room for the aesthetic question, or for any question.

Today you step out of a motor, while a couple of lorries thunder by in a cloud of dust. You find the approaches defended by walls. You enter by leave of a porter, and are greeted, on reaching the platform, by a light railway, a neo-German hostel, and a code of academic malice controlled from Chicago. These useful additions clarify the intelligence. You may persuade yourself, in spite of them, into a mood of romance. But the mood they invite is that of a critic at an exhibition. This is the penalty of greater knowledge. It isn't my fault. No one would have been more pleased than I to leave the brain idle in a dream of history and landscape and light and wind and other impalpable accidents. But if circumstances insist on showing me more than I want to see, it is no good telling lies about it.

The columns, therefore, can be disposed of in a word. They are surprising, as Sir Gilbert Scott's town hall in Bombay is surprising because it combines Hindu themes with Gothic. Like mules, these crosses are infertile. They have no bearing on the general course of architecture, and hold no precepts for it. You may like them in a casual way, if they happen to agree with some current of contemporary fashion. The columns at Persepolis don't.

The columns jump to the eye first. Other architectural features are the stairs, the platform, and the palace doors. The stairs are fine because there are so many of them. The platform is fine because its massive blocks have posed, and solved, an engineering problem. Neither has any art. But the doorways have. They, and they alone, boast a gleam of true invention; they suggest ideas, they utter a comment, with regard to other doorways. Their proportions are narrow and thick, thus inviting a perpetual to and fro; whereas our doors ask the figure to pause and frame itself. Like the arches at Stonehenge, they are made of monoliths, one for each side and one on top. But their mouldings and angles are as sharp and delicate as if cut by a machine.

Then comes the decoration. Those reliefs hold a horrid shock for anyone who has known them in photographs. Where they have been exposed to the weather, their line and rhythm emerges poetically from the black-mottled stone. The ones inside the doorways, and the ones that Herzfeld has dug up, have exactly the same line and rhythm. But their stone, owing to its extreme hardness, has proved impervious to age; it remains a bright smooth grey, as slick as an aluminium saucepan. This cleanness reacts on the carving like sunlight on a fake old master; it reveals, instead of the genius one expected, a disconcerting void. I see only too well what Christopher meant when he said the sculptures were 'unemotional without being intellectual'. My involuntary thought, as Herzfeld showed me the new staircase, was: 'How much did this cost? Was it made in a factory? No, it wasn't. Then how many workmen for how many years chiselled and polished these endless figures?' Certainly they are not mechanical figures; nor are they guilty of elaboration for its own sake; nor are they cheap in the sense of lacking technical skill. But they are what the French call *faux bons*. They have art, but not spontaneous art, and certainly not great art. Instead of mind or feeling, they exhale a soulless refinement, a veneer adopted by the Asiatic whose own artistic instinct has been fettered and devitalized by contact with the Mediterranean. To see what that instinct really was, and how it differs from this, one can look at the Assyrian reliefs in the British Museum.

A lesser shock is administered by the crenellations along the parapet and balustrades of the staircase. Herzfeld found them in almost perfect condition; each has three steps and looks as if it had been built from a child's box of bricks. These jagged excrescences adorned all the palaces; Krefter has reproduced them with care on his. They are ugly enough in themselves. But adjacent to the reliefs, their clumsy iteration and angular shadows spoil the delicacy of the carving as well. Herzfeld said: 'They give it life.' They do. But it isn't a pretty life and it kills everything else.

Abadeh, 3 March Ali Asgar couldn't bear the tea-house any more. We left Persepolis after lunch.

A newly planted avenue led off the Isfahan road to Cyrus's tomb, a sarcophagus of white marble on a high, stepped plinth, standing by itself among the ploughed fields. It looks its age: every stone has been separately kissed, and every joint stroked hollow, as though by the action of the sea. No ornament or cry for notice disturbs its lonely serenity. Enough that Alexander was its first tourist. There used to be a temple round it. One can still see how this stood from the bases of the columns.

Since then, it has become the Tomb of the Mother of Solomon. In deference to this transformation, a miniature mihrab and an arabic inscription have been carved on one of the inside walls. Across the mihrab hangs a bunch of rags and bells; leaves of an old Koran were blowing about the floor. The ground inside the temple boundary is occupied by Mohammadan graves.

Half a mile further on stood a platform of the Persepolis type, supporting one plain white pillar; and near this, the ruin of a tomb-house like the one at Naksh-i-Rustam. At length, while the sun's last rays spurted from a bank of rain clouds, I trudged over the plough to that solitary marble stele which bears the four-winged effigy of Cyrus. Now indeed I could imagine how the visitor to Persepolis used to feel; and so dreaming was lost in the dark, till rescued by the flash of the car's headlights.

Isfahan. 5 March finds me staying with Wishaw, the 'captain of the oil'; in other words, manager of the Anglo-Persian Oil Company's local branch.

The name of the Governor of Isfahan is Mr Trump-of-Raphael. Before calling on him, I asked one of Wishaw's clerks to translate my letter of recommendation:

H.E. The Governor-General, ·
                    Isfahan.
Mr Birn, one of the learnedmen of England, is proceeding yours to pay visit to the History Buildings etc. of that districts, who will also take photos of the said buildings.
    Please issue necessary instructions to the Authorities concerned to render him any assistance he may require.
    Sgd – MAHMOOD JAM
    (*Sealed*) MINISTRY OF INTERIOR

Mr Trump-of-Raphael told me his plans for improving the Maidan. The first instalment of them has got him into trouble, since Marjoribanks disapproves of the new tank on the ground that it may breed the anopheles mosquito. Nevertheless he will proceed with the rest. The arcaded walls are to be enriched with tilework. And where the road cuts across in front of the bazaar entrance at the north-east end, it will pass under big tiled archways on either side. The architect is a German who works under a supervising committee consisting of Herzfeld, Godard, and other savants.

Isfahan, 9 March Muzaffar the painter, who exhibited at the London exhibition and afterwards did a picture for the Queen, takes one back to the days before artistic temperament, when artists did as they were told. He comes of generations of painters, and has inherited their craftsmen's attitude; in fact he started by decorating pen-boxes. I asked him to do a miniature of me. Certainly, he said, if I would give him a photograph to copy. That, I replied, was just what I would not do, as my purpose in giving him the commission was to see if he could draw from life. He can. He has done a portrait, and got a likeness, quite in the Persian style. But I had to design the picture, say how the head must be spaced on the paper, and decide if the background should be plain or enriched. His pupils do the backgrounds and borders from a repertory of traditional patterns.

He prides himself on having two manners, Persian and European. I have seen some miniatures he did from photographs; they were simply the photographs themselves, only tinted. The other day he designed an appalling poster of two peacocks for a brand of local cigarette. 'There!' he announced proudly. 'I can do miniatures and I can do this. Rubens couldn't have done both.'

Why Rubens? Why Rubens particularly?

Isfahan, 13 March Christopher is now a prisoner in the Residency at Bushire, according to news from Teheran. Ayrum, the Chief of Police, still says it is the fault of the General Staff. The Minister of Foreign Affairs says it is due to Ayrum's personal orders.

Mrs Budge Bulkeley, worth £32,000,000, has arrived here accompanied by some lesser millionairesses. They are in great misery because the caviare is running out. Altogether, they are travelling in much less comfort than I do. A dozen couriers (they have two) on their dignity are not worth one servant who can cook and can turn a pigsty into one's ordinary bedroom at five minutes' notice – for such is Ali Asgar.

One of the party was heard to say of Mrs Moore, who is on her way here by aeroplane: 'Rich? Why she could buy us all up four times over.'

Mr Trump-of-Raphael gave a tea-party for them. I sat between the English bishop and a Kajar prince.

'Why are you out here?' asked the bishop angrily.

'Travelling.'

'What in?'

Isfahan, 16 March Yesterday was Marjoribanks' birthday. As Persian custom ordains, the Governor held a reception the night before.

This sudden use brought the Chihil Sutun to life again, transforming it from a stale summerhouse into the stately pleasure dome it originally was. Spread with carpets, lit with pyramids of lamps, and filled with several hundred people, the verandah looked enormous; its wooden pillars and painted canopy towered away into the night; the glass niche at the back, glittering through its gold filigree, seemed infinitely distant. The Persians sat in black rows, with their hands folded and their feet under their chairs. Dr Wolff, the German dentist, wore a bowler hat. In the front stood tables heaped with cakes and tangerines. Waiters handed endless cups of tea.

Mr Trump-of-Raphael arrived in a dinner jacket, over which flapped a mackintosh. He was so evidently pleased to see everyone there that everyone was pleased to see him. He shook hands with all he could reach, and acted the host instead of the official dummy, as an English governor would have done.

A brass band of Armenian boys from Julfa struck up, and we moved to the front to watch the fireworks. These exploded beside the long tank, rockets, catherine wheels, and the rest, till at last two lines of golden fountains were pouring into the black water, and Marjoribanks himself spluttered vengefully into flame at the further end. The band played the National Anthem and that was the end of the first reception.

The second was more select. About fifty people collected in a long vaulted room, beneath those languid Safavid frescoes which have vied with Omar Khayam to give the world a false idea of Persian art and sentiment. The German bank manager's wife acted as hostess. Another band from Julfa played jazz inside a glass cupboard. At the end of the room was a cold buffet, which dispensed red cup from large bowls. Being composed of three parts arak and one Julfa wine, it was not so innocent as it looked.

No Persian would venture to entertain a single guest, much less give a party, without carpets. When dancing began, the floor rose like an angry sea, and not until several couples had been wrecked were nails employed to quiet the woollen breakers. At the buffet, Kajar princes hobnobbed with their official enemies the Governor and Chief of Police. Their faultless smokings and Cartier studs would have made my borrowed suit feel shabby but for the German element, which can be relied on anywhere to make other nationalities feel smart. One of them, seven feet high, wearing a tail-coat, a collar without an opening four inches deep, and a buff hunting waistcoat, had the audacity to leer at my cummerbund.

It was a pleasant evening, and when Mr Trump-of-Raphael in a touching manner asked me what I thought of it I honestly applauded his good taste. There was nothing pretentious, no self-conscious nationalist antiquarianism or self-conscious Persian modernity, to spoil the guests' enjoyment. Persians have a gift of social ease. This taste of it made me feel quite affectionately towards the old monster whose life we had been celebrating. Besides, not everyone can say he has danced in the Chihil Sutun.

The whole Char Bagh was illuminated as I walked back to Wishaw's house over the river. Tiers of lamps and candles were ranged at intervals under the trees, great wedding cakes of light thirty feet high, draped in red and backed with gilt mirrors. In the midst of all this blaze, put forth by the Municipality at much trouble and expense to prove its loyalty, the mullahs of the College had quietly gone one better. From the parapet of the great portal they had let down three cut-glass chandeliers, whose pale candles, flickering against the back void of the arch, revealed three globes of goldfish suspended between them.

The next afternoon there was a procession. Having spent the morning decorating the Anglo-Persian car, I fell asleep after lunch and missed it. Wishaw missed it too, because all his employees had gone out and he had to stay behind to guard the store-yard.

Isfahan, 18 March The beauty of Isfahan steals on the mind unawares. You drive about, under avenues of white tree-trunks and canopies of shining twigs; past domes of turquoise and spring yellow in a sky of liquid violet-blue; along the river patched with twisting shoals, catching that blue in its muddy silver, and lined with feathery groves where the sap calls; across bridges of pale toffee brick, tier on tier of arches breaking into piled pavilions; overlooked by lilac mountains, by the Kuh-i-Sufi shaped like Punch's hump and by other ranges receding to a line of snowy surf; and before you know how, Isfahan has become indelible, has insinuated its image into that gallery of places which everyone privately treasures.

I gave it no help in doing so. The monuments have kept me too busy.

One could explore for months without coming to the end of them. From the eleventh century, architects and craftsmen have recorded the fortunes of the town, its changes of taste, government, and belief. The buildings reflect these local circumstances; it is their charm, the charm of most old towns. But a few illustrate the heights of art independently, and rank Isfahan among those rarer places, like Athens or Rome, which are the common refreshment of humanity.

The two dome-chambers of the Friday Mosque point this distinction by their difference. Both were built about the same time, at the end of the eleventh century. In the larger, which is the main sanctuary of the mosque, twelve massive piers engage in a Promethean struggle with the weight of the dome. The struggle in fact obscures the victory; to perceive the latter demands a previous interest in mediaeval engineering or the character of the Seljuks. Contrast this with the smaller chamber, which is really a tomb-tower incorporated in the mosque. The inside is roughly thirty feet square and sixty high; its volume is perhaps one third of the other's. But while the larger lacked the experience necessary to its scale, the smaller embodies that precious moment between too little experience and too much, when the elements of construction have been refined of superfluous bulk, yet still withstand the allurements of superfluous grace; so that each element, like the muscles of a trained athlete, performs its function with winged precision, not concealing its effort, as over-refinement will do, but adjusting it to the highest degree of intellectual meaning. This is the perfection of architecture, attained not so much by the form of the elements – for this is a matter of convention – but by their chivalry of balance and proportion. And this small interior comes nearer to that perfection than I would have thought possible outside classical Europe.

The very material is a signal of economy: hard small bricks of mousy grey, which swallow up the ornament of Kufic texts and stucco inlay in their puritan singleness of purpose. In skeleton, the chamber is a system of arches, one broad in the middle of each wall, two narrow beside each corner, four miniature in each squinch, eight in the squinch zone, and sixteen above the squinches to receive the dome. The invention of Firuzabad has expanded; and will expand much further before Persian architecture dies in the eighteenth century. Here we catch it in the prime of youth and vigour. Even at this stage, the system is repeated or varied in many other buildings: the tomb-tower at Maragha for instance. But I doubt if there is another building in Persia, or in the whole of Islam, which offers so tense, so immediate an apparition of pure cubic form.

According to the inscription round the dome, the tomb-tower was built by Abul Ghanaim Marzuban, the Minister of Malek Shah, in 1088. One wonders what circumstance at that moment induced such a flight of genius. Was it the action of a new mind from Central Asia on the old civilization of the plateau, a procreation by nomadic energy out of Persian aestheticism? The Seljuks were not the only conquerors of Persia to have this effect. The Ghaznavide dynasty before them, the Mongol and Timurid dynasties after them, all came from north of the Oxus, and each produced a new Renascence on Persian soil. Even the Safavids, who inspired the last and most languid phase of Persian art, were Turks originally.

It was this last phase which gave Isfahan the character it has today, and which produced, curiously enough, its other great masterpiece. In 1612, Shah Abbas was occupied with the Royal Mosque at the south-west end of the Maidan, whose huge blue bulk and huge acreage of coarse floral tilework form just that kind of 'oriental' scenery so dear to the Omar Khayam fiends – pretty, if you like, even magnificent, but not important in the general scale of things. In 1618, however, he built another mosque on the south-east side of the Maidan, which was called after his father-in-law Sheikh Lutfullah.

This building stands at the opposite pole of architectural virtue to the small dome-chamber in the Friday Mosque. The latter is remarkable because, apart from its unique merit, that merit is of a kind which most people have regarded as the exclusive property of the European mind. The Mosque of Sheikh Lutfullah is Persian in the fabulous sense: the Omar Khayam brigade, to whom rational form is as much anathema as rational action, can wallow in it to their hearts' content. For while the dome-chamber is form only, has no colour, and obliterates its ornament by the intentness of its construction, the Mosque of Sheikh Lutfullah hides any symptom of construction or dynamic form beneath a mirage of shallow curved surfaces, the multitudinous offspring of the original squinch. Form there is and must be; but how it is created, and what supports it, are questions of which the casual eye is unconscious, as it is meant to be, lest its attention should wander from the pageant of colour and pattern. Colour and pattern are a commonplace in Persian architecture. But here they have a quality which must astonish the European, not because they infringe what he thought was his own monopoly, but because he can previously have had no idea that abstract pattern was capable of so profound a splendour.

As though to announce these principles as soon as possible, the outside of the mosque is careless of symmetry to a grotesque degree. Only the dome and portal are seen from the front. But owing to the discrepancy between the axis of the mosque and that of the Ali Gapu opposite, the portal, instead of being immediately under the dome, is set slightly to one side of it. Yet such is the character of the dome, so unlike is it to any other dome in Persia or elsewhere, that this deformity is hardly noticeable. Round a flattened hemisphere made of tiny bricks and covered with prawn-coloured wash runs a bold branching rose-tree inlaid in black and white. Seen from close to, the design has a hint of William Morris, particularly in its thorns; but as a whole it is more formal than pre-Raphaelite, more comparable to the design of a Genoese brocade immensely magnified. Here and there, at the junction of the branches or in the depths of the foliage, ornaments of ochre and dark blue mitigate the harshness of the black and white tracery, and bring it into harmony with the soft golden pink of the background: a process which is continued by a pervading under-foliage of faint light blue. But the genius of the effect is in the play of surfaces. The inlay is glazed. The stucco wash is not. Thus the sun strikes the dome with a *broken* highlight whose intermittent flash, moving with the time of day, adds a third texture to the pattern, mobile and unforeseen.

If the outside is lyric, the inside is Augustan. Here a still shallower dome, about seventy feet in diameter, swims above a ring of sixteen windows. From the floor to the base of the windows rise eight main arches, four enclosing right-angles, four flat wall-space, so that the boundaries of the floor form a square. The space between the tops of the arches is occupied by eight pendentives divided into planes like a bat's-wing.

The dome is inset with a network of lemon-shaped compartments, which increase in size as they descend from a formalized peacock at the apex and are surrounded by plain bricks; each is filled with a foliage pattern inlaid on plain stucco. The walls, bordered by broad white inscriptions on dark blue, are similarly inlaid with twirling arabesques or baroque squares on deep ochre stucco. The colours of all this inlay are dark blue, light greenish blue, and a tint of indefinite wealth like wine. Each arch is framed in turquoise corkscrews. The mihrab in the west wall is enamelled with tiny flowers on a deep blue meadow.

Each part of the design, each plane, each repetition, each separate branch or blossom has its own sombre beauty. But the beauty of the whole comes as you move. Again, the highlights are broken by the play of glazed and unglazed surfaces; so that with every step they rearrange themselves in countless shining patterns; while even the pattern of light through the thick window traceries is inconstant, owing to outer traceries which are several feet away and double the variety of each varying silhouette.

I have never encountered splendour of this kind before. Other interiors came into my mind as I stood there, to compare it with: Versailles, or the porcelain rooms at Schönbrunn, or the Doge's Palace, or St Peter's. All are rich; but none so rich. Their richness is three-dimensional; it is attended by all the effort of shadow. In the Mosque of Sheikh Lutfullah, it is a richness of light and surface, of pattern and colour only. The architectural form is unimportant. It is not smothered, as in rococo; it is simply the instrument of a spectacle, as earth is the instrument of a garden. And then I suddenly thought of that unfortunate species, modern interior decorators, who imagine they can make a restaurant, or a cinema, or a plutocrat's drawing-room look rich if given money enough for gold leaf and looking-glass. They little know what amateurs they are. Nor, alas, do their clients.

Yezd (4100 ft), 20 March   The desert between Isfahan and Yezd seemed broader, blacker, and bleaker than any, despite the warm spring sun. Its only relief was the ventilation mounds of the kanats, strung out like bowler hats in rows of ten and twenty miles, and enormously magnified by the clear shimmering air. I remember Noel's telling me he had calculated that one-third of the adult male population of Persia is perpetually at work on these underground water-channels. So developed is the sense of hydrostatics in successive generations that they can construct an incline of forty or fifty miles through almost flat country without any instruments, and at never more than a given number of feet below the ground.

I had a frightful misadventure this morning. Last night, on going to the English mission for an injection, I was thankful to accept their kind suggestion that, since the doctor was away, I should sleep in his bedroom. In the middle of the night the poor man came back unexpectedly, and seeing a strange head on his pillow, was obliged to sleep on a sofa. But worse followed. When at last he did venture into his own room to fetch some clean clothes, he caught me in an orgy, sitting on his bed over a bottle of wine and a cigar. Knowing I should be out all day, I was lunching early. I tried to put a bold face on it by offering him some wine, but he formed an unfavourable impression.

I was worried, on arriving here, that I had no letters of recommendation. 'I shall be your letter,' said Ali Asgar gravely, explaining that he had been servant to the present Governor of Yezd for ten years, when the latter was Mayor of Isfahan; in fact, just before I engaged him in Shiraz, the Governor had telegraphed asking him to come back, and he had refused. Now, as we entered the Governor's office, here he was! The Governor jumped out of his chair with a cry. Ali Asgar, who at his brightest has the aspect of an ageing curate, stood with folded hands and sagging knees, smirking and fluttering his eyelids with the modesty of a Victorian miss. Eventually, as he had prophesied, the Governor turned his warmth to me, asking Ali Asgar might be free to have supper with him and talk over old times.

This settled, I had every facility to explore, accompanied by an intelligent and obliging police-officer. The throw-off of a monument-hunt in a virgin town like Yezd must take place from a convenient height, whence it is possible to see which domes or minarets, by their form or material, give promise of good work beneath. Today, clue after clue yielded treasure, till at the end of the day we were almost too tired to walk home.

Sir Percy Sykes is the only writer who has noticed the buildings here, and he but shortly. Do people travel blind? It is hard to imagine how the portal of the Friday Mosque could escape anyone's notice. It stands over 100 feet high, and its narrow tapering arch is almost as spectacular as the chancel arch at Beauvais. After this, the court inside is a disappointment, a parochial little enclosure. But not the sanctuary, whose walls, dome, and mihrab are covered with four-teenth-century mosaic in perfect condition. This is the best decoration of the kind I have seen since Herat. It differs from the work there. The colours are colder, the designs more lucid and precise, but not so gorgeous.

An extraordinary series of simple, egg-domed mausoleums now lured us across the town – extraordinary in that, being built of a brick that was hardly distinguishable from mud, they might have been expected to contain nothing but wreckage. Yet one after another they revealed walls, vaults, and domes painted with bold, plaited Kufic in a style so rich, and at times so distorted, as to lack any known precedent. The most elaborate of them is the Vakht-i-Sa'at, which was built in 1324. Some of the others must be earlier. The Shrine of the Twelve Imams, for example, has a frieze of Kufic in the same style as that inside the Pir Alam Dar at Damghan, which dates from the eleventh century.

We came on another curiosity in the bazaar, one of the old city gates known as the Darwaza Mehriz. Its massive wooden door is reinforced by iron plates which are stamped with primitive signs of the Zodiac. Such things have an appearance of incalculable anti-quity. But primitive forms make unreliable calendars. They may be just a symptom of artistic ineptitude.

Yezd is unlike other Persian towns. No belt of gardens, no cool blue domes, defend it from the forbidding wastes outside. Town and desert are of one colour, one substance; the first grows out of the second, and the tall wind-towers, a witness of the heat, are such a forest as a desert might grow naturally. They give the place a fantastic outline, though not so fantastic as those of Hyderabad in Sind. The wind there always blows from the sea, and the towers project canopies to meet it. The towers of Yezd are square, and catch the wind from all four quarters by means of hollow grooves, which impel it down into chambers beneath. Two such chambers at either end of a house set up a draught through the length of it.

At present, though the Governor has ambitious plans, only one boulevard has been driven through the old labyrinths. Lovers of the picturesque deplore even this. But it is a boon to the inhabitants, who now have somewhere to walk, breathe, meet each other, and survey the distant mountains.

Going to the garage in search of transport to Kirman, I fell into conversation with an ex-deputy, who told me that Kavam-al-Mulk has been in prison, but is now released, while the fate of Sardar Assad and the other Bakhtiari brothers is still unknown. He was bitter against Marjoribanks, and I wondered why, till he recounted how his uncle, an old man of seventy-four and blind in one eye, has been two years in prison for refusing to let Marjoribanks have his rice-growing estates in Mazandaran. That inimitable ruler has been seizing estates all over the country, and making a fortune out of them, since the other Naboths have not been so obstinate. I was astonished at the man's indiscretion. But I suppose he thought I should not betray him. I shan't, I hope. This happened before I got to Yezd, and he wasn't an ex-deputy.

Bahramabad (5200 ft), 22 March   Breakfasting here on the Kirman road, after all night in a lorry.

Today is *No-Ruz*, 'New Day', in other words the first of the Persian New Year and a public holiday. Ali Asgar, with some reason, has just uttered a small complaint: 'no bath, no shave, no clean clothes'. And then, driving home the point in English: 'No-Ruz Persian Kissmas, Sahib.'

I produced the proper present.

*

Kirman (5700 ft), 24 March   A furious dust-storm hid the town as we arrived. It gets up every afternoon between two and four. There was another yesterday.

'In view of its isolation, the improvements in Kirman are comparatively few,' says Ebtehaj's guide-book priggishly. They are more than Yezd's. There are several wide streets, and also a cab, which I had the good fortune to meet, and, learning it was the only one, to engage for the day. It took me out of the town to the Jabal-i-Sang, a domed octagonal shrine of the twelfth century, interesting because it is built of stone instead of brick.

Otherwise, although Kirman has never been archaeologically explored, I found only two objects of note. One was the mihrab-panel in the Friday Mosque, of fourteenth-century mosaic, which appears to have been done by artists from Yezd. The other was the College of Ganj-i-Ali Khan, an ugly building, and not so old, but retaining patches of mosaic. These depict dragons, cranes, and other creatures unusual in Persian iconography, forming a kind of chinoiserie, though how Chinese ideas ever penetrated to this remote city is a mystery.

The Kuba-i-Sabz, which Sykes mentions, has fallen down. It was a shrine with a tall blue dome, in the Timurid style. I found its ruin incorporated in a modern house.

The wine here is red and is made by the Zoroastrians. Ali Asgar bought a bottle, but it was too sweet, and I sold it to the hotelkeeper.

A Persian acquaintance has lent me the volume on Persia in the Modern World Series. Persians hate all books that mention them, but he says they hate this one because the flattery is *too* thick. This is a wonderful feat from a man so in love with his own integrity as Sir Arnold Wilson.

Mahun (6300 ft), 25 March   Travellers from the Indian frontier, Christopher among them, have thought they were in paradise when they arrived at Mahun after crossing the Baluchistan sand-desert. Even on the way from Kirman, this desert impinges a sinister presence. There are sand drifts on the road, and these must mean the end of Persia, since Persian deserts are stony.

*

The Shrine of Niamatullah brings a sudden reprieve, a blessing of water and rustle of leaves. The purple cushions on the judas trees and a confetti of early fruit-blossom are reflected in a long pool. In the next court is another pool, shaped like a cross and surrounded by formal beds newly planted with irises. It is cooler here. Straight black cypresses, overtopped by the waving umbrellas of quicker-growing pines, throw a deep, woody shade. Between them shines a blue dome crossed with black and white spiders' webs, and a couple of blue minarets. A dervish totters out, wearing a conical hat and an embroidered yellow sheepskin. He leads the way past the tomb of the saint below the dome, through a spacious whitewashed hall, to a third and larger court, which has a second and larger pair of minarets at the far end. A last formal pool, and a mighty plane tree gleaming with new sap, stand outside the last gate. The country round is covered with vineyards, fields of ninepins full of clay cones to support the vines, as mulberries support them on the Lombardy Plain. A high range of mountains in a dress of snow and violet mist bounds the horizon.

While the cadent sun throws lurid copper streaks across the sand-blown sky, all the birds in Persia have gathered for a last chorus. Slowly, the darkness brings silence, and they settle themselves to sleep with diminishing flutterings, as of a child arranging its bed-clothes. And then another note begins, a hot metallic blue note, timidly at first, gaining courage, throbbing without cease, until, as if the second violins had crept into action, it becomes two notes, now this, now that, and is answered from the other side of the pool by a third. Mahun is famous for its nightingales. But for my part I celebrate the frogs. I am out in the court by now, in the blackness beneath the trees. Suddenly the sky clears, and the moon is reflected three times, once on the dome and twice on the minarets. In sympathy, a circle of amber light breaks from the balcony over the entrance, and a pilgrim begins to chant. The noise of water trickling into the new-dug flower-beds succeeds him. I am in bed at last. The room has ten doors and eleven windows, through which a hurricane of wind and cats in search of chicken bones whistles and scutters. Still the frogs call each other; that vibrant iridescent note makes its way into my sleep; I wake to find a cat opening my food-box with such fury that were I a safe-breaker I should engage it for an assistant. The draught shakes the bed. I hope Ali Asgar is warmer with the dervishes, but dare not grumble to him in the morning, as

General Sykes told him Mahun *was* paradise fifteen years ago. Morning impends, lifts its grey veils, arrives – and as though at the beat of a martinet conductor, the birds strike up again, a deafening, shrieking hymn to the sun, while a flock of crows on the other side of my room, not to be forgotten, set up a rasping competition. Now, and as suddenly, silence has fallen again, while the first rays of sunlight steal on to the stage. Outside the door, Ali Asgar and the dervish are fanning a tray of charcoal and coaxing the samovar. Footsteps pass: 'Ya Allah!" The dervish answers 'Ya Allah!' The pilgrim chants his morning prayers from the balcony, using long-drawn nasal semitones that remind me of Mount Athos. An arc of gold lights the blue dome and the sky is fleeced with pink. Here comes Ali Asgar with a tray of tea.

Yezd, 28 March Approaching Yezd in the early morning, after another all-night journey, we met a Zoroastrian funeral. The bearers were dressed in white turbans and long white coats; the body in a loose white pall. They were carrying it to a tower of silence on a hill some way off, a plain circular wall about fifteen feet high.

This afternoon I drove out to a village in the country, to see a garden. This village has 1000 houses, and is worth about £62,500 as a property, including its water-supply. The rent-roll is £2250: not a large interest on the capital. Violets and almond blossom were in flower in the garden, and a stocky white iris with a strong smell. The owner showed me a tree that had been twice grafted, so that plum, peach, and apricot were all in flower on it together. His other treasures were a pipless pomegranate, for which Kew has been searching; and an orange house in a sunk court twenty-five feet deep, where the main kanat broadens into a pool. He spoke with feeling of the pistachios he gets in summer from Ardekan, which is warmer than Yezd and has the brackish water they like.

Isfahan, 31 March Christopher is here.
He has been allowed provisional liberty to collect his things in Teheran. So now, God willing, we shall go to Afghanistan together.

I stopped at Nayin on the way back, to see the mosque, which dates from the ninth century and is one of the oldest in Persia. Its stucco ornament is filled with bunches of grapes, and suggests a transition of Hellenistic ideas through Sasanian art into Mohammadan. Thence to Ardistan, where stucco is used in a new way, to form a kind of filigree over the brickwork. This mosque is Seljuk, dating from 1158, and has the same purity of form, though not in the same degree, as the small dome-chamber in the Friday Mosque at Isfahan.

Teheran, 2 April A mountain freshet had cut the road outside Isfahan. With the help of twenty peasants we pushed the car through water up to the waist. By the time we had changed our clothes, changed oil, petrol, and plugs, and dried the cylinders, the water had gone down, and the other cars, which had been passively waiting, went on ahead of us. British initiative looked rather foolish.

We are staying at the Legation. I came down to find the house full of children dressed as fairies. A children's play is in rehearsal.

Teheran, 4 April Sardar Assad has 'died of epilepsy' in the hospital at Kasr-i-Kajar.

Kasr-i-Kajar is a fortress which dominates Teheran from a height. It was from here that Russian guns demolished the constitutional movement before the War. Marjoribanks has converted it into a model prison, and lest this homage to Progress should escape notice, gave a treat there for foreigners, who were much impressed by the kitchen and sanitary fittings. But, as an American said to me yesterday, 'the death-rate among the upper-class prisoners is curiously high'.

Yesterday was a day of alarums. It was enough to meet Marjoribanks in the street, and hear his subjects' nervous clapping. On my return to the Legation, an apocalyptic rumble heralded a runaway horse and cart, which came pelting down the drive, scattering the benches it had been unloading for the children's play. Not feeling heroic, I stepped out of the way. The porter shut the gate, and the horse, unable to break through it, was precipitated up the bars like a gorilla, while the cart disintegrated underneath it. Though shocked, the horse was unhurt.

Then the play took place, and was followed by tea.

*

R. B.: 'Won't you have another cake?'

Shir Ahmad (*mf*): 'Thank you, no, I have eaten. (*f*) I am full, (*dim*) not to here, (*touching his throat, cr*) but to here (*touching his forehead*). I have eaten (*f*) everything. I have eaten every dish on table. (*p*) You know, my name is Shir Ahmad. And Shir, you know, means loin. (*Roaring, ff*) When I ATTACK, (*whispering, pp*) it is terrible.'

Behind the scenes, a proper incident has developed out of Christopher's detention. Repeated inquiries have now elicited a reason for it, which is – to use the actual words of the Minister for Foreign Affairs – that 'Mr Sykes talks with peasants.' We imagine this must be a covert allusion to his conversation with Marjoribanks' gardener at Darbend. It is not very convincing, but will probably be enough to restore the London Foreign Office to its usual state of slavish acquiescence in the maltreatment of British subjects. Their protest in this instance has been couched with such exquisite tact that the Persians have now decided to expel Father Rice from Shiraz. Perhaps the Vatican will defend him better. The Nuncio is in a rage.

Christopher called on Shir Ahmad this morning.

Shir Ahmad (*mf*): 'You stay long time in Teheran?'

Christopher: 'I am leaving in a fortnight, and apart from the pleasure of seeing Your Excellency (*both bow*), I came to ask permission to leave by Afghanistan.'

Shir Ahmad (*pointing at Afghanistan, and roaring ff*): 'YOU SHALL GO.'

Christopher: 'It is kind of Your Excellency to say so. But I feel it my duty to tell you first that I have been under suspicion of spying in south Persia, and that the result—'

Shir Ahmad (*p*): 'I know.'

Christopher: 'What makes it more absurd is—'

Shir Ahmad (*pp*): 'I know. I know.'

Christopher: 'If they had told me earlier, I could have—'

Shir Ahmad (*pp*): 'I know. But it does not matter.'

Christopher: 'Excuse me, Your Excellency, it does matter. I am very angry.'

Shir Ahmad (*laughing, mf*): 'You are angree, ha, ha – it is wrong.

Your Minister he angree – it is wrong. The Persians, ha, ha, they are right, (*cr*) they are right.'

Christopher: 'Surely Your Excellency has more sense than to believe—'

Shir Ahmad (*mf*): 'The Persians they are right. Why do they make you go away?'

Christopher: 'They say I talk with peasants.'

Shir Ahmad (*triumphantly*, *f*): 'Then they are right. I will tell you how they are right:

'In Persia, in Afghanistan, in Irak, in Orient, (*pp*) there are no mysteries. (*f*) In England, in Russia, in Alleman, (*pp*) great mysteries. (*f*) In England, mystery of the ships, in Russia, many millions peoples, mystery of the armies, in Alleman, in France, mystery of the guns. (*p*) In Afghanistan, in Persia, (*violent gesture of dismissal*) no mysteries. No armies. No ships. (*mf*) This is the history of the kingdoms.'

Christopher: 'But I don't understand why—'

Shir Ahmad (*mf*): 'I tell you. Let me speak. It is simple. (*cr*) You shall hear:

'(*mf*) There was an old donkey, poor old ass, he carry too many stones, very tired. One day, the animal with much hair, much nose, much teeth, how is he called? he barks like dog.'

Christopher: 'A wolf?'

Shir Ahmad (*ff*): 'NOT a wolf.'

Christopher: 'A jackal?'

Shir Ahmad (*f*): 'A jackal! . . . One day jackal come to poor old donkey. (*pp*) Donkey he very tired, very sad. (*mf*) Jackal say, "Excuse me, sir, will you be king, will you be Shah-in-Shah, over our jungle?"

'(*mp*) Donkey he answer, "It is never possible."

'(*mf*) Jackal he say, "Yes, yes, I want it. You must stand on this hillock."

'(*mp*) Donkey he say, "I do not want. I must not be king. Let me carry my stones."

'(*mf*) Jackal tell him, "Never mind. Stand always on this hillock and put on these coats."

'Jackal give him loin's coats. Donkey he put them on and stay on hillock.

'(*pp*) In jungle jackal meet a (*ff*) LOIN. (*mf*) He say, "Your Majestee, there is another Shah on the hills, high Shah, higher than Your Majestee."

'(*pp*) Loin very angree. He answer (*roaring literally, ff*) "Grrrr! How you dare! Where is he? I shall eat all of you!!" (*Eyes blazing, teeth gnashing.*)

'(*mf*) Loin go to hillock quick. He see donkey in loin-coat. It is too big. Ass-loin too big, too high. Loin fears, he go away. (*Laughing, cr*) Then all animals fall in front of donkey. He is Shah-in-Shah over jungle. (*Pause.*)

'(*pp*) One day little (*cr*) pick come—'

Christopher: 'Little what?'

Shir Ahmad (*mf*): 'A pick . . . ha, a pig . . . come look at ass-loin. He make (*grunting f*) honk, pig-noise. Ass-loin very angree. He stamp feets like Shah-in-Shah and make (*indescribable sound*), donkey-noise. (*ff*) Then all animals, lipards, loins, tigers, great beasts, see Shah-in-Shah on hillock is only poor old donkey. Pouf! Finish! Poor old donkey he dead.

'(*mf*) You hear, Mr Sykes? I tell you, it is same in Orient. Afghanistan and Persia two old donkeys. But Persia donkey in loin's coat, ass-loin. It is good. Persia very proud, very high. But if you (*cr*) talk to him like pig did, if you (*ff*) TALK to him, (*mf*) he very angree, because all animals, all peoples, see he is donkey. So you must go away.'

Shir Ahmad continued on the theme of Persian pride, and presently told of an interview with Marjoribanks arising out of the murder of some Persian police on the Afghan frontier.

'(*mf*) Shah he very angree. I tell him, "How do you do, sir? Are you well? How are you feeling?"

'Shah he say, (*ff*) "Grrrr!"

'(*mf*) I tell him, "Sir, why are you starting? (*cr*) Stop starting."

'(*mf*) Shah he say, (*ff*) "Grrrr!"

'(*mf*) I ask him, "Why are you angree?"

'Shah he say, (*ff*) "Where are the murderer Afghans?"

'(*mf*) I tell him, "We do not know. (*p*) We are very sorry."

'(*mf*) Shah he say, (*ff*) "Grrrr!"

'(*mf*) I ask him, "What do you want to do?"

'Shah he say bad things for Afghans, he say he will send soldiers to kill Afghans.

'I tell him, "No, sir, this is wrong that you tell me."

'Shah he say, (*roaring ff*) "How wrong? Your Excellency tell me I am wrong?"

'(*mf*) I tell him, "Go to Afghanistan, Your Majestee. Kill many Afghans, (*cr*) many. (*p*) They are wicked mens. (*mf*) But first kill your Chief of Police, General Ayrum. He also wicked man. In Naderi bath last week some mens do bad things to a woman. Then they cut her head (*appalling gesture, cr*) off! and leave body with much blood. (*dim*) General Ayrum cannot find murderers. We cannot find murderers. He is very sorry. We are very sorry. So kill General Ayrum, and (*ff*) then go to Afghanistan. (*mf*) But first I must see General Ayrum (*cr*) dead! killed! with much blood also!"

'(*mf*) Shah he laugh. "Your Excellency must not be angree. It is all right." '

Teheran, 11 April The new Legation photograph contains eighty-four people, including children, translators, and messengers. Not all sleep on the premises, but they can all be found there at midday. Such is the weight of Persia in our diplomacy.

Last night Young, the librarian of the American College, took us to a Zur Khana. He first became aware of this institution by hearing his pupils disparage Swedish drill in favour of it. It dates from pre-Mohammadan times, and may have developed out of a Zoroastrian rite.

A tall room in the bazaar quarter greeted us with a smell of bodies and a white light. Its walls were covered with portraits, some drawings, some yellowed photographs, which gave it the same look as those cabinets of aristocracy, Dempster's at Eton and Madame Sacher's at Vienna. They showed the champions of the past, *pahlevan* they are called, an ancient title which is applied to such mythical warriors as Rustam, but signifies strength alone rather than any moral virtue. Above the pictures hung other souvenirs of 'the fancy', a row of embroidered trunk-hose worn in wrestling contests, and a number of iron bows to which, instead of strings, were attached loose chains festooned with iron discs. An adjoining room was stacked with wooden clubs and square wooden shields.

In the middle of the floor was a pit three or four feet deep and thirty square, filled with fine sand, trodden hard, on which lay a foot's depth of straw, tightly packed to make it springy. This was occupied by a dozen men of various ages, naked but for a towel round the waist, and extended at full length on their bellies: the *pahlevan* of the future. A tray of charcoal stood on a table in the corner, over which the orchestra was warming his drum to make it resonant. When the drum struck up, the performers raised and lowered themselves, up and down, faster and faster, till the orchestra began to sing, and suddenly, with a succession of clashes on bell and drum alternately, ping, ping, pom...pppom, pppom...PING, PING, brought the act to a close.

Twirling of clubs followed, one man at a time, one club in each hand, and each club so heavy that it was as much as I could do to lift one off the floor with both hands. Then more body exercises. Then whirling, with the arms outstretched, brought to such a speed that I could distinctly see two profiles and a front-face on one performer at the same moment. The orchestra of drum, voice, and bell played throughout, slackening and quickening its rhythm, so that the performers were visibly responding to a musical impulse, faces and bodies were vivid with enjoyment, and the contrast with Swedish drill, as it transforms the hope of Europe into ranks of gesticulating automata, became even more painful to us than to Young's Persian pupils.

The last act was occupied with the iron bows, each held above the head, while chain and discs clanged to and fro from shoulder to ear. The champion of this exercise eventually did a dance, hopping in and out of the bow in the style of Tex McLeod and his lasso, except that owing to the weight of the instrument he was so exhausted at the end of it that he could hardly pick himself out of the pit. Meanwhile, new arrivals were undressing, to take their turn at the next session.

When the first was over, the performers put on their clothes and we saw what kind of people they were. Most were merchants or shopkeepers. One was an air force officer. And there was also a scholar who is at present translating the *Encyclopaedia Britannica* with the help of four assistants. The first volume of this labour would have been published immediately had he not realized, just in time, that the alphabetical order of the English differed from that of the Persian.

The proprietor, who presides over each act to see that no one overstrains himself, explained the organization. Each Zur Khana is a club, and most of them are situated, like this one, at the junction of the bazaar and residential quarters, so that business men can call in for exercise on their way home. The subscription is three tomans, that is 7s. 6d., a month. Occasionally there are competitions between different Zur Khanas.

I met a young Swede at dinner, whose expensive jewellery and talk about his father's estates made me wonder why he was living in Teheran.

Swede: 'I am in the business of cases.'
R. B.: 'Cases?'
Swede: 'Cases for sausages.'
R. B.: 'Tins do you mean?'
Swede: 'No, cases for the sausages themselves made from sheep's intestines. Some people think it is not a nice business. I do not always talk about it.'
R. B.: 'I thought those cases were made of rice-paper or some such material.'
Swede: 'Not at all. Every sausage has a gut case.'
R. B.: 'What happens, ha, ha, with a sausage six inches across?'
Swede (*seriously*): 'We use not only sheep's guts, but also ox guts. The big intestine of the ox will hold the biggest sausage manufactured.'
R. B.: 'But have Swedish cattle no intestines? Why come to Persia for them?'
Swede: 'Persian cases are of high grade. The first grade comes from the Kalmuckian steppe in Russia. The second from Australia and New Zealand. The next from Persia. It is an important business for Persia. Cases are one of the largest exports under the Swedish-Persian trading agreement.'
R. B.: 'What made you choose cases as a profession?'
Swede: 'It is my father's business.'

Hence the estates, I supposed.

Sultaniya (c. *5900 ft*), *12 April*   A last visit to Uljaitu's mausoleum. It was the first great monument I saw in Persia, but I had no standard of comparison then, and I was afraid it might disappoint me now.

It does not.

There are two smaller monuments not far away, an octagonal tomb-tower of the thirteenth century known as that of Sultan Cheilabi, and an octagonal shrine, squatter and later, which shelters the grave of Mullah Hassan. The brickwork of the first, still pointed as though built yesterday, excels the best work of those masters of European brick, the Dutch. The second is remarkable for a domed stalactite ceiling painted red and white. ·

A narrow path led to the later shrine through a brown and thorny scrub. 'What a pity you can't come back in summer,' said the peasant with me wistfully. 'The rose-avenue is so beautiful then.'

Teheran, 14 April Stopping at Kazvin on the way back, I discovered the local white wine and bought the whole stock of the hotel. How comfortable that hotel seems now! I remember after we had stopped there on the way from Hamadan, warning the Charcoal-Burners in Baghdad to avoid it at all costs.

Almost all visitors to Persia travel either by Resht or by Hamadan, and all who do must pass the outside of the Friday Mosque at Kazvin. Yet, except for Godard, the French Director of the Antiquities Service, I believe I am the first person to have noticed the Seljuk stucco in the sanctuary, a lovely scheme of panels, cornice, and arabesque frieze, which dates from 1113. The inscriptions are all interspersed with those graceful trailing flowers, roses, tulips, and irises, which are generally thought to have been invented by the Safavids four centuries later.

Teheran, 20 April Still here.
We ought to have left this morning, but were prevented by a deluge of rain.

Thrush, a schoolmaster, is also on his way to Kabul, by the southern road. He told the Afghan Embassy he was looking for adventure, at which Shir Ahmad, always anxious to oblige, suggested he should pose as a Russian spy and then save himself from being shot by producing a letter which Shir Ahmad would give him for the purpose. Christopher and I met him this morning, as we were discussing the importance of comfort on our journey. He said he preferred discomfort, revelled in it. I know the type: they die on one out of sheer inefficiency.

This afternoon I called on Assadi, the Mutavali Bashi of the Shrine at Meshed. This is a court appointment, whose holder controls the shrine's revenues amounting to £60,000 a year. He was anxious enough for me to see the hospital he is building with those revenues. But I could not pin him to a promise to insinuate me into the shrine.

As a person, more is known of Gohar Shad than I thought.

Teheran, 21 April   Still here.

This time we stopped to see Upham Pope, who arrived yesterday. Some of my photographs and information may be useful to his forthcoming *Survey of Persian Art.*

He came in an aeroplane with Mrs Moore, a matriarch in a shawl, more than seventy years old and worth as many millions. Her two sisters, three maids, and a 'manager' made up the party. We met them at tea at the American College. Christopher was appalled at the toadying that went on, but he has no sympathy with people whose work depends on private benefactions.

Part V

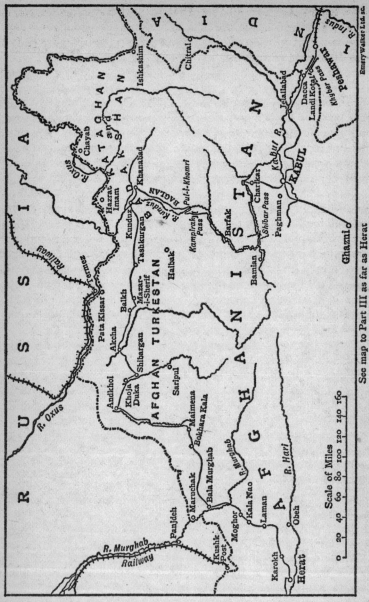

See map to Part III as far as Herat

Emery Walker Ltd. sc.

Scale of Miles

0   20   40   60   80   100   120   140   160

Shahi (c. 300 ft), 22 April   The first evening of our long-planned journey.

Lady Hoare and Joseph got up early to breakfast with us under the wistaria. The winter aspect of the Legation compound, resembling a Victorian asylum, was now almost hidden by blossom and young leaves. And as we drove away, I remembered with infinite gratitude the kindness I had found in those ugly little houses, and among the English community in general. Such kindness is easy to forget and impossible to repay: it needs a rich man to offer the same degree of hospitality in England as two clean sheets and a bath represent after a journey in Persia. Worse than that, he who writes is apt to repay it with injury, in the form of political indiscretion, which makes life for the residents more difficult than it is already. But this, I must admit, leaves me impenitent, regrettable as it is from the personal point of view. To asperse a sunset in these days is a political indiscretion; and equally so, to praise it, if there happens to be a cement-factory in the foreground that ought to be praised instead. Somebody must trespass on the taboos of modern nationalism, in the interests of human reason. Business can't. Diplomacy won't. It has to be people like us.

Once more the Khorasan road, poignant with memories! In spite of the spring, it was snowing at the pass which leads over the edge of the plateau down to the Caspian coast. Under the white blizzard occurred an extraordinary transition. In five minutes we had escaped from a world of stone and mud and sand and everlasting drought which had endured since Damascus, into one of wood and leaves and moisture, where the hills were clothed with bushes, the bushes grew into trees, and the trees, as the snow stopped, gathered into a glowing forest of bare trunks whose leafy vaults shut out the sky. The oppression of the plateau was suddenly remitted. It was only now I knew what a penalty had been levied on the spirit by the bare wind-swept deserts, the threatening mountains and the tumbledown villages. The relief was actually physical. Our bodies seemed to undergo a change of gravity, a return to normal buoyancy.

These feelings were interrupted by a piercing whistle and a puff of white smoke. In the bottom of the valley Marjoribanks's new railway was creeping up towards the plateau. There, after surmounting the second step of the Elburz at Firuzkuh by a tunnel in the form of a triple spiral, it should arrive at Teheran in three years' time. It can never pay. The taxation imposed by the first two hundred miles of it is already depriving the peasants of their only luxuries, tea and sugar. But its purpose is a question of psychology rather than economics. For the modern Persian it is the symbol of national self-respect; it provides at last a fresh diet for that unconquerable vanity which has subsisted during two thousand years on the exploits of Darius. To us, after all we have suffered at the mercy of the internal combustion engine, the grunt of steam seemed as companionable and old-fashioned as the rattle of a four-wheeler. We felt twice befriended by the trees and the train.

When we first crossed the pass, the lumber-shoots down the hills and the shingled eaves of the houses reminded me of Austria. Out on the coastal plain, where the fields are divided by hedges and brambles, and bracken and clumps of nettles flourish on the grass banks beneath them, we might have been in England on a wet afternoon – till we saw a tiger skin hanging outside somebody's front door. Among these pastoral surroundings, the bare-footed Mazandarani shepherd-boys in their black fleece hats looked curiously exotic. They have an air of effete savagery which seems to have been produced by the action of a semi-tropical environment on people who must once have been nomads.

Shahi is a pioneer town called into existence by the railway. Four main streets from nowhere converge on an asphalt circus, which is dignified with pavements and shop windows. The hotel is crowded with Russian, German, and Scandinavian engineers.

Asterabad (300 ft), 23 April   There is a road from Shahi to Asterabad, but it has been allowed to fall into disrepair for the benefit of the railway. We could only drive as far as Ashraf.

Two gardens and a palace still mark this royal pleasaunce, where Shah Abbas received Sir Dodmore Cotton in 1627. Seen from a distance, the palace on its wooded hill looks like an English country house. But it is really very small, its tilework is coarse, and it is planned with the incapacity to make convenient use of a given space usually found in Persian secular buildings. Its main peculiarity is that by some strange coincidence the windows are of a type which Ruskin transferred from Florentine Quattrocento palaces to the suburbs of Oxford. The two gardens are more romantic. Long stone waterways proceed through gently sloping meadows, negotiating each fall in level with a flat stone glissade in the Mogul style. Wherever this style originated, in Persia, India, or Oxiana, it is proper to a barren landscape only. Here, framed in grass and bracken, it becomes slightly excessive, as an Italian garden is in Ireland.

The larger garden illustrates the same scale of ideas as Shah Abbas put into effect at Isfahan. From the hill at the back, where pink orchids were flowering in the undergrowth, a cypress avenue descends through a walled enclosure of several acres, which is dotted with other cypresses in the manner of an English park. The waterway runs inside the avenue, and like that of the Villa Lante, passes between two pavilions, which are joined by a roofed arcade that acts as a bridge. At the bottom of the avenue stands a gate-house. Beyond this, a road carries on the line of the trees through the village of Ashraf and across a strip of cultivated plain, till the eye is brought to rest by the glinting horizon of the Caspian.

Looking for somewhere to lunch, we chose one of the square pools, now dry, which used to receive each water-glissade and whose copings are carved with holes for fairy lights in the form of wicks floating on oil. I took up the picnic-bag and jumped down into the long grass at the bottom. But the place was already occupied. Five feet of cinnamon-coloured snake, luckily more frightened than I was, lashed its way round my legs to a crevice in the masonry.

When the train arrived the car was attached on a truck, and the servants remained in it, while we consorted with a crowd of holiday-makers from Teheran, come to inspect the new marvel. Five pro-hibitions in each carriage informed them of railway etiquette. At Bandar Shah, the new Caspian port where the railway ends, a regular seaside crowd met the train. Among them were the local Chief of Police and a representative of the War Office, who asked us where we were going.

Gumbad-i-Kabus?

Certainly. And we could also, if we liked, motor on to Meshed by the new military road through Bujnurd and the Turcoman country.

This was a welcome surprise. When I asked for permission to visit Gumbad-i-Kabus in Teheran, Jam, the Minister of the Interior, sent me a private message begging me to withdraw the request, since the place was in a military zone and he could not grant it. Hearing this, Pybus, our Military Attaché, offered to put in a word for us with the General Staff. But he had had no answer when we left, and we had come thus far on chance. It was Diez's picture of Gumbad-i-Kabus that decided me to come to Persia, and I would sooner, as far as I know, have missed any other building in the country.

Even in the dark, we could perceive the steppe. The headlights died in space, finding nothing to reveal but a passing boar. There came a scent of sweet grass, as on a night in June at home before the hay is cut. At Asterabad the populace were celebrating Mohurram, marching through the streets behind a draped coffin and bearing aloft triangular banners of lights. Many wept and groaned, and such as had their hands free were tearing their clothes and beating themselves, as Shir Ahmad had described. We are staying with an old Turk, who used to be British vice-consul here, and offers to arrange a tiger-shoot for us.

Gumbad-i-Kabus (200 ft), 24 April After following the Bandar Shah road a little way back, we turned to the right down a track between wattle fences. High reeds obscured the view. Suddenly, as a ship leaves an estuary, we came out on to the steppe: a dazzling open sea of green. I never saw that colour before. In other greens, of emerald, jade, or malachite, the harsh deep green of the Bengal jungle, the sad cool green of Ireland, the salad green of Mediterranean vineyards, the heavy full-blown green of English summer beeches, some element of blue or yellow predominates over the others. This was the pure esssence of green, indissoluble, the colour of life itself. The sun was warm, the larks were singing up above. Behind us rose the misty Alpine blue of the wooded Elburz. In front, the glowing verdure stretched out to the rim of the earth.

Bearings, landmarks, disappeared, as they would from a skiff in mid-Atlantic. We seemed to be always below the surrounding level, caught in the trough of a green swell. Sitting down, we might see for twenty feet: standing up, for twenty miles – and even then, twenty miles away, the curve of the earth was as green as the bank that touched the wheels, so that it was hard to tell which was which. Our only chart was by things whose scale we knew: groups of white-topped kibitkas, dotted like mushrooms on a lawn – though even in their case it needed an effort of reason to believe they were not mushrooms; and droves of cattle, mares with their foals, black and brown sheep, kine and camels – though the camels were deceptive in the opposite sense, seeming so tall that it needed another effort to believe they were not antediluvian monsters. As the huts and animals varied in size, we could plot their distances: half a mile, a mile, five miles. But it was not this that conveyed the size of the steppe so much as the multiplicity of these nomadic encampments, cropping up wherever the eye rested, yet invariably separate by a mile or two from their neighbours. There were hundreds of them, and the sight, therefore, seemed to embrace hundreds of miles.

As plans of cities are inset on maps of countries, another chart on a larger scale lay right beneath our wheels. Here the green resolved, not into ordinary grass, but into wild corn, barley, and oats, which accounted for that vivid fire, as of a life within the green. And among these myriad bearded alleys lived a population of flowers, buttercups and poppies, pale purple irises and dark purple campanulas, and countless others, exhibiting all the colours, forms, and wonders that a child finds in its first garden. Then a puff of air would come, bending the corn to a silver ripple, while the flowers leaned with it; or a cloud shadow, and all grow dark, as if for a moment's sleep; though a few feet off there would be no ripple and no darkness; so that this whole inner world of the steppe was mapped on a system of infinite minute recessions, having just those gradations of distance that the outer lacked.

Our spirits had risen when we left the plateau. Now they effervesced. We shouted for joy, stopping the car lest the minutes that were robbing us of the unrepeatable first vision should go faster. Even the larks in this paradise had lost their ordinary aloofness. One almost hit my hat in its inquisitiveness.

We found the Gurgan river in a cutting thirty feet deep, whose bare earth cliffs traced a gash of desolation through the green. It was as wide as the Severn in its upper reaches, and we crossed it by an old brick bridge on tall pointed arches. This was defended, on the north bank, by a gate-house, whose overhanging upper storey had a broad-eaved tiled roof such as one sees in the Apennines. From here smooth green tracks began to radiate over the steppe in all directions, and we could hardly have found the way but for the occasional traffic of riders on horses and camels and high-wheeled gigs who pointed it out to us. They were all Turcomans, the ladies in red chintz covered with flowers, the men in plain red or more rarely in gorgeous multi-coloured silks woven with lightning zigzags. But there were not many fleece hats. Most of the men wore Marjoribanks's substitute, or at least a cardboard peak attached to a fleece cap.

The Elburz now began to curve round in front of us, enclosing a green bay. In the middle of this, twenty miles away, a small cream needle stood up against the blue of the mountains, which we knew for the tower of Kabus. An hour later, steering by this point, we reached a small market town, whose broad straight streets recall the Russian occupation of the district before the War. The tower stands on the north of the town, helped into the sky by a green hillock of irregular shape, but artificial, and of great age.

A tapering cylinder of café-au-lait brick springs from a round plinth to a pointed grey-green roof, which swallows it up like a candle extinguisher. The diameter at the plinth is fifty feet; the total height about a hundred and fifty. Up the cylinder, between plinth and roof, rush ten triangular buttresses, which cut across two narrow garters of Kufic text, one at the top underneath the cornice, one at the bottom over the slender black entrance.

The bricks are long and thin, and as sharp as when they left the kiln, thus dividing the shadow from the sunshine of each buttress with knife-like precision. As the buttresses recede from the direction of the sun, the shadows extend on to the curving wall of the cylinder between them, so that the stripes of light and shade, varying in width, attain an extraordinary momentum. It is the opposition of this vertical momentum to the lateral embrace of the Kufic rings that gives the building its character, a character unlike anything else in architecture.

There is nothing inside. The body of Kabus used to hang there, suspended from the roof in a glass coffin. He died in 1007. For more than a thousand years this lighthouse has announced his memory, and the genius of Persia, to the nomads of the Central Asian sea. Today it has a larger audience, which must wonder how the use of brick, at the beginning of the second millennium after Christ, came to produce a more heroic monument, and a happier play of surfaces and ornament, than has ever been seen in that material since.

[Superlatives applied by travellers to objects which they have seen, but most people have not, are generally suspect; I know it, having been guilty of them. But re-reading this diary two years later, in as different an environment as possible (Pekin), I still hold the opinion I formed before going to Persia, and confirmed that evening on the steppe: that the Gumbad-i-Kabus ranks with the great buildings of the world.]

The military Governor called at dinner time, and told us of the tradition that something used to flash from the roof of the tower; it was of glass or crystal, and was believed to hold a lamp. The Russians, he said, took it away; though he did not explain how they reached it. This tradition may contain a distorted reference to Kabus's glass coffin, which seems to have been genuine fact, as it was recorded by the Arab historian Jannabi soon after Kabus's death.

The country round here is covered with antiquities, if only we had time to stop and look for them. 'Alexander's Wall' is only a few miles north of the Gurgan, and the swamps along the river to the east are said to be crowded with ruins that no one has explored. There are also prehistoric remains. Not long ago some Turcoman families found a tumulus filled with bronze vessels, which they abstracted and put into domestic use. Then bad luck overtook them, and ascribing it to their desecration of a grave they returned to the tumulus and re-buried the vessels. One imagines the rush of professors to this archaeological Klondyke, if they knew where it was.

The Governor also brings us the bad news that the road to Bujnurd is blocked by rain and landslides. We might get through, but a lorry has just crawled in here half wrecked, after spending five days on the journey, and we dare not risk the car, with Afghanistan before it. In consequence, we are considering a ride over the mountains to Shahrud, while the car goes back by Firuzkuh.

*

Bandar Shah (sea-level), 26 April Under arrest! I am writing on a bed in the police-station.

We are in the wrong, which makes it the more annoying. Having waited at Gumbad-i-Kabus till four o'clock, when there were still no horses to be had, we decided to go back with the car, and avoiding Asterabad, reached here at ten o'clock. There was nowhere to sleep but the station, and the station-master, a wilting young man, was not pleased at our disturbing him so late. The train this morning was due to leave at seven. He told us to have the car ready by the siding at six. It was. But the truck for it did not arrive till ten to seven, and we suddenly saw that the station-master, out of spite, had sent the train off without us. The pent-up irritation of seven months exploded: we assaulted the man. There were loud shrieks, soldiers rushed in, and pinioning Christopher's arms, some struck his back with the butts of their rifles, while their officer, who was scarcely four feet high and had the voice of a Neapolitan tenor, repeatedly slapped his face. I escaped these indignities, but we share the confinement, to the bewilderment of the police, who find us a nuisance.

They threaten us with an 'inquiry' into the 'incident' in Teheran. We must grovel to avoid this at all costs. It would take weeks. I wonder – we both wonder – what madness came over us to jeopardize our journey in this way.

Samnan (4000 ft), 27 April The 'incident' was settled by the German superintendent of the repair shops, an imperturbable old man, who lounged into the police-station, said, 'What's this?' and after seeing us shake hands with the station-master, took us off to his house for the night. This was the kinder of him, because his daughter and son-in-law, a Danish bank manager, had arrived unexpectedly from Teheran, and since there was only one spare room we had to put up our beds in the parlour.

This morning as we left Shahi it was raining, and the road up to the pass was slippery and dangerous. Round the corner came a lorry out of control. We hit it broadside, lurched towards the precipice above the valley ... this was the end; but no, we stayed on the road, and had only to deplore that my suitcase, which had been attached to the step, lay crushed by the lorry's front wheel into a thin blue sandwich, extruding clothes, films, and drawing paper. The insurance, which had lasted eight months, ran out last week.

At Amiriya they said it had rained for fifteen days consecutively, and that such weather at this time of year had never been known before.

Damghan (3900 ft), 28 April   More disasters.

Twenty miles from Samnan the back axle broke. We had a spare one, but it took five hours to fit, while Christopher and I, unable to help, wandered forlornly about the sodden, glistening desert, consoling ourselves with the yellow dwarf tulips just coming into flower, and occasionally scrambling eggs in a ruined tea-house.

'What language are you talking?' asked Christopher of the youth in charge.

'I talk Chakapakaru, the language of Samnan. Don't you?'

We don't. But it may be a treasure for the philologist.

The rain fell like a bath-waste. For miles at a time the road was a river, the desert a flood, and every mountain a cataract. But by some freak of Nature, a *river-bed* which ran beside the telegraph poles, and which was several feet below the level of the surrounding country, remained completely dry.

In one torrent a couple of lorries were already embedded without hope. The local population hauled us through, exacting the toll of wreckers before doing so, else they would have led the car into the deepest part and left it. Henceforth the road improved, and we were travelling at forty miles an hour on the straight when a small water-course, three feet wide, two deep, and as sharp as a coffin, flashed across our sight . . . it was the end again; but no; we jumped it, fell into a bog, and landed up alive with a shattering bump against a heap of gravel.

The front wheels were the shape of duck's feet, but the axle had held, and we could just waddle into Damghan, where the blacksmith is now straightening it. Here we saw Pybus' Indian orderly, who told us that his master, returning from Meshed, had stuck in a river on the other side of the town. Pybus himself appeared soon after, at the head of a procession carrying his luggage. This included an old woman, bent double with rheumatism and shrouded in blue checks, who was laboriously salving a minute portfolio.

We cheered Pybus up by telling him of our own misfortunes. Three bottles of Shahi wine, an orange salad, and Wishaw's cigars have cheered us all up.

Abbasabad (c. *3000 ft*), *29 April* Even on my other two journeys, this accursed windy spot where they sell cigar-holders of green soapstone and the men wear red blouses, seemed the peak of misery. Now we have to spend the night here.

The river flowed right over Pybus' car. It was a new limousine. This morning it looked like Neptune's cave. After two lorries had failed to pull it out with chains, we went on.

It was still raining. Beyond Shahrud we ran into soft sand, which flew up into a paste on the windscreen, so that I had to drive with my head outside it, though never at less than thirty miles an hour or we should have stuck. The inky jagged hills and cloud-wracked skies of Khorasan were still the same. But a new vegetation had sprung up over the black water-logged desert: the sparse green of camelthorn, strange asphodels, and a kind of stocky yellow cow-parsley, three feet high and as thick as a tree: an ugly, sinister flower.

They said here there was water four feet deep on the way to Sabzevar. We therefore stopped, and I have gone to bed with Gosse's *Father and Son*. Christopher has been buying a red blouse with as much fuss as if it was from Schiaparelli.

Meshed, 1 May 'Just in time for the ball!' shouted Mrs Gastrell, as we staggered up the steps of the Consulate.

Does the whole Indian Political Service travel about Asia with dressing-up boxes? Mrs Gastrell was a Negress in black skin-tights and a top hat; Gastrell, who is seven feet high, danced a Scottish reel as Bluebeard, wearing cloth of gold and a caerulean beaver. Rose, of the same service, appeared as a Kate Greenaway schoolboy.

Mrs Hamber was a shepherdess, Hamber a Bokhara grandee in silks of a pattern larger than the human body. Before I could say how pleased I was to see them again, they were transforming me into a charwoman; while Christopher, pinioned by the Gastrells, was whisked into the regalia of an Arab sheikh. The missionaries were out in force. Mr Donaldson, having spent half his life studying Shiah pilgrims, had very properly become one. When I asked him if it wasn't a sacrifice to have all his hair shaved off for one evening, he said, 'Oh no, it fits very well. I always travel bald and am starting on a journey tomorrow to visit the Georgian villages between Abbasabad and Kuchan. The people are Mohammadans of course, but they still have a tradition of superior education.'

The charwoman forgot herself so far as to stab the Bokhara grandee in the back with a parasol during an apache duet.

Meshed, 2 May Lee of the Bank says he has been doing more business lately than for some time past. I asked him if this were due to the expulsion of the Jews from Afghanistan. He said it might be.

Those Jews had the lambskin trade in their hands, and I remember at Christmas Lee had been interested in my account of their exodus; though neither he nor I knew at the time that it was due to a government order. The reason of his interest was that formerly a large proportion of this trade went through Meshed, to the profit of the town and the Bank. But when Marjoribanks started his policy of economic nationalism, this stopped. All trade stopped more or less, till at last the Khorasan customs service could not even pay its wages out of its receipts. But now that many of these Jews have entered Persia, they may have brought the lambskin business back with them.

One always hears of 'Persian' lamb, and when I was in Afghanistan before I did not realize the economic significance of the trade to that country; though there was much conversation about lambskins in the Herat bazaar. Persia, it is true, exports lamb enough. But the fine fur, for which milliners in London and Paris pay up to £7 a skin, is a monopoly of Oxiana. This is due to a peculiar dry herbage which grows on the Oxus plain and makes the wool curl more tightly than it will elsewhere. Thus the really profitable part of the lambskin trade is shared between Russia and Afghanistan. But why the Afghans must needs get rid of the people who conduct their part of it, and so make Persian middlemen a present of the profits, is a mystery we have still to unravel.

Meshed, 6 May   A possible light on this mystery was vouchsafed us yesterday by my old friend the Afghan consul. We were discussing an announcement in the paper that the Afghan Government had decided to rebuild Balkh, and I asked him what the point was, since Mazar-i-Sherif, the capital of Afghan Turkestan and a flourishing city, is only seventeen miles away. He answered that Balkh was a historical city, the *Home of the Aryan Race*.

This mania must have spread from Germany. Till a year ago the Afghans claimed that they themselves were Jews: the lost tribes of Israel. But nothing is too fantastic for Asiatic nationalism.

The days have passed pleasantly here. We ought to be off, but two things detain us. One is the arrival of a spare axle from Teheran. The other is the shrine. In point of coloured mosaic, no building in Persia that I have seen or heard of can compare with the Musalla at Herat, except possibly the shrine here, which was built by the same woman; in which case, being more or less intact, it is probably the finest example of colour in the whole of Mohammadan architecture. I had not grasped this probability when I was here before; I supposed that the faience at Isfahan would equal or surpass that of the Musalla. It does not. Sheikh Lutfullah is more gorgeous, but only as St Peter's is more gorgeous than the Tempio at Rimini; the vernal inspiration of a Renascence is lacking. I will not leave this town without seeing Gohar Shad's only complete building.

We have cleared the ground. Our first move was to visit the new hospital, the apple of Assadi's eye, in order to be able to praise it to him when he returned from Teheran. This piece of tact put him in a good humour, but no more; he was still disinclined to take official responsibility for the safety of a foreigner inside the shrine. Nevertheless, our call on him led indirectly to acquaintance with an amiable young schoolmaster in suède gloves, who offered to help us for the fun of the thing – for the fun, that is, of striking a blow for knowledge against the forces of ecclesiastical darkness. We met him last night to discuss matters, having first taken a room at the hotel so as to keep our plans secret from the Consulate. By the time he arrived I had become a Persian; at least he thought so, greeting me in Persian fashion and being astonished when the seedy Oriental with eyes cast down and hands folded in his sleeves burst into a rude guffaw. This clinched it. He will take us tonight.

This morning we drove out to Chinaran, along the road to Askabad and the Russian frontier. From here a cart track took us to within six miles of the tower of Radkan. We walked the rest of the way, at first over springy turf cropped short by droves of horses, then through a series of sticky saline marshes. Our guide was a furious little peasant with enormous whiskers.

'Do you know the way to Radkan?'

'How should I not know it?' he vociferated indignantly. But he only knew the way to Radkan village, and his anger passed all bounds when we dragged him through those marshes to the tower instead.

It was worth the effort: a massive cylindrical grave-tower with a conical roof, ninety feet high, and dating from the thirteenth century. The outside wall consists of columns two feet thick, which touch one another. Their brickwork, rusty red in colour, is arranged in tweed patterns, which give the building a sort of shine, as of a well-groomed horse. Unlike the Gumbad-i-Kabus, this tower has a staircase in the thickness of the wall.

On the way back, we turned off the main road to visit Tus. I was saying to Christopher that apart from the old bridge and mausoleum there, he ought to see the Firdaussi memorial, because it proved that a breath of architectural taste still lingered in modern Persia. The words froze on my lips: a crowd of workmen were busy demolishing it. Iron railings hid the pool. Municipal flower-beds lay ready for cannas and begonias. And at the end, instead of the pleasant unostentatious pyramid I admired in November, rose half-built copies of the bull's-head columns at Persepolis.

I apologized for my enthusiasm and we drove away. Marjoribanks, it appears, saw a photograph of the first memorial, and said it was too plain.

Meshed, 7 May   Last night, excusing ourselves from the Consulate, we dined at the hotel. Christopher observed that an up-to-date guide to Meshed might contain a sentence such as: 'Visitors intending to inspect the Shrine of the Imam Riza usually dine and make up at the Hotel de Paris.' We finished with vanilla ices, and primed ourselves with a miserable sour Caucasian burgundy. At eight o'clock, I had just applied the last shred of cork to the nape of Christopher's neck when our friend the schoolmaster arrived with an Armenian lady, who had come to see the heroes start. She saw them into a broken-down victoria. This drove to the main gate of the Shrine, where we dismounted, but instead of entering, turned to the right up the circular avenue. 'Are you ready?' said the guide, and dived into a dark tunnel. We followed like rabbits, found ourselves in a little yard, scurried down a lighted bazaar full of booths and purchasers, and came out into the great court of the Mosque of Gohar Shad.

Amber lights twinkled in the void, glowing unseen from the mighty arch before the sanctuary, reflecting a soft blaze over the gilded entrance to the tomb opposite, and revealing, as the eye adapted itself, a vast quadrilateral defined by ranks of arches. An upper tier rose out of reach of the lights, and, passing through a zone of invisibility, reappeared as a black parapet against the stars. Turbaned mullahs, white-robed Afghans, vanished like ghosts between the orbits of the lamps, gliding across the black pavement to prostrate themselves beneath the golden doorway. A sound of chanting was heard from the sanctuary, where a single tiny figure could be seen abased in the dimness, at the foot of its lustred mihrab.

Islam! Iran! Asia! Mystic, languid, inscrutable!!

One can hear a Frenchman saying that, the silly fool – as if it was an opium den in Marseilles. We felt the opposite; that is why I mention it. Every circumstance of sight, sound, and trespass conspired to swamp the intelligence. The message of a work of art overcame this conspiracy, forcing its way out of the shadows, insisting on structure and proportion, on the impress of superlative quality, and on the intellect behind them. How this message was conveyed is difficult to say. Glimpses of arabesques so liquid, so delicately interlaced, that they looked no more like mosaic than a carpet looks like stitches; of larger patterns lost in the murk above our heads; of vaults and friezes alive with calligraphy – these were its actual words. But the sense was larger. An epoch, the Timurids, Gohar Shad herself, and her architect Kavam-ad-Din, ruled the night.

*

'Please blow your nose,' whispered our guide to Christopher.

'Why?'

'I ask you, blow it, and continue to blow it. You must cover your beard.'

Our guide was well known to the mullahs and policemen on duty. They greeted him without noticing the shabby plebeian at his side or the sneezing consumptive at his heels. We walked twice round the quadrangle, very slowly, bowing to the Tomb each time; then quickened our pace through the other two great courts, an ethereal vision of silver-white niches in double tiers.

'Now,' hissed our guide, 'we are coming to the main gate. I shall talk to you, Mr Byron, when we go out. You, Mr Sykes, please blow your nose and walk behind.'

Guards, porters, and ecclesiastics stood up respectfully as they saw him come. He seemed entirely preoccupied with his own conversation, which took the form of a charwoman's monologue and sounded so remarkable in Persian that I had no need to simulate interest: 'So I said to him rumble rumble rumble rumble Rumble he said rumble Rumble? I said I said and rumble rumble Rumble rumble he said to me I said Rumble! rumblerumblerumblerumble . . .' Everyone bowed. Our guide cast an eye over his shoulder to see that Christopher was following, and we were out, got a cab, and were soon scrubbing our faces at the hotel before returning to the Consulate.

We thanked him profusely. But in the same breath I was obliged to tell him that having seen this much, no amount of gratitude could prevent my begging him to take me again by daylight. Noticing his reluctance, Christopher offered not to come, as his beard was evidently an embarrassment. This relieved our guide. He arranged to call for me at two o'clock today.

This morning, when I entered the hotel, the bedroom attendant brought me a plate of corks and charcoal without being asked for them. It was another thing to make up for daylight with these crude materials: my moustache looked green instead of black, and turned out brindled; my eyes were still blue, inside lashes semi-black and sore with scrubbing. But the costume was subtle: brown shoes with tight black trousers four inches too short; grey coat; gold stud instead of a tie; our servant's mackintosh; and a black Pahlevi hat which I aged by kicking it – these components created the perfect type of Marjoribanks' Persia. Alas! my work of art was hardly complete before a telephone message informed me that our guide had funked at the last minute.

Not daring to take a cab by myself, I had to walk the mile and a half to the Shrine. The sun was at my back; I sweated under the mackintosh as I invented a quick Persian-looking trot of short high steps that would prevent me from tripping over uneven paving-stones; but no one looked at me. The goal grew nearer. There was the main gate. There the little tunnel. Without looking round, I was in it, found the yard, realized there were trees there, and then saw that the further exit was completely blocked by a group of mullahs, my potential assaulters, who were discussing the wares of a small bookshop.

Everything depended on my pace. I was keyed to it, and by it. If it faltered, I was exposed. So I kept to it, and clove that group of mullahs as a torpedo cleaves the waves. By the time they noticed me, grumbling at such ill manners, there was only my back to notice.

I hastened down the dark bazaar, found the dome where I turned to the left, and was greeted, on coming out into the court, by such a fanfare of colour and light that I stopped a moment, half blinded. It was as if someone had switched on another sun.

The whole quadrangle was a garden of turquoise, pink, dark red, and dark blue, with touches of purple, green, and yellow, planted among paths of plain buff brick. Huge white arabesques whirled above the ivan arches. The ivans themselves hid other gardens, shadier, fritillary-coloured. The great minarets beside the sanctuary, rising from bases encircled with Kufic the size of a boy, were bedizened with a network of jewelled lozenges. The swollen sea-green dome adorned with yellow tendrils appeared between them. At the opposite end glinted the top of a gold minaret. But in all this variety, the principle of union, the life spark of the whole blazing apparition, was kindled by two great texts: the one, a frieze of white *suls* writing powdered over a field of gentian blue along the skyline of the entire quadrangle; the other, a border of the same alphabet in daisy white and yellow on a sapphire field, interlaced with turquoise Kufic along its inner edge, and enclosing, in the form of a three-sided oblong, the arch of the main ivan between the minarets. The latter was actually designed, it says, by 'Baisanghor, son of Shah Rukh, son of Timur Gurkani (Tamerlane), with hope in God, in the year 821

(AD 1418)'. Baisanghor was a famous calligrapher; and being the son of Gohar Shad also, he celebrated his mother's munificence with an inscription whose glory explains for ever the joy felt by Islam in writing on the face of architecture.

This vision was a matter of seconds. Simultaneously I began to feel insecure. I had intended to follow last night's plan of walking slowly round the court, but was prevented by two crowds, one listening to a preacher before the main ivan, one praying before the Tomb opposite; so that either way I was threatened by religious etiquette. Other pilgrims were squatting along the walls, many of them Afghans, all quite different in clothes and manner from my lower middle-class Persian self, and eyeing me, so I imagined, with hawk-like scowls as I walked to and fro between the two crowds. At last it was no longer imagination: my gaping inquisitiveness attracted notice. I scuttled back into the bazaar. The mullahs were no longer in the passage. Out in the street stood Christopher, leering wantonly as I passed him with eyes averted. Now, on the way back, the sun was in my face, and people turned to look at me as I passed. There was something wrong. Whatever it was, Mrs Gastrell did not jump to it. She was drying her hair by the fire, and was highly incensed when her privacy was abused by an unknown native.

I have learned what I wanted to know: first, that the use of coloured mosaic out of doors reached its climax at the Timurid Renascence; and second, that the beauty of it in the shrine here is nevertheless surpassed on six of the seven minarets at Herat, whose remains have an even finer quality and purer colour, and are not interrupted by plain brickwork. The few travellers who have visited Samarcand and Bokhara as well as the Shrine of the Imam Riza, say that nothing in those two towns can equal the last. If they are right, the Mosque of Gohar Shad must be the greatest surviving monument of the period, while the ruins of Herat show that there was once a greater.

I tremble to think that of the four finest buildings in Persia, the Gumbad-i-Kabus, the small dome-chamber in the Friday Mosque at Isfahan, the Mosque of Gohar Shad here, and the Mosque of Sheikh Lutfullah at Isfahan, my acquaintance with two was postponed till my last fortnight in the country.

*

Kariz (3000 ft), 8 May We meant to stop at Sengbest to examine
an eleventh-century mausoleum and minaret which are visible a
mile off the road. But a rainy sky made us push on to Turbat-i-
Sheikh Jam. The shrine there was disappointing. So was our lunch.
It was in Isfahan I decided sandwiches were insupportable, and
bought a blue bowl, which Ali Asgar used to fill with chicken
mayonnaise before starting on a journey. Today there had been
treachery in the Gastrells' kitchen, and it was filled with mutton.
Worse than that, we have run out of wine.

Then began that end-of-the-world feeling which I had noticed
before on the plain where Persia and Afghanistan meet, and which
now struck Christopher too. Fields of opium poppies surrounded the
infrequent villages, shining their fresh green leaves against the
storm-inked sky. Purple lightning danced on the horizon. It had
rained here already, and out in the desert we could smell the aromatic camel-thorn as if it was on fire. Yellow lupins mingled with
big clumps of mauve and white iris. Kariz itself was pervaded by an
overpowering scent, as sweet as bean-flowers, but more languid,
more poetic. I walked out to try and place it. The opium flowers
called me, glowing in the dusk like lamps of ice. But it was not from
them.

Kariz, 9 May It rained in the night. We tried to start, but came
back after five hundred yards.

Kariz, 10 May This morning we took horses to inspect the road
and try out our army saddles. I mounted a bay mare, old, small, and
starved; Christopher a white stallion, young, big, and wall-eyed.
The difference in sex ensured all the pace that could be got out of
them.

At the Persian block-house in no-man's-land we found an officer
who had only been two days in command there and was already
depressed beyond speech by the companionship of his few troopers,
a savage dog, and a yardful of scraggy mares with their new-born
foals. Not a tree nor a stream nor any hint of garden warded off the
sodden yellow cow-parsleys of the desert. We offered him some cake,

and said we must be getting on, to see the worst of the road where it crosses the marsh.

He demurred, maintaining it was unsafe, but, seeing we were determined, came with us for the sake of company, riding with a rifle under his left thigh. A couple of troopers came too, and the whole party scattered out in line to reconnoitre all possible tracks. We had gone a kilometre or so, when the officer shouted to me to observe a sleeping shepherd. Another of his scares, I thought, when I saw flies – too many of them – on the bare legs. A blue-brown mask, swollen to the size of a pumpkin, was cricked backwards: the eyes were shut, the black lips open.

The officer was distraught. How could the man have died so near the block-house? When had he died? And what had caused his death? Did we think he could have been run over by a motor? Looking round at the plain dead level for ten miles in every direction, and remembering that the average traffic was one lorry a day, we did not think so: thus dashing our Persian's last hope of pretending that a corpse in our path, if untoward, was still a sign of Progress.

At length he took courage, dismounted, and lifted the body up. Its contents rattled. The limbs were crook'd and rigid. It had a bullet wound over the left eye, and another over the left breast. The man was a Kazak. His greying beard was thin enough to count the hairs. His knobbled stick had fallen where he fell, and seemed, as it lay there, a more human thing than the rotting hulk beside it.

The officer said he must go back at once, to write a report. When we answered, of course, but we must go on, he grew frantic. The dilemma was solved by the appearance on the horizon of a solitary cavalier from the direction of Islamkillah. Christopher and I rode off to meet him. The officer followed, groaning. The stranger was an Afghan horse-coper, and told us that even his horse had got into difficulties on the road across the marsh; the mud had come up to his belly, as we could see. This was all we needed to know. After drinking tea at the block-house, we left the officer composing his report, and started to ride back by an alternative road.

This led us, after an attack by dogs from a nomad encampment which took the stallion on its blind side and made it snort with fear, to the garrison town of Yusufabad, where an officer entertained us with sugar cakes in a clean carpeted room overlooking a garden of flowering broom and acacias. He was a handsome young fellow, smartly turned out, and had the politeness to sympathize with our interest in his country's monuments.

'Vous avez raison, messieurs. Cette tour de Gumbad-i-Kabus, je la trouve unique dans le monde entier. Vous avez été à Isfahan? Naturellement. C'est épatant, n'est-ce pas? Il y a encore des antiquités ici ... oui, toutes proches.' And he described the minaret of Kerat, which Diez illustrates and whose whereabouts all maps and inquiries had so far failed to elicit. If that was too far – as unluckily it was – there was the Maulana at Tayabad only a mile away, which was 504 years old.

He also told us of a second road across the frontier to Islamkillah, which runs south-east from Yusufabad till it reaches the hills, thus avoiding the marsh. We may try it, as it seems that the ordinary road will need three or four days' sun to dry it. The sky was cloudier than ever as we rode back to Kariz.

AFGHANISTAN: Herat, 12 May   Dear old Herat!

Again I inhabit a square bare room with white walls and a blue dado and a ceiling of poles. The clang of the metalsmiths below brings back a memory of gloomy autumn days, of waiting, waiting. A curious procession reintegrates: the Noel party, the Indians, the Hungarian, the Punjabi doctor and the Charcoal-Burners, all menaced by winter and the closing of the roads. Now we have summer before us; yet the air blows chill through the open doors as I lie in bed watching the early-morning bustle of the street. There is a new car in the town, a dark blue Chevrolet, 1933 model. But the royal barouche is there too. The Commander-in-Chief is standing at the corner. Fewer people are carrying rifles than formerly, though everyone grasps a rose, or has one in his mouth. Perhaps roses have displaced rifles. There is certainly no sign of that 'trouble in the spring'.

I have just been down to get some tea, and seen the minarets in the dawn light from the roof at the head of the stairs. That light has altered. Five months ago it was a mournful gleam, waning day by day, weighing on my spirits even more than dawns when there was no light and rain uttered its hopeless patter on the tin roof. Now it will be stronger every morning. We can walk to Mazar if we want, instead of racing the winter and losing by a day.

*

Our arrival here last night surprised ourselves as much as our hosts. Yesterday morning, about half-past ten, Christopher and I rode off to Yusufabad in a leisurely mood, intending to spend the day at the Maulana at Tayabad. On our way back the night before, we had noticed various low-lying points on the road that were still too deep in water for a car to pass them. Now they were almost dry. Simultaneously we saw a new storm rolling up behind us from Persia. It looked as if we must cross the frontier at once or endure another three days' wait. We were better mounted than the day before. Christopher galloped back to fetch the car and luggage. I galloped on, found the Faulana, which had a beautiful stucco inscription backed by turquoise glaze, and reached Yusufabad again one minute before the car. Bundling in my saddle and saddle-bags, we set off under the guidance of a peasant who wore a long crimson blouse sprigged with white leaves and whose hair was cut to the bob and fringe of a medieval page. There were no difficulties as far as Hajiabad, a small village near the hills. But after that, as we made our way along their lower slopes, we came to loose sand and could not have found the track without our guide. Monstrous cow-parsleys standing upright in the middle of it showed it had borne no other traffic this season. After a time we could see Islamkillah, a solitary fortress in the blue distance of the plain below, and eventually came out on the Herat road two miles beyond it, but dutifully drove back to comply with the frontier regulations. They gave us a dish of poached eggs as a reward.

The hotel in Herat had been warned by telephone that foreigners were coming, and Seyid Mahmud was standing on the threshold. When he saw me, his eyes nearly fell out of his head, and he struck up a sort of antique chorus: 'Mister-é-Bairun mariz bud, Mister-é-Bairun was ill. He has come back. Was ill, was ill. Came back, came back. Mister-é-Bairun was ill, came back, was ill, came back,' etc., till Christopher, not knowing the signs of Afghan affection, thought he was in a mad-house. Do I flatter myself? Moss-roses were placed in our button-holes, the best carpets in our rooms, and pots of geraniums on our tables. Two kinds of sherbet were brought out. Sponge cakes and my favourite jam would be ready tomorrow. The luggage was up in a twinkling.

'Thank God for a country where things are done with gusto again,' said Christopher.

*

Our delay at Kariz had one advantage: Thrush has gone on to Kandahar. He wrote a testimonial in Seyid Mahmud's book, saying that by European standards the hotel was rather a pity, but by Afghan ones he supposed he had no complaints. This is the man who revels in discomfort.

Herat, 13 May The municipal improvement mania has spread here from Persia. A small bandstand now shelters the policeman at the crossroads, from which, if a cab totters round the corner, he intimidates it with a red truncheon and a whistling fit to scare the Chicago underworld. They are also pulling down the bazaar, and replacing it by a series of little piazzas for the different trades. This really is an improvement. The old tunnel is a fearsome place, desperately cold in winter, and of no architectural value.

Nature has made other alterations. At Gazar Gah, where I last saw marigolds and petunias, the pool in the outer court is overhung with single white roses growing as thick as snow; instead of the whistle of the autumn wind, doves are fluttering about the pines and families making holiday in the decagonal pavilion. And seen from the terrace outside, the whole plain between the mountains and the Hari river is now a sea of varying greens and silver streams.

Walking out to the Musalla with this diary under my arm, in search of peace to write it, I recognize each field, each bank, each twinkling ditch – but only as one recognizes a face in strange clothes. Even the minarets have changed; their blue has grown more vivid, as if in answer to the landscape's challenge. The huge round bases, that rose before out of the bare earth, rise now from lush emerald corn, in whose depths flourishes a bright purple monkshood; or from the shining white and filling grey-green pods of the opium crops; or from those low trees, scattered with gold when I first saw them, and bare as bones when I left, that have now turned into bushy deep-green mulberries. The sun dispenses a temperate heat from a sky of temperate blue. And over all presides that elusive languid scent which first met us at Kariz, borne from its petalled cave on the caressing summer breeze.

People are talking on the other side of the Mausoleum. There is a platform there, facing the mountains, where I was intending to sit.

But no; some mullahs have taken it. Books are spread out on the ground, and a group of downy-bearded novices are receiving instruction; while two others are sitting on a wall near by, reading to themselves. A frown from the mullah who is declaiming, and whose white turban is wound round a purple cone, asks me to keep away. I find a place opposite them, at a respectable distance, from which the tall black entrance and the big blue melon-dome above it dwarf the pied group on the platform. It is a pity they are so preoccupied. I might ask them else why they choose this site for lessons. Is it in honour of the people who are buried there? And if so, what do they know about them? Stories of Gohar Shad were still common talk here in the last century.

It is not her beauty these stories recount; still less her patronage of the arts. To the people of Herat, who knew her for sixty years, she was a personality. The versatility of her life and the violence of her death made her the type of her age, an age when Herat was capital of an empire stretching from the Tigris to Sinkiang.

One thinks of our own queens, Elizabeth and Victoria. Women of this kind are rare in Mohammadan annals. That is why, perhaps, Mohun Lal heard her still described, four hundred years later, as 'the most incomparable woman in the world'. But the Timurids, though leaders of Mohammadan society, were Mongols by birth and tradition; their ideas of domestic life came from China, that paradise of masterful women. Timur's first wife rode at her husband's side through his early hardships and adventures. And later, in the palmy days at Samarcand, Clavijo records how his other wives and his daughters-in-law gave parties independently of their husbands, at which their chief amusement was to make the men drunk. Gohar Shad, herself the daughter of a Jagatay noble, took advantage of Mongol custom to indulge more serious tastes.

Her father was the Emir Ghiyas-ad-Din, whose ancestor had saved the life of Jenghis Khan. She was married to Shah Rukh, probably in 1388, certainly before 1394 when their son Ulugh Beg was born. It was a successful marriage, according to the ballads of Herat, which sing of Shah Rukh's love for her. But little is known of their first forty years together, except what concerns her buildings. She founded the mosque at Meshed, for instance, in 1405, and took Shah Rukh to see it in August 1419, when he praised the patterns and workmanship and dedicated a gold lamp to the tomb of the saint. It is only later she comes to the front of the stage, first as the consort of Shah Rukh's old age, and then as his widow.

I was right about the single minaret over there, in thinking it was part of her college. A sketch done by Major Durand of the Boundary Commission in 1885, just before the demolition, shows the quadrangle of the college standing adjacent to the Musalla, and this minaret attached to its main gate. So I imagine it, overlooking the royal foundress and her two hundred ladies, as they arrived from the town on that visit of inspection that had such amiable consequences for the students of the college. On account of the ladies, whose emotions were liable to get the better of them, the students had been sent out; all except one, who had fallen asleep – it may have been a scented summer afternoon like this. On waking up, and looking from his window to see what the noise was, he caught the eye of 'a ruby-lipped lady', who hastened to his room, but was betrayed, on rejoining the royal party, by the 'irregularity of her dress and manners'. To prevent further incidents of this kind, or rather to bless them, Gohar Shad forthwith married all her two hundred attendants to the students, who had previously been ordered to avoid the society of women. She furnished each student with clothes, a salary, and a bed. And she ruled that husband and wife should meet once a week, on condition that the former attended to his studies. 'She did all this,' adds Mohun Lal piously, 'to arrest the progress of adultery.'

Shah Rukh had eight sons, of whom Ulugh Beg, the eldest, and Baisanghor, the fifth, were also sons of Gohar Shad. Intellectually, these two fulfilled the promise of their parentage; they and their mother became the central figures of the Renascence. Ulugh Beg leaves the stage of Herat for that of Transoxiana. In 1410 his father made him Viceroy of Samarcand, and ten years later his mother visited him there to see his new observatory. His astronomical calculations led him to reform the calendar, and brought him posthumous honour at Oxford, where they were published in 1665.

Baisanghor, living beside his parents in Herat, played no part in politics beyond that of president of his father's council. His court was of poets and musicians, and he extended his mother's passion for building to painting and book-production. A corps of forty illuminators, binders and calligraphers worked under his immediate eye. Among the latter he himself held an eminent place, and that this was not accorded him out of flattery can be seen from his inscription at

Meshed, which I must compare one day with the other specimens of his hand in the library there and the Serai at Constantinople.

Like so many of his family, this talented prince failed to discriminate between the pleasures of the mind and the body. He died of drink in 1433. Forty days' mourning were decreed, and a vast concourse lined the route of the funeral cortège from his residence of the White Garden to his mother's college. There, in the college quadrangle, Gohar Shad had built a mausoleum. The college has disappeared, all save that one minaret. But looking across the fields, I see that the mausoleum is still a scene of theological study, and that the happy band of students who married Gohar Shad's ladies have been followed by others down to the present time.

Gohar Shad by now was rising sixty, and had another quarter of a century to live. It was her affection for Baisanghor's son, Ala-ad-Daula, that brought her into politics. For the rest of her life she worked to secure his interest in the succession, to her ultimate undoing.

Her partiality made enemies of those it aimed to exclude, particularly of her other grandson Abdullatif, son of Ulugh Beg, who had been brought up at his grandparents' court in Herat. Furious at the attentions lavished on Ala-ad-Daula, he removed himself to his father in Samarcand, at which Shah Rukh, who adored him, was inconsolable. Gohar Shad, therefore, to please her ageing husband, set out to bring him back, travelling up the road we shall take tomorrow, in the heart of winter. Abdullatif may have had reason for his flight. For the old lady, having fetched him back, turned her spleen instead on Mohammad Juki, Shah Rukh's youngest son, to such effect that he expired, as Khondemir puts it, of mortification. He also was buried in the mausoleum.

Two years later occurred the misfortune for which she had been preparing. She had persuaded her husband, despite his failing powers, to lead an army into Persia, and had herself accompanied him. After marching nearly as far as Shiraz, Shah Rukh settled for the winter at Ray, where Teheran is now. And there, on 12 March 1447, he died, aged sixty-nine years. The first period of the Timurid Renascence was over. For the arts cannot flourish without political, or at least civic stability, and during the next twelve years Herat fell prey to ten successive rulers.

The anarchy opened inauspiciously for Gohar Shad, who was

caught in her own trap. Ala-ad-Daula, the grandson she trusted, had been left in charge of Herat. Abdullatif, the grandson she suspected and had forced to accompany the army in order to watch him, now had her in his power. He left her in no doubt of it, seizing not only her baggage, but all her animals as well; so that while the body of the dead king was on its way back to Herat in a litter, his widow, the most famous woman of the age and more than seventy years old, was compelled to follow it on foot across the wastes of Khorasan; 'with an ordinary linen scarf thrown over her head, and a staff in her hand', says Khondemir. She was rescued from this predicament by Ala-ad-Daula, who captured Abdullatif and put him in the citadel (where I got into trouble over the artillery park). On learning this, Ulugh Beg, who had started from Samarcand with an army to claim the empire also, renounced his claim in favour of Ala-ad-Daula on condition that his son was set at liberty.

For a moment Gohar Shad's plans had triumphed. But a dispute arose with Ulugh Beg over the other terms of the agreement, and he continued his advance on Herat. There he got news that a party of Uzbeg raiders had sacked the suburbs of Samarcand and destroyed many of his favourite works of art. To replace them he carried off as many treasures as he could from Herat, including a pair of bronze doors from Gohar Shad's college. He also took away the body of his father Shah Rukh out of the mausoleum, and deposited it at Bokhara on his way back to Samarcand. Meanwhile, Abdullatif's morbid fancy must needs start brooding on his father's supposed preference for his younger brother; regardless of the fact that but for his father's renunciation of the empire, he would still have been in prison. He crossed the Oxus from Balkh, defeated his father at Shahrukhiya, and had him executed by a Persian slave. So perished Ulugh Beg on 27 October 1449, the most amiable of all his family and the only scientist among them.

Six months later the parricide was assassinated by one of Ulugh Beg's servants.

For the next seven years Abulkasim Babur reigned in Herat. He too was a son of Baisanghor, and seems to have lived in peace with his grandmother. But Ala-ad-Daula, Baisanghor's youngest son, was still her favourite. And when Abulkasim Babur died in 1457, of drink like his father, she summoned her last energies to the support of her great-grandson Ibrahim, Ala-ad-Daula's son.

She was now more than eighty years old. That July Abu Said, the great-grandson of Timur and ancestor of Babur, arrived before Herat. Only the citadel held out for Ibrahim. But Abu Said, though he directed operations in person, could not take it. Infuriated by this hindrance to his plans, and believing that its resistance was being secretly encouraged by Gohar Shad, he had the old lady put to death.

She was buried in her own mausoleum. On her tombstone was written: 'The Bilkis of the Time'. Bilkis means Queen of Sheba.

A year later both Ala-ad-Daula and Ibrahim were laid beside her. But another great-grandson, also of the seed of Baisanghor, survived in the person of Yadgar Mohammad. In 1469 he was living with Uzun Hassan, the Chief of the White Sheep Turcomans, when that ruler was attacked by Abu Said. The attack failed. Abu Said was captured, and Uzun Hassan handed him over to his guest, then a boy of sixteen. The boy, having given the necessary order, retired to his tent; Abu Said was immediately executed. Thus was Gohar Shad avenged by the posterity of Baisanghor.

It is cold. The sun has gone down. The mullahs have gone in, and their pupils with them. The lustre has gone from the blue towers and the green corn. Their shadows have gone. The magic scent has gone. The summer has gone, and the twilight brings back the spring, cold and uncertain. I must go.

Goodbye, Gohar Shad and Baisanghor. Sleep on there under your dome, to the sound of boys' lessons. Goodbye, Herat.

Moghor (c. *3000 ft, 120 miles from Herat*), *17 May*, and smoking the last of Wishaw's cigars, bless him; I wish at moments I were back in that secure and comfortable domicile, among those sweet blue domes and sweet mauve mountains. Still, our present situation has the compensation of grass and rolling downs. And at least we have passed Kala Nao, so that I now, as well as Christopher, am in new country.

We left Herat in the early afternoon three days ago, sped by a bottle of sherbet from Seyid Mahmud. At Karokh a lawn had sprung up under the pines; the fish were still swimming in their netted pool, for ever upstream to keep themselves out of the net. Our inclination was to stay the night, and discretion counselled it, as there was a mackerel sky. But arguing that if we did stop, and it did rain, we might be held up for several days, we resolved to cross the pass that night. It was a risk, and if anyone had told me six months ago that I should ever take that risk again, I should have called him feeble-minded – instead of myself.

The earth gradient leading up to the pass, where we had such trouble with the lorry, presented no difficulty when dry. Again the spare gnarled junipers and the great view greeted us at the top; again there were storm clouds over Turkestan. The worst was over, we thought; when we noticed that the north face of the mountains was still damp. Half a mile down the car stuck.

Our joint strength could not move it, though the gradient was about one in three and the bonnet was pointing steeply at the valley below. The undercarriage was impaled on a boulder. For an hour and a half, ankle-deep in freezing slush, we levered away the rocks; it sank the deeper. As dark fell, two white-cloaked shepherds came by with their flock. We begged them to wait and help us. They said they dared not, owing to the wolves. But one of them, at his own suggestion, lent us his rifle and two remaining bullets to see us through the night.

We discussed what to do. Jamshyd the chauffeur wanted Christopher and me to walk to the nearest village for help, while he stayed behind with the gun. Christopher wanted us all to go to the village. I, knowing the village was five miles off, wanted us all to stay in the car, arguing that such a walk would be an indescribable bore, that the village in question was inhospitable and thievish enough when awake, that it would be more so if disturbed when asleep, and that in any case it would give us no help till morning. Christopher replied that it was nonsense to suppose the wolves would be deterred by headlights or the engine running, and that if we stayed in the car, they would raven their way through the side curtains and pick our bones clean. To this I averred that whether it was nonsense or not, we should stand a better chance in the car than out of it, and that anyhow the dogs of the village were more savage than wolves. 'For God's sake', I said, 'get into the car, drink this whisky, and let us be cosy.'

We were. Quilts and sheep-skins replaced our mud-soaked clothes. The hurricane lantern, suspended from a strut in the hood, cast an appropriate glow on our dinner of cold lamb and tomato ketchup out of the blue bowl, eggs, bread, cake, and hot tea. Afterwards we settled into our corners with two *Charlie Chan* detective stories. Jamshyd fell asleep in the front. I listened for a while to the wind soughing in the junipers and an owl hooting in the distance; then I too slept. Christopher stayed awake with the gun on his knee, thinking every rustle a wolf or a brigand.

At half-past two he woke me with a word more sinister than any wolf: 'Rain.' There came a patter on the hood; it increased to a steady drumming. At dawn, Jamshyd set off down the road for help.

Still in our quilts, we started breakfast, and were spreading some Herat jam on slabs of bread and butter when, looking up, we beheld a man on horseback. It was the shepherd of the gun. We returned it, and the bullets, with grateful thanks. He spoke not a word, but vanished among the dark rain-soaked trees.

Jamshyd came back leading a gang of turbaned road-makers, who had been sent out on a corvée because a visit from Abdul Rahim was expected. The rain was dropping in sheets; every angle of the mountains was occupied by a cataract. If anything, the descent was worse than in November. Then at least it was dry below the snow-line. Now, along that narrow ledge whence the red pinnacles rose into the clouds above, and whole ranges could be seen emerging from the clouds below, the car pursued its agonizing progress, generally quite out of control, often broadside, and never less than two feet from the edge. At one point, a red boulder, dislodged by the rain, had blocked the ledge and a shelf had to be built out round it. At length we reached the roadmakers' tent. From there, they said, the road was good – newly dug, that is; for digging is the equivalent of resurfacing in this country. It led us out on to the open slopes, now covered with pasture. On and on we slithered and bumped through the driving rain, digging the car every quarter of a mile out of ruts that would ordinarily have needed half a dozen men, but were now so slippery that one spade and our feeble shoves sufficed.

I walked most of the way, looking at the flowers in the long grass by the road's edge, small scarlet tulips, dwarf irises of cream and yellow, a kind of purple onion flower that pursued me from my buttonhole with a stink of bad meat, poppies, campanulas, and a strange plant with the leaves of a tulip, whose flower, the colour of pink blancmange, had square separated petals growing upwards in a cup. Crops began after a time, clover and wheat, as low as they would be in England at this season. The village of Laman was already in sight when the car fell into a ditch from which we had no hope of removing it unaided.

The village at this time of year looked a pretty little place, shaded by poplars, enlivened by a rushing stream, and overhung by red cliffs upholding tables of green grass; very different in fact from the last view I had of it through the white mist of a December dawn. Christopher had gone ahead, and been met by boorishness and ill-humour. But by the time I arrived, the headman had telephoned to the Governor of Kala Nao about us, and received us hospitably, lighting a bonfire in the middle of his floor to dry our clothes. That night the Governor of Kala Nao sent us a pilau on horseback.

This morning there was not a cloud in the sky. After giving the road an hour or two to dry, we set off down the valley, crossing the river every ten minutes and generally having to dry the magneto after-wards. Half-way we met the Governor of Kala Nao on his grey horse, followed by a picturesque retinue in whose tail I espied the secretary that had wanted my pen. He said he had ordered a room to be ready for us if we wanted it. But no, we said; we should reach Murghab tonight.

The valley widened. In its grass recesses appeared the same encamp-ments of kibitkas, whose flocks impeded, dogs resented, and children mocked our passage. The salukis, I noticed, were still rugged. All the grass, even high up on the cliff-tops, was stained with patches of vermilion poppies. Occasionally, by the roadside, a burst of royal blue burrage in their midst produced a curiously artificial effect, as if both had been planted out of patriotism. We drank some milk at Kala Nao, forsook the river at last, and continued along the bottoms of a rolling down country, making good pace and confident of being in before dark. The road was crawling with tortoises, which Jamshyd called lobsters. We also met two snakes. They were four feet long, pale green, and probably harmless. But with true Indian hatred, Jamshyd stopped the car and solemnly murdered them.

Twenty miles from Kala Nao, the front axle struck a hummock. There was a slight jar, and the engine petered out.

*

One of those sordid, anxious periods ensued in which we fiddled and twiddled, changed the coil, micturated into the battery, and tested everywhere for sparks. The engine refused to cough. It was nearly evening, the country was deserted, and this particular stretch of road was notorious for brigands.

At this juncture a bearded gentleman wearing a blue turban and mounted on a long-bodied black horse, trotted round a corner of the downs. He was followed by two attendants carrying rifles on their saddle-bows. One had a beard also. The other's face was veiled.

'Who are you?' asked the leader.

'I know who this gentleman is,' interrupted the unveiled follower, pointing at me. 'He came to Kala Nao in the winter and fell ill there. Your health is better now, aga, by the grace of God?'

'By the grace of God it is. I remember you too. You are in the employ of His Excellency the Governor of Kala Nao, and brought me food when I was ill.'

Reassured by this mutual recognition, the two parties became more confiding. Christopher explained our predicament.

'My name,' announced the man in the blue turban, 'is Haji Lal Mohammad. I am a pistachio merchant, who had business in Murghab and am now returning to India. This is a bad stretch of road to be out on after dark; a man had his throat cut here not long ago. The nearest robat is only one farsakh off. If you will mount these gentlemen's horses, we will ride on there, and tell the people to send out other horses for your chauffeur and luggage.'

We mounted, and the guards with their rifles hopped up behind us. The veiled enigma clasped his hands round my stomach.

'What do you think of him?' Haji Lal asked me.

'I don't know what to think of a man when I can't see his face.'

'Ha, ha, he is very young, but a great killer. He has already killed five men. Too young for so many, don't you think?'

The enigma giggled coyly under his draperies and tickled me in the ribs.

'I presume you are followers of Jesus,' remarked Christopher's pillion-mate.

'Certainly.'

'And were in Herat three days ago?' broke in Haji Lal. 'Therefore you can tell me what the exchange is between Kabuli and Indian rupees. Also the price of Karakulis.' By these he meant lambskins.

'Are you married?' he continued. 'How many children have you, and how much money? I sometimes think of visiting London. How much does it cost to spend the night there?'

'That depends,' answered Christopher, 'on what sort of night you want to spend.'

This reminded Haji Lal of a more pressing matter. 'Have you any medicines in your luggage?'

'Yes.'

'Will you give me one? I want the kind that will make me please the ladies in Herat.'

'I'm not sure that we have that kind.'

We jogged along in silence for a little.

'That car of yours,' said Haji Lal suddenly. 'What's wrong with it?'

'I don't know.'

'Will it ever go again?'

'I don't know.'

'What will you do if it doesn't?'

'Go on by horse.'

There was a further silence.

'Will you sell it?' asked Haji Lal.

The words fell like music. But Christopher was careful not to show it.

An hour's ride brought us to the robat of Moghor. Robat is the Afghan term for caravanserai, and is also used as a measure of distance, since the main highways have these establishments every four farsakhs or sixteen miles. This one consists of the usual court-yard, with stabling below and a range of rooms over the entrance. But the parapets are crenellated for serious business, and the gates shut earlier than in Persia.

The people of the place agreed that the open road was no place for Jamshyd and the luggage at this time of day, and sent out to fetch them as soon as possible.

Moghor, 18 May   Christopher has accepted Haji Lal's offer for the car, which is about fifty pounds. He only gave sixty for it originally. One of the guards has gone off to Kala Nao to fetch part of the money, and the rest is arriving in sacks from the neighbouring villages; our friend must be a man of credit. Ten pounds are being deducted for the black horse, which Christopher has taken a fancy to. I am hiring one for myself, in case we find motor transport later.

A lorry has just passed on its way to Herat containing the secretary to the Russian Consulate in Maimena. Having seen our car being dragged in by oxen, he stopped to ask if he could help, which was friendly of him. He said that lorries run from Maimena to Mazar-i-Sherif almost daily.

After he had gone, an Afghan walked into the room and addressed me as 'Tovarish'. 'Good God,' I said, 'don't comrade me. I'm English.' It took a long time to persuade him that not all fair people were Russians. But when we succeeded in doing so, it transpired that he was an escaped Russian subject and in fact had nothing to say for the Bolsheviks.

There is a river near the robat where we went this evening to wash our plates. Seeing a village on the other side of it, we asked a passing youth if he could get us any milk there. He could, he said, if he had anything to put it in; so we handed him a thermos. But instead of going to the village, he stood still and open-eyed, fingering the glittering object, till we had finished washing up. Then, as we started to go back to the robat, he ran after us, and taking off his turban presented it to us as a security for the thermos.

Later. Everyone thinks Christopher has been swindled over the car, whose value in this country seems to be greater than we thought. I forgot to mention the most curious part of the bargain. This was that we should give Haji Lal a letter to enable him to see over the buildings at New Delhi. I have done my best, though I know no one in the Public Works Department there.

One should study first aid before starting on this kind of journey. We have just had one man asking help for a sprained thumb, another for worms. The least one can do is to make a show of treating them. But instead of masquerading as a witch doctor, it would be pleasanter to know they would be cured.

*

Bala Murghab (1500 ft, c. 45 miles from Moghor), 20 May   We left
Herat six days ago. If we had started in the morning instead of the
afternoon, we should probably have arrived here the same night.

Our caravan from Moghor consisted of six horses, three for the
luggage, one for me, one for the 'gunman' who escorted us, and
Christopher's black. The last turned out to be a remarkable pacer,
putting its near and off legs forward alternately with the speed of a
machine gun. We forsook the motor road, and cutting across the
downs, came to higher hills, still grass-covered, but dotted with out-
crops of rock and occasional pistachio bushes which I mistook for
wild fig trees till I saw the clusters of reddening nuts. From the top
of this range we had a last view of the Paropamisus behind us, still
half hidden by rain clouds. In front, and nearer, rose the main range
of the Band-i-Turkestan.

A broad valley, hot and stony, intervened, where the desert flora
reappeared and a solitary traveller, seeing us from afar, hid himself
in a gulley till we had passed. On the other side of the valley, as we
were preparing for a new ascent, a river came in sight and was flowing, to our astonishment, straight towards the mountain wall. Its
behaviour was explained by a pair of rocky gates, each crowned by
a watch-tower, which passed it through the mountains. We followed
it, crossing from the west bank to the east by means of a dilapidated
bridge, of whose two stone arches one had been washed away and
replaced by a wooden suspension. The motor road, which must have
joined the river further south, uses this bridge. According to the
Russian who called on us at Moghor, both it and the towers were
built by Alexander.

The river in question was the Murghab, which rises in the Hindu
Kush and frays out to lose itself in the desert round Merv. Here it
was about the size of the Thames at Windsor, though the current was
stronger, flowing between low grass banks lined with reeds and
bushes of pink spiraea. On the other side, groups of black tents were
dotted over the green foothills.

Having ridden more than thirty miles, and Murghab being still
another twelve, we stopped for the night at a robat. The people were
stupid and disobliging; our room was an airless cell, and crowded
with flies, which showed we must have dropped during the day; and
we were glad to be gone early this morning, leaving the valley at last

and emerging into a cultivated plain encompassed with grassy rounded foothills. Here it was much hotter. The cropped grass by the road already had a brown tinge, and the corn was standing high, full of pink veitches. Yet on some of the hills men were ploughing; perhaps for a second crop. As usual, the town looked like a wood from a distance, but reminded me of an Irish market town once we were in it. The front doors lead straight out of the street into one-storey houses, so that instead of the ordinary blank walls and intervening courtyards one catches sight of the life within.

Central Asia is beginning. Conversations in Turki assailed us, uttered by hirsute, slit-eyed men wearing striped and flowered gowns. Turcomans in busbies and red robes were pacing up and down, having mostly escaped over the Russian frontier, which is only twenty miles away. We saw a party of their women, all dressed in different reds and squatting over their food in an open court; with their tall hats nodding as they ate, they looked like a bed of geraniums and sweet-williams. To our surprise we also saw various Jews seated unconcernedly before their shops.

Our gunman took us to the Governor's house, which stands in a walled garden by the river. Outside it, on a bluff above the water, perches the old castle, now containing a small garrison. From this to the garden, the bank is lined with mulberry trees, beneath which the townsmen spread their leisure conversing, reading, praying, washing and grazing their horses. Christopher joined them with his.

The Governor was eating, but ordered us to be his guests; we have a room at the back of his secretary's office. They tell us he is seventy years old, has a long white beard, and is much loved for his suppression of robbers. Some of the robbers were clanking about in fetters on the other side of the garden; they seemed cheerful enough. He appears to enjoy the position of a hereditary khan, and may perhaps be the last representative of those numerous independent rulers who flourished between the Oxus and the Hindu Kush till eighty years ago, when the Emir Dost Mohammad incorporated their dominions in the Afghan state. His son, who has the face of a Spanish noble-man and is dressed in top-boots, a shooting suit, trench coat, stiff white collar, and turban cocked over one eye, certainly does the honours with the air of a Crown Prince. The whole atmosphere is patriarchal. Turcomans, Tajiks, and Uzbegs, of both sexes, keep coming up the garden path to seek justice at the secretary's window.

A black Labrador retriever and a doubtful spaniel are also wandering about the garden, both bred in Russia.

Maimena (2900 ft, c. 110 miles from Murghab), 22 May   Turkestan!

I have been reading Proust for the last three days (and begin to observe the infection of uncontrolled detail creeping into this diary). His description of how the name *Guermantes* hypnotized him reminds me of how the name *Turkestan* has hypnotized me. It started in the autumn of 1931. The Depression was in full swing, Europe insupportably gloomy, one asked if Communism was the solution, and the only way of escape seemed to be a villa at Kashgar out of reach of the post. I consulted the London Library, the library of the Central Asian Society, and the School of Oriental Studies; but architecturally and historically it appeared that Russian Turkestan, if not so remote, would offer more than Chinese. I gave up Kashgar, made friends with a secretary at the Russian Embassy, collected the members of a possible expedition, and went to Moscow to ask leave for it to start. To no purpose: in every department I was met by the argument that when Russian scientists, or even a single tea-taster, were allowed in India, I might go to Bokhara. In 1932 I reverted to the original plan. Another party was formed, and applied to the India Office for permission to travel up the Gilgit road to Kashgar. This application, after eliciting a curious sidelight on the sort of information confided to the India Office archives concerning peers who visit India, was forwarded to Delhi and Pekin. But before it could be answered, the government in Kashgar collapsed, civil war invaded the whole of Sinkiang, and the Gilgit road was closed to travellers. There remained a third, an Afghan, Turkestan. For it, another expedition was formed, but preferred, at the last moment, to undertake a research into the combustive properties of charcoal. I tried by myself, failed, have tried again, and now have hopes of succeeding. But though we have crossed the provincial frontier, we are still only halfway to Mazar.

When he actually met his duchess, Proust's image was shattered; he had to build another, to correspond with the woman instead of the name. Mine has been confirmed, enhanced. In the last two days, all the novelty and pastoral romance implied in the name Turkestan have come true; already a whole chapter of history has been transferred from the printed page to the mind's eye. I owe this fulfilment to the luck of the season. It was Mme de Guermantes' complexion that failed Proust. We have found Turkestan in the full bloom of early summer.

Three cars stood in the Governor's garden at Murghab. One was the lifeless body of a grey Ford coupé. The others were Vauxhalls, new, dark red, and closed; when it rained, they were covered with tarpaulins. Early in the morning after our arrival, the Governor and his son drove away in the Vauxhalls, to Maruchak on the Russian frontier. We looked forlornly at the Ford's engine scattered over the surrounding vegetable-beds and ordered horses.

'I can take you to Maimena in the car if you like,' said a Persian boy named Abbas, plucking the radiator out of a bush. 'We will start in an hour.'

The likelihood of covering more than two or three of the intervening hundred miles in this preposterous vehicle seemed so remote that we took none of the usual precautions before starting, prepared no food, disdained, if only out of courtesy to the driver, to count the car's spare parts, and even went so far as to wear our so-called best suits. The luggage was put into the back, where it reached to the ceiling. When Christopher and I stepped into the front, the chassis subsided a foot, as if we had been the mother-in-law in a slapstick film. Abbas was winding the crank handle. Suddenly his arm flew over his head, the noise of a blackmith's shop proceeded from the now collected engine, and we bounded across the Governor's flower-beds, while Abbas, in flying pursuit, just reached the wheel in time to turn us through the gate. Down the main street the population fled; in a minute we were through the town and tearing up a deserted valley. The luggage fell out of the unglazed windows. The radiator, playing fountains to the sky, first declined to the earth in front, then fell backwards on top of the engine, entangling itself in the fan, till we roped it up with our bedding cord. The sound of the machinery became apocalyptic, clanking and fizzing without any sort of rhythm till at last, with a final deafening cannonade, it ceased altogether and Abbas beamed at us with the expression of a conductor laying down his baton after an applauded symphony. A sympathetic report from the near hind tyre, though a beat late, announced that it also needed rest for the moment. We had come ten miles.

There was no spare tyre. Gathering up the shreds of the outer cover, Abbas produced a patching outfit, while Christopher and I, still determined that fate should look after us, lowered our best suits on to the grass some way off. The afternoon shadows were lengthening. It remained to bring the engine to life. But this was quickly accomplished by a few random blows with a hammer, as one beats a child, and we jumped in just in time. We now began to realize that the kangaroo paces of our vehicle, though not so comfortable as the glide of the old Chevrolet, were taking us over a road which the Chevrolet could never have tackled at all.

The valley we were following was about two miles broad. A river ran along it on the west, confined in an earth cutting. On either side rose earth hills, whose boneless green contours, rounded and polished by the weather, had the glossiness of a horse's flanks; though those on the west grew so steep towards the bottom that they met the valley with bare cliffs, revealing the body underneath, where the green vesture had no hold. Valley and hills alike were covered with a pasture of waving golden green, so rich that we could scarcely believe it had not been specially sown; until, when we came to crops, they seemed bare and thin by comparison. This wonderful country, with not a pebble in it to impede the plough or seedling, was hardly inhabited.

Not a pebble assisted the surface of the road either. When we left the valley, turning from north to north-east, the track was marked simply by two ditches, dug for that purpose, which wound in and out of the troughs of the downs. The grass which had looked so smooth from a distance was full of holes and hummocks; every bump threatened to annihilate us. But imperceptibly the distance to Maimena grew less, and we had come about forty miles when Abbas, seeing two turf pillars by the road, suggested that though his headlights left nothing to be desired we should stop here for the night. Feeling we had tempted fate enough for one day, we agreed.

A side track from between the pillars led us over several hump-backed bridges to a solitary house and yard overlooked by a grove of poplars. Its owner came out to greet us, a man of middle height dressed in white with a white turban, whose smile, framed by a curly dark brown beard, had the innocence of a child's. He showed us to a carpeted room furnished with a sliding wooden window, a fireplace, and a lot of old books in a niche over the door; it had the smell of an English drawing-room, exhaled by a pot-pourri of rose-leaves that were drying in another niche. Children staggered in with the luggage. Others brought us tea as we sat in the grass outside, gazing at the cool serpentine shadows among the green hills smeared with gold, above which rose the abrupt lilac peaks of the western Hindu Kush.

By supper-time, horsemen were arriving from the neighbouring villages to have their ailments treated. One had fever, one sores on his nose, which had been slit as a punishment; one headaches and vomiting in the morning; one a pestilent skin-disease all over his back, which had lasted a year and looked like syphilis: but what could we do for him? We doled out aspirin, quinine, and ointment, all we had, and now deliberately assumed the witch doctor's air of mystification, saying the medicines would not work, at least in the case of the sores, unless accompanied by repeated washings in boiled water – yes, *boiled*, we hissed, as though it had been a toad's liver. This morning there were more of them.

I went for a walk after breakfast in the poplar grove. Sparrows were twittering in the upper branches. Below, it was shady and damp and smelt of an English wood, which caused me a stab of homesickness. Then our host took us to see his walled garden, a vineyard with a watch-tower in the middle where he sits to enjoy the view and see who is arriving. A dank dell in one corner contained a tangle of big crimson roses, of which he picked us an armful each.

We asked if we could pay for our shelter, or at least for the food we had eaten. 'No,' he said, 'you cannot. My house is not a shop. Besides, you gave the people your medicines.'

'He is a holy man,' explained Abbas as we drove away, 'who receives all travellers on this road. That is why he puts up these things' – pointing to the grass pillars – 'so that they shall know his house is there. The name of the place is Kariz.'

The car smelt of roses as we crossed the frontier into Turkestan.

The road was now a dug road again, but offered frightful obstacles on its way through the hills. We crossed two river beds three hundred yards wide, playing musical chairs with the boulders; the gradient out of the first was so steep that we ran backwards into the water at thirty miles an hour. In every cutting the rain had cleft great fissures in the soft earth surface. Eventually we changed to the old horse-road, where engineering had not interfered with the drainage. It ambushed us instead with a regular pit, which the Ford jumped in and out of like a tennis ball.

Twelve miles before Maimena, we stopped at a pool and a group of trees in the plain of Bokhara Kala to watch a partridge fight. The spectators formed a ring, the birds were unloosed from their wicker domes; but one turned tail after a few minutes, and scuttling through our feet, fled into the landscape pursued by us all. The road was more populous now. Most of the travellers were mounted on horses of a miniature hunter type, as though the Chinese and Arab breeds had met here; with their gay turbans, flowing beards, flowered robes, and carpets rolled up behind them, they might have stepped from any Timurid painting, but for the rifles slung across their backs. There were animals too, many snakes and tortoises, Indian jays as bright as kingfishers popping out of holes as we passed, and a species of earth-bound squirrel, light buff in colour, whose rudimentary bush of a tail, only two inches long, was the natural concomitant of a country without forests. Near Maimena the hills were more culti-vated, and we noticed that as far as the plough had reached, often to the very top of each green escarpment, poppies had sprung up; so that even the peaks were dappled with scarlet among the golden green.

The Governor of Maimena was away at Andkhoi, but his deputy, after refreshing us with tea, Russian sweets, pistachios and almonds, led us to a caravanserai off the main bazaar, a Tuscan-looking old place surrounded by wooden arches, where we have a room each, as many carpets as we want, copper basins to wash in, and a bearded factotum in high-heeled top-boots who has laid down his rifle to help with the cooking.

It will be a special dinner. A sense of well-being has come over us in this land of plenty. Basins of milk, pilau with raisins, skewered kabob well salted and peppered, plum jam, and new bread have already arrived from the bazaar; to which we have added some treats of our own, patent soup, tomato ketchup, prunes in gin, chocolate, and ovaltine. The whisky is lasting out well. But the library unfortunately is down to the classics and I am now reading Crawley's translation of Thucydides while Christopher is back at our much-battered Boswell.

We also have with us a work by Sir Thomas Holdich called *The Gates of India*, which gives a summary of Afghan exploration up to 1910 and describes the journey of Moorcroft, who died at Andkoi in 1825. In this I find, on page 440: 'Moorcroft's books (thirty volumes) were recovered, and the list of them would surprise any modern traveller who believes in a light and handy equipment.' What surprises me is that considering he was away five years, there should have been so few. A light and handy equipment! One knows these modern travellers, these overgrown prefects and pseudo-scientific bores despatched by congregations of extinguished officials to see if sand-dunes sing and snow is cold. Unlimited money, every kind of official influence support them; they penetrate the furthest recesses of the globe; and beyond ascertaining that sand dunes do sing and snow is cold, what do they observe to enlarge the human mind?

Nothing.

Is it surprising? Their physical health is cared for; they go into training; they obey rules to keep them hard, and are laden with medicines to restore them when, as a result of the hardening process, they break down. But no one thinks of their mental health, and of its possible importance to a journey of supposed observation. Their light and handy equipment contains food for a skyscraper, instruments for a battleship, and weapons for an army. But it mustn't contain a book. I wish I were rich enough to endow a prize for the sensible traveller: £10,000 for the first man to cover Marco Polo's outward route reading three fresh books a week, and another £10,000 if he drinks a bottle of wine a day as well. That man might tell one something about the journey. He might or might not be naturally observant. But at least he would use what eyes he had, and would not think it necessary to dress up the result in thrills that never happened and science no deeper than its own jargon.

What I mean is, that if I had some more detective stories instead of Thucydides and some bottles of claret instead of tepid whisky, I should probably settle here for good.

*

Maimena, 24 May   The court of our robat becomes a market in the mornings. We are woken by the sound of hoofs, the dump of bales and a chaffering in Persian and Turki. Beneath our verandah bobs a sea of turbans, white, deep blue, pink, and black, some flat and broad, some tight and pumpkin-shaped, some wound anyhow as if they had come out of a mangle. These merchants are mainly Uzbegs, aquiline-featured and iron-bearded, all dressed in long robes of chintz or silk which bear designs of flowers, or stripes, or the big jazz-lightning effects in red, purple, white, and yellow which used to be made in Bokhara and are now thought old-fashioned. The tall leather boots have toes like canoes, high heels, and embroidery round the top. Other races throng the bazaar: Afghans from the south, Persian-speaking Tajiks, Turcomans, and Hazaras. The Turcomans are those of the Oxus, and are distinguished from the western tribes by a different hat: instead of the black busby, they sport a lambskin cone surrounded by a ring of coarse buff fur which comes, we are told, from the *sag-abi*, water-dog; is this an Oxus otter? The Hazaras, who are of Mongol stock, descend from Timur's armies and live mainly in the mountains, supposedly in great poverty. Those we see here are the picture of prosperity, well-built people with handsome oval faces of a Chinese cast and complexion, who dress in short embroidered jackets not unlike those of the Levant a hundred years ago. Single exotics pick their way through the crowd: a Hindu merchant; a dervish with a live black snake, four feet long and poisonous, coiled round his neck; a little man in white ducks and a black cloth cap, who is the Russian consul. The women as usual are invisible, but the small girls wear saris and nose jewels in the Indian way. Even the soldiers fail to strike a discord. A regiment marched through the bazaar this morning, skull-faced morbid-looking fellows when deprived of their turbans; but every other rifle had a rose in the muzzle. Perhaps Nur Mohammad was among them. There is a large garrison here to which he was returning when I said goodbye to him that morning in Kala Nao.

The town has no architectural character. Its only feature is a ruined castle. Inside this rises a mound, which used to have buildings on it, as heaps of bricks show, but is now occupied by a solitary sacred grave.

Outside the town, where the bazaar ends, lies a spacious meadow, which might be an English cricket field, against a horizon of poplars. Every evening a brass band plays there in front of the Commander-in-Chief's villa, a mud house of one storey defended by a hedge of roses. In the tea-houses near the road, someone plucks a guitar; the men put down their cups and murmur a melancholy song. A stream beside them turns a little mill, and a flock of white doves have gathered on its bank under a plane tree. The band strikes up again in the distance.

Men with roses in their mouths are sauntering across the grass to watch the wrestling matches. Each wrestler wears a pointed skull-cap and keeps on his long gown, but is swathed round the waist with a red sash, which gives the other man a grip. Before the contest is decided, a partridge match is announced, and the ring breaks up to reform itself round the birds. Eventually a bird escapes, and the whole audience, boys and greybeards alike, tucking up their gowns above the knee, scatter in frantic pursuit.

Against the darkness of a coming storm, the pale orange sunset lights up the green earth-mountains, the waving poplars silvered by the breeze, and the multi-coloured dresses of the sporting populace.

Andkhoi (1100 ft, 82 miles from Maimena), 25 May   We have hired a lorry to take us to Mazar-i-Sherif. It is a new Chevrolet, and its accessories, self-starter, milometer, etc., work. This is the way to travel here. We sprawl over the benches with all our necessaries, food, water-bottles, cameras, books, and diaries about us, while the heavy luggage rides on top. The chauffeur is an Indian, a Peshawari, and consequently most respectful, but he stutters, and when he and Christopher get stuttering together conversation moves slowly. Besides him, we have old Puss-in-boots with his rifle, from Maimena, and a couple of Turcomans, one resembling a Guards' officer, the other an Etruscan Apollo.

For travelling, Puss-in-boots wears a brown lambskin hat, a frock coat of black felt, and breeches of the same which are left undone in front; there is another pair underneath, but the effect is arresting. His name is Ghapur.

From Herat to Maimena we were travelling mainly north-east. On leaving Maimena we turned due north up a valley such as one finds among the Wiltshire uplands, where the villages are lined in close succession along a small nameless river meandering through orchards and fields: orchards in this case of mulberries and apricots; fields of pale-blue flax flowers. After Faizabad, the chief of the villages, the hills grew lower, the ground barren, and the air warmer; we began to skid in sand. A flat horizon opened out, a sinister hot breeze struck us, and the sky grew the colour of lead. We had reached the Oxus plain, and felt the presence of the river fifty miles away as one feels the presence of the sea before seeing it. At length we sighted a flat-topped mound, on top of which, at the head of a steep stairway guarded by yellow plaster lions, stood a hideous brick bungalow. Here we found the Governor of Maimena, a giant of a man with spectacles, a small black beard and a feminine voice, to whom we presented a letter from Shir Ahmad.

'Yes,' he said, 'the ground is all *cooked* between here and Mazar, but it is green again near the Jihun', employing this word for the Oxus, and not understanding our reference to it as the Amu Darya. He gave orders for our lodging in Andkhoi, which was still two miles off.

Andkhoi is the centre of the lambskin trade. At the depot in the bazaar, which was also stacked with Russian petrol and galvanized iron pails, we watched the skins being cured in a solution of barley and salt, laid out on the roofs to dry, and heaped into bales for packing. The manager said that the Jews had been deported from here to Herat in order that the trade should be no longer in the hands of 'foreigners'. Most of the flocks, he added, were owned by Turcomans. The Andkhoi skins were the best of all, those of Akcha nearly as good, and those of Mazar, where the ewes lamb three or four weeks later, not so good. Every year he sent a lakh (7500) of skins to London.

Christopher asked if he could buy some skins. Fine ones, of course. 'This quality,' said the man, producing a pelt large enough for a pair of doll's cuffs, 'costs 70 Afghanis (£1.15s.). The best quality, suitable for a good hat, is worth 100. But we don't get many of them.'

It is Friday evening, and people are celebrating the holiday at tables under the mulberry grove outside the bazaar. I am writing among them, drinking whisky with snow in it and waiting for a pilau.

*

Mazar-i-Sherif (1200 ft, 122 miles from Andkhoi), 26 May   I must confess that for me our arrival here this evening was a solemn occasion. I left England in August with two hopes: one, to see the monuments of Persia; the other to reach this town. Neither was very formidable, but they have taken some time to fulfil.

We were out of Andkhoi by five o'clock in the morning. Espying a flock of sheep when the sun was up, we stopped the lorry and walked towards it over the sparse crackling pasture that makes the wool curl. The shepherd was an Uzbeg, and would have no truck with us at first, supposing we were Russians. He excused his ill manners later by explaining that three years ago the Russians had stolen sixty thousand of the best sheep, which made us wonder if the disgraced Jews might not have been concerned in some transaction of this kind. His flock consisted of two breeds: Karakulis, which give the finer fur, and Arabis; catching a ram of one and an ewe of the other, he showed us how to distinguish them by the tails. Both grow fat tails, but while the Arabis' are round or kidney-shaped, the Karakulis' dangle a pendant from the middle.

Further on, we found a Turcoman encampment. The men were out, but the dogs attacked us, and as the women would not call them off, it needed twenty minutes' studied resolution to make the snarling beasts retire. Two old witches, presumably widows, came out to greet us dressed in loose ugly robes of grey-blue sackcloth, though they kept the tall head-dress. The younger women, who stayed at a distance, were a beautiful sight moving hither and thither among their black beehives, sweeping the ground with pink-and-white draperies, and making a show of modesty behind long veils of rich saffron yellow that fell from their tall pink hats. These veils often take the form of coats. We passed some women later in the day, still dressed in red, whose faces were framed in coats of deep cornflower blue embroidered with flowers.

I approached a mother and two children. They fled into a kibitka, and I turned to a younger woman of magnificent carriage who was clasping a baby. Placing it behind a wattle screen, she grabbed a pole, traced a circle in the dust in front of it, and came at me like a mediaeval knight. Her face was screwed up with anger, and there was something in the tone of her denunciations that made me uncomfortable, as if I were meanly taking advantage of her man's absence. The two old witches chuckled at the scene. But our guard, a new one who had joined us at Andkhoi, was ashamed, and said that Afghanistan was like that. He had on a sophisticated Western mackintosh, and was always taking snuff from a silver-mouthed gourd with a ruby in the lid.

One kibitka was empty, a guest-house perhaps, and we could examine it unthreatened. A dado of trellis-work on the inside, and another of rush-matting on the outside, enclosed the bottom of the black felt dome. This was stretched over a frame of bent wood, which was attached, at the apex, to a sort of circular basket open to the sky and serving as a chimney. Beneath the basket hung a festoon of black tassels. Double doors opened from a stout wooden frame; both were slightly carved. There was felt on the floor, and the furniture consisted of carved and painted chests. The general effect was not at all squalid or savage. As we left, we saw one of the kibitkas being dismantled. The struts of the frame, when folded up, resembled a bunch of thin skis. But the basket apex, as big as a cartwheel, swayed uneasily on the camel's hump.

It was an evil day, sticky and leaden: Oxiana looked as colourless and suburban as India. A green patch of pasture at Khoja Duka tempted us to stop again, to watch a drove of brood mares and their foals, among which cavorted a raw-boned old stallion of sixteen hands, which is big for these parts. Christopher said a group of ragged children sitting on a wall reminded him of the clients at Sledmere. Then we came to Shibargan, a ruined place overlooked by a castle, whence a road goes south to Saripul. It was near Saripul that Ferrier noticed a Sasanian rock-carving. So he says. But we could hear no corroboration of it between Maimena and Andkhoi, and he is too unreliable for us to have gone in search of it without.

Akcha was more flourishing. We met an ice-cream barrow under the castle walls whose owner put a table in the lorry for us to eat lunch off, and brought a pail of snow to cool our drinks.

After Akcha, the colour of the landscape changed from lead to aluminium, pallid and deathly, as if the sun had been sucking away its gaiety for thousands and thousands of years; for this was now the plain of Balkh, and Balkh they say is the oldest city in the world. The clumps of green trees, the fountain-shaped tufts of coarse cutting grass, stood out almost black against this mortal tint. Sometimes we saw a field of barley; it was ripe, and Turcomans, naked to the waist, were reaping it with sickles. But it was not brown or gold, telling of Ceres, of plenty. It seemed to have turned prematurely white, like the hair of a madman – to have lost its nourishment. And from these acred cerements, first on the north and then on the south of the road, rose the worn grey-white shapes of a bygone architecture, mounds, furrowed and bleached by the rain and sun, wearier than any human works I ever saw: a twisted pyramid, a tapering platform, a clump of battlements, a crouching beast, all familiars of the Bactrian Greeks, and of Marco Polo after them. They ought to have vanished. But the very impact of the sun, calling out the obstinacy of their ashen clay, has conserved some inextinguishable spark of form, a spark such as a Roman earthwork or a grass-grown barrow has not, which still flickers on against a world brighter than itself, tired as only a suicide frustrated can be tired.

Yet by degrees the country became greener, pasture covered the adamant earth, trees multiplied, and suddenly a line of bony dilapidated walls jumped out of the ground and occupied the horizon. Passing inside them, we found ourselves amid a vast metropolis of ruins stretching away to the north; while on the south of the road, the shining greens of mulberries, poplars, and stately isolated planes were balm to eyes bruised by the monstrous antiquity of the preceding landscape. We stood in Balkh herself, the Mother of Cities.

Our guard, surveying the ruins, which were mostly left in this state by Jenghis Khan, remarked: 'It was a beautiful place till the Bolsheviks destroyed it eight years ago.'

Half a mile more brought us to the inhabited core of the place, a bazaar, shops, serais, and a crossroads. Out of the trees to the south rose a tall fluted dome, moonlit-blue against the deep-toned verdure and the slaty frown of a storm on the Hindu Kush. We walked to this building, while the chauffeur went in search of rooms; and on emerging from behind it were surprised to see our acquaintance the Governor of Maimena in the middle of an open space. Near him stood a Frank, whose polished pea-shaped pate announced him for a German. A squad of four soldiers was drawn up on one side, a knot of officers and secretaries had gathered on the other. Between them, in front of a tent approached by carpets, the German was explaining the lie of the ground to a dignified man wearing a fur hat, neatly trimmed black beard, open cricket shirt, and three fountain pens in his breast pocket.

This man to whom the Governor of Maimena presented us, was Mohammad Gul Khan, Minister of the Interior for Turkestan. He had driven over from Mazar to see about the rebuilding of the city. There were pegs in the ground, and a clearance has already been made between the front of the domed shrine and the ruined arch of a college opposite. The German told us he had been three years in Afghanistan and six months in Mazar, where he acts as maid-of-all-work for bridges, canals, roads, and building in general.

The storm was approaching. Mohammad Gul, after hoping we had not been overwhelmed by the inconveniences of the road, mounted his car and drove away. His mention of a hotel in Mazar, where he expected us to be comfortable, decided us to follow him instead of stopping in Balkh. It was another fifteen miles. The deluge and the dark descended as we reached the capital.

'Where is the guest-house?' we asked, using the ordinary Persian word.

'It is not a guest-house. It is a "hotel". This way.'

It is indeed. Every bedroom has an iron bedstead with a spring mattress, and a tiled bathroom attached, in which we sluice ourselves with water from a pail and dry our feet on a mat labelled BATH MAT. The dining-room is furnished with a long pension-table laid with Sheffield cutlery and finger-bowls. The food is Perso-Afgho-Anglo-Indian in the worst sense of each. The lavatory doors lock on the outside only. I was about to point this out to the manager, but Christopher said he liked it and wouldn't have them touched.

We pay 7s. 6d. a day, which is not cheap by local standards. Judging from the excitement of the staff, we must be the first guests they have had.

Mazar-i-Sherif, 27 May This town owes its existence to a dream.

In the time of Sultan Sanjar, who reigned in the first half of the twelfth century, a report reached Balkh from India that the grave of Hazrat Ali, the fourth caliph, lay near by. This was denied by one of the mullahs of the place, who believed, as most Shiahs still do, that

240

his grave was at Nejef in Arabia. At this, Ali himself appeared to the mullah in a dream and confirmed the report. The grave was found, and Sultan Sanjar ordered a shrine to be erected over it, which was finished in 1136 and provided the nucleus of the present town.

This shrine was destroyed by Jenghis Khan. In 1481 it was replaced by another at the instance of Hussein Baikara, who had been campaigning in Oxiana the year before. Thenceforth Mazar became a place of pilgrimage, and gradually ousted the fever-stricken ruins of Balkh as the chief town of the district, just as Meshed, by the same process, ousted Tus in Khorasan.

There is not much to be seen of Hussein Baikara's building from the outside; though its two shallow domes, indicating an inner and an outer sanctuary, suggest that the plan was copied from Gohar Shad's Musalla. The exterior walls were entirely retiled in the last century with a coarse geometric mosaic of white, light blue, yellow, and black. Even since Niedermayer was here, there have been additions; the Italian balustrades of turquoise pottery along the main parapets do not appear in his photograph. All the same, the group as a whole is not unpleasing; it might be described as a cross between St Mark's at Venice and an Elizabethan country house translated into blue faience.

Outside the big shrine stand the ruins of two smaller ones. Their domes have fallen, but each retains panels of mosaic round the drum, ugly in colour owing to an excessive pinkish ochre. Like the mausoleum at Herat, the easterly one contains an inner dome, a shallow intermediate structure resting on the wall of a gallery inside the drum. Above this can still be seen the curved brick buttresses which supported the upper dome as it rose from the outside of the drum.

As at Meshed, there has been a clearance of houses round the shrine, so that it can be seen from a distance completing the vistas of various streets. Indeed the whole town has been smartened up lately. The bazaars are new and whitewashed, and their roofs are supported on piles which let in light and air underneath. In the new town, where the hotel and Government offices stand, the roads are edged with neat brick gutters. The traffic is shared between the Indian gharry, with an awning, and the Russian droshky, with its high wooden yoke over the horse's neck. After Murghab and Maimena we feel in contact with the outer world again, and wish we had stayed longer in those places. Still, it would be churlish not to admit that the town is the pleasanter for these improvements. We are certainly enjoying the hotel.

There seem to be objections to our visiting the Oxus. The Governor and the Mudir-i-Kharija are both away at Haibak, and we have had to deal with the latter's deputy, a callow pompous young man, who received our proposals disdainfully. But he evidently has no power of decision in the matter. We must ask assistance of the Vazir, as Mohammad Gul is called.

Mazar-i-Sherif, 28 May   There is a public garden outside the hotel, growing sweet-williams, snapdragons, hollyhocks, and evening primroses. Between the beds little benches have been placed, and more popular rush-mats, where people sit and drink while the music plays. There are two bands. One stands in the sun, a row of old men with brass instruments; they know three European tunes, and are accompanied by two young men behind, who strike every beat on the triangle and drum. The other sits lackadaisically on a dais under a tree and plays Indian music on a guitar, various drums, and a small harmonium. We listen from our rooms, whose French windows open on to a verandah behind the garden.

Each afternoon, as the clouds gather on the mountains, an irresistible lassitude descends. Flies and a sticky warmth fill the room. The sound of partridges clucking turns my dreams into a September afternoon at home, till I remember they are waiting to be fought. Why these clouds? It is hot enough, but the summer ought to have set six weeks ago. Such a year has never been known. The rain that fell the night we arrived has closed the road to Kabul for a month; a whole village has fallen into the gorge at Haibak. If we ride on from here, as may be necessary, we shall have to camp out, and apart from designing a couple of mosquito nets, we have been too lazy to see about an outfit. Water is the main difficulty of such a journey, as sufferers from syphilis of the throat, who are numerous, are apt to choose the wells to spit in.

Our hopes of the Oxus have been further discouraged.

The Muntazim of the hotel, a fat elderly disagreeable man, acts as our gaoler. This morning he followed us protesting to Mohammad

Gul's office, where we learnt that the Vazir would be asleep till eleven. At eleven he followed us back there. The Vazir was still asleep. He then followed me to the telegraph office, puffing and sweating in the heat; the more he puffed, the quicker I walked. The Muntazim-i-Telegraph, whom I had been told of by his fellow in Herat, said he had forgotten all his English in the stress of speaking Russian; there was a Russian in the office with him. He suggested I should go to the doctor instead. On the way to the hospital I jumped into a pony cart, leaving the Muntazim-i-Hotel in the road. But the driver, it appears, will have to complete the report of my movements.

The doctor, Abulmajid Khan, proved to be a Cambridge graduate, a charming and cultivated man, whose natural reserve, so rare in Indians, soon expanded into geniality. He has been here eight years, and, seeing my surprise, explained that he had had to leave the Indian Medical Service owing to an incident connected with the Non-Cooperation Movement. He spoke rather wistfully of this youthful indiscretion, which had wrecked his career, and added that the Non-Cooperation Movement seemed to be dead now, as if to imply that the effort which had cost him so much had been given to a lost cause. But there was no bitterness in his voice, and none of that embarrassing defiance which Indian nationalists often assume towards an Englishman. I tried to convey, without seeming fulsome, that the nationalists had my sympathy and that of many more Englishmen today than ten years ago. There was no bitterness either in his remarks about Afghanistan. He is fond of the people and of his work, in which he differs from the other Indians I have met in this country.

It is not easy work. He has to run the hospital on 10,000 Afghan rupees a year, the equivalent of £250. The beds are contained in two or three one-storey pavilions, which stand in a shady garden full of twittering birds. They looked rough, but clean and well ordered. The patients suffer mainly from cataract, stone, and syphilis.

I told the doctor of our wish to visit the Oxus and of our attempts to see Mohammad Gul. He said the latter's attack of sleeping sickness was merely a polite intimation that he did not wish to discuss the matter with us. I asked him what further steps we could take. He suggested we write the Vazir a letter in English, but so elaborate in style as to be beyond the powers of the Muntazim-i-Telegraph to translate. In that case, one of the resident Indian merchants will be summoned, who may put in a good word for us.

The result of this suggestion has been as follows:

His Excellency Mohammad Gul Khan,
  Minister of the Interior for Turkestan.

Your Excellency,
Knowing from personal experience that Your Excellency's day is already too short for the public welfare, it is with signal reluctance that, in the absence of Their Excellencies the Wali and the Mudir-i-Kharija at Haibak, we venture to lay before Your Excellency a trifling personal request.

In undertaking the journey from England to Afghan Turkestan, whose tedium and exertions have already been thrice repaid by the spectacle of Your Excellency's beneficent administration, our capital object was to behold, with our own eyes, the waters of the Amu Darya, famed in history and romance as the river Oxus, and the theme of a celebrated English poem from the sacred pen of Matthew Arnold. We now find ourselves, after seven months' anticipation, within forty miles of its banks.

Understanding from the secretary of His Excellency the Mudir-i-Kharija that an extraordinary permission is necessary to visit the River, we request this permission for ourselves, confident that Your Excellency will not be deluded into imputing a political motive to what is but the natural curiosity of an educated man.

The fact that others, in their lesser wisdom, may be victims of this delusion, reminds us that Afghanistan and Russia are not the only countries in the world to be separated by a river. We dare observe that an Afghan traveller, sojourning in France or Germany, would encounter no regulations to prevent his enjoying the beauties of the Rhine.

There are indeed some countries where the Light of Progress has yet to pierce the night of mediaeval barbarism, and where the foreign visitor must expect to be obstructed by ill-conceived suspicions. But we consoled ourselves, during our stay in Persia, by the consideration that we should soon be in Afghanistan, and should thus escape from a parcel of vain and hysterical women to an erect and manly people, immune from ridiculous alarms, and happy to accord that liberty to strangers which they justly demand for themselves.

Were we right? And on returning to our country, shall we say that we were right? The answer lies with Your Excellency. Certainly, we shall tell of the hotel in Mazar-i-Sherif equipped with every comfort known to the great capitals of the West; of a city in course of reconstruction on lines that London itself might envy; of bazaars stocked with all the amenities of civilization. But are we then to add that though Your Excellency's capital holds everything to delight the visitor, nevertheless the chief, the unique attraction of the district is denied him? that, in short, he who comes to Mazar-i-Sherif will be treated as a spy, a Bolshevik, a disturber of the peace, if he asks to tread the shores where Rustam fought? We believe that Your Excellency, jealous of your country's good name, would deprecate such statements. We believe also that when you have read this letter, they will not be necessary.

We had hoped originally to make a journey by horse along the River from Pata Kissar to Hazrat Imam. If this is inadvisable, we should be content simply to ride or drive from here to Pata Kissar, and back. All we desire is a sight of the River, and any point will serve this purpose if Your Excellency cares to suggest another. We have mentioned Pata Kissar because it is the nearest point, and because from there can be seen the ruins of ancient Termez on the opposite bank.

With apologies for troubling Your Excellency with so long a letter in a foreign tongue.

We are, etc., etc.

The invention of this grotesque document has afforded us almost too much amusement. Mohammad Gul must be a greater fool than he looks if his vanity is deceived by it.

Mazar-i-Sherif, 29 May The letter has at least provoked an answer. Refusal.

It appears that Mohammad Gul is not simply being disagreeable. High policy is involved, which lays down that permission for foreigners to visit the river must be got from Kabul; so that even if he wished, Mohammad Gul could not let us go without a correspondence that might take a month now that the telegraph is cut at Haibak. Apart from this, there is also a local obstacle. In the last six months, huge bands of Turcomans have crossed the river from Russia and settled themselves in the jungle on the south bank. Their lawlessness alone would prevent our proposed ride to Hazrat Imam. It would also give cover to any Bolshevik agents who might think it their duty to prevent two Englishmen from reconnoitring the frontier. This last reason might sound unnecessarily imaginative if it did not correspond with information given us in Meshed.

According to the doctor, who visited Tashkent some years ago and was not well received there, we shall miss nothing by not seeing Pata Kissar, which consists of two tents, one for the customs officer and one for the guard; there used to be some buildings, but they were swept away by a flood. He agrees, however, that the ride to Chayab or Hazrat Imam would have been interesting, taking us through a beautiful country renowned for its pheasants; though there are no tigers there as I thought.

All the same, I should like to have seen the ruins of Termez; Yate describes them as looking very impressive from the south bank, and there is an early minaret among them which Sarre illustrates. But it is precisely Termez, I suppose, that those putative agents would object to our seeing. The railway from Bokhara ends there, and the place is held by a regiment from European Russia. It is the Peshawar of Russian Turkestan.

The Russian forces on the Oxus are not there for ornament. They actually invaded Afghanistan at the time of Amanullah's dethrone- ment. It was not a very serious invasion, though sufficient to explain our guard's remark at Balkh; the whole force consisted of about 300 men, three guns, and a small medical service. At one moment they were shut up in the fort of Dehdadi, a large walled enclosure which we passed on the road between here and Balkh and noticed because the walls, instead of falling to bits, were in good repair. Here they were besieged by hordes of Turcomans, whom they held off by dragging their guns from one side of the walls to the other. But the Turcomans, who are said to have numbered more than 20,000, put up a wretched fight.

One imagines the hysteria that must have shaken the Government of India when it heard of this incursion, regardless of the fact that, as far as I can see, the Russians were only doing what we do every year on the North-West Frontier: smothering tribal unrest before it could spread over the border. No doubt, if opportunity had arisen, the Russian troops would have acted in Amanullah's interest, just as ours, in similar circumstances, might have acted in King Nadir's. But the broad issue is clear. If the Afghans can't keep their own house in order, the Russians will be liable to do it for them on the north, just as we do on the south. They showed this then; they were ready to show it again last November, when I was in Herat. No wonder the Afghans are nervous, particularly up here. It is only eighty years since this part of Turkestan was incorporated in the Afghan state. Access from Kabul is difficult owing to the Hindu Kush. The local Turcomans, swollen by disaffected refugees, are regarded by the Russians as a potential source of anti-Bolshevik infection. Naturally, the province's real safeguard lies in the fact that the Russians are not anxious to embroil themselves with the British, and that Afghanistan intact, if quiet, is useful to both Powers as a buffer. But the Afghans think it humiliating to admit this. None the less, they know well enough that the way to keep the Russians at arm's-length is to keep their own country peaceable, and that the best means of doing this are telegraphs and roads: the former to summon troops, the latter to convey them, to the scene of any rising. We have seen something of their efforts in this respect. But the national communications will need a lot of improvement before they cease to be at the mercy of the weather.

As we suspected after our conversation with the Uzbeg shepherd, it was fear of Russian penetration, economically if not by force, that led to the expulsion of the Jews last winter. There were always a few Jews in Afghanistan, squalid ill-bred people, unprosperous and unimportant. These Jews have stayed behind; we saw some of them in Murghab. The ones I met at Kala Nao in such distress were Bokhara Jews – I thought perhaps they were – who only came to Afghanistan after the Revolution, when they were assisted to escape by an Afghan consul in Tashkent who could be bribed for visas. But as Jews always will, having settled in a new country, they still kept up a connection with the parent community, and the Afghans began to fear that most of the profits of the lambskin trade were being surreptitiously diverted to Russia; not to mention the sheep themselves. The Jews have not been the only sufferers from this kind of jealousy. Ten years ago there were about 400 Indian traders in and around Mazar. Since then, particularly since the advent of Mohammad Gul, they have been systematically blackmailed out of business, till only five or six are left, and the Government of India, having done nothing to help them, is supposed to be in its dotage.

Poor Asia! Everything boils down to the inevitable nationalism, the desire for self-sufficiency, the wish to cut a figure in the world and no longer be called interesting for lack of plumbing. Afghan nationalism is not so undignified as Persian because the officials have learnt, thanks to Amanullah's bowler, that the people they seek to inspire with it are still prepared to fight before throwing away tradition for a mess of technical pottage. But it goes its way in silence, sometimes sensibly in the direction of public benefits such as roads and posts, sometimes in that of such extravagant eccentricities as the hotel here and the rebuilding of Balkh. These are Mohammad Gul's personal schemes; they reveal the extreme nationalist, who cares more for symbols than utility, the Afghan de Valera who would even go so far as to change the official language from Persian to Pushtu. All the same, Mohammad Gul is more than a froth-blower; our conversation at Balkh brought us into contact with a singular man. He was educated in Turkey, became an associate of Enver Pasha, and was with him near Bokhara when he was killed by the Russians. In his own country he enjoys a unique reputation for incorruptibility and disinterestedness; this is the secret of his power, which extends beyond the boundaries of Turkestan. In fact, we hear that this is why he is kept in Turkestan.

Mazar-i-Sherif, 30 May   We spent today at Balkh.

The shrine in the inhabited part of the town was put up to the memory of Khoja Abu Nasr Parsa, the son of a more famous saint, Khoja Mohammad Parsa, who brought religion to the poet Jami when he was five years old and died at Medina in 1419. Abu Nasr Parsa became a theological lecturer in Herat, at the college founded by Firuza Begum, the mother of Hussein Baikara. Later he seems to have settled at Balkh, for in 1452 he came forward there to advise Babur, son of Baisanghor, against crossing the Oxus and attacking Abu Said. He died in 1460.

The body of the building is a plain brick octagon, which is concealed, and overtopped, by a tiled façade flanked with glistening corkscrew pillars. From behind the façade, standing on the octagon, the fluted dome rises to a height of eighty feet. Two minarets also stand on the octagon, clumped in between dome and façade.

The colours of the façade are confined to white and dark and light blue, reinforced by discreet touches of black. It is the absence of purple and other warm tints which produces the silvery effect that struck us on first arrival. This effect is continued by the dome, whose fat round ribs are covered with tiny bricks glazed with greenish turquoise; where the glaze has worn off, at the top, the ribs are white and look as if they had received a fall of snow. Like the other two domes of this type at Herat and Samarcand, that of Abu Nasr Parsa has a monumental pride. But the building as a whole is unsubstantial and romantic. An unknown force seems to be squeezing it upwards. The result is fantasy, and in some lights, an unearthly beauty.

We could not enter; but on creeping into one of the sixteen window embrasures that surround the drum, were assailed by the sound of a village choir-practice. This arose, as usual, from a mullah and his pupils.

There is another shrine outside the east gate known as that of Khopa Agacha. Who St Agacha was I don't know. Hussein Baikara had three grasping mistresses of that name, and Babur a wife. They came of an Uzbeg family.

It is not an interesting building. The dome has disappeared. Round the drum runs a glazed Kufic inscription. Near by lies another of those crouching artificial platforms to which Balkh owes its archaeological fame.

We lunched under a plane tree among a crowd of turbaned navvies. The plan of the new city is as ambitious as Canberra, but no one who can help it will come from Mazar to this fever-stricken air; one might as well rebuild Ephesus in the hope of displacing Smyrna. Later, I was drawing the shrine when a black-bearded person in Kabuli dress came up, muttered after my health, and stated that while photographing was permitted, drawing was not, and that my sketch was therefore his. At this I was seized by such a paralysing anger that I could not speak for several minutes. When I could, the words were taken out of my mouth by one of the servants from the hotel who, as he put it, 'made fight' with the officious brute and learned that he was employed in the rebuilding scheme. By the time they had finished, my drawing and I were out of sight.

Doctor Abulmajid came this evening to give me an injection. He had to ask leave to do so, and thought it more discreet not to dine with us. But we managed to give him a cold whisky and soda, having secured four bottles of soda water from the photographer's and put them in a pail of snow. It was a triumph for all of us. But I could see that the taste of a 'burra peg' again reminded him sadly of his youth and promise. I went to his house the day before yesterday, one of the ordinary mud houses of the place, and found he had had his chairs and sofa covered with loose frilly chintz in the English country way.

He told us that until Foucher came here a few years ago and bought them all up, the old Greek coins of Bactria were still in circulation. Since then, people have begun to think them priceless and ask twenty or thirty times the museum value for them.

Fruit has begun: delicious apricots, and now some cherries, but these are of the Morello kind, so bitter that we have had them made into jam.

Mazar-i-Sherif, 1 June Yesterday morning Christopher called at the Mudir-i-Kharija's office to ask permission to visit the Russian Consulate. His excuse was that we needed some visas, of which there is in fact no hope, though it is tantalizing to think that Bokhara is only fifteen hours from Termez by train. However, he had no chance of using this excuse, since even the Mudir-i-Kharija's deputy is asleep to us now. He therefore went by himself, breasted his way through a post of Afghan soldiers who presented their bayonets at him, and at length reached M. Bouriachenko, a small intellectual man who was sitting under a tree reading.

'You want visas for Samarcand?' said M. Bouriachenko. 'Of course you do. I will telegraph to Moscow at once to say that two Oxford professors of Islamic culture' – (God forgive us, we both left Oxford without degrees) – 'have arrived here and are waiting for permission to cross the Amu Darya. No, there is nothing to see at Termez. The place you ought to go to is Anau. Professor Simionov has just written a book on the Timurid monuments there. I wish I could give you the visas at once, but I'm afraid it will take a week or so to get a reply. Anyhow you are *here* for a bit, that's the main thing. We must have a party. Will you come?'

'When?' asked Christopher, forgetting to say thank you in his surprise.

'When? I don't know when. What does it matter? This evening? Would that suit you?'

'Perfectly. What time?'

'What time? Seven, is that all right? Or six? Or five to four? We can start now if you like.'

It was half-past eleven, and a blazing hot morning. Christopher said perhaps the evening would be nicer.

*

At half-past six we tiptoed out of the hotel so that the Muntazim should not hear us, reached the gate of the Consulate, where the guard brandished their weapons as before, and found ourselves in a series of courtyards shaded by trees; in the front yard stood a number of lorries and cars, including a red Vauxhall. M. Bouriachenko received us in a cool room free from icons of Lenin and Marx, and lit by a private electric light plant. I said, I supposed by his name that he must come from Ukraine. 'Yes, from Kiev, and my wife from Riazin.' She walked in, a young woman plainly dressed in dark purple, whose good-natured face was framed in hair drawn flat from a parting in the middle. Others followed her: an enormous wallowing man, slightly scented, from whose pitted face came the voice of a dove; his wife, a blonde with red lips whose golden hair was brushed straight back from her forehead; Master Bouriachenko, aged five and the spit of Chaliapin; a boy and girl belonging to the second couple; the doctor, a tubby little fellow with a black moustache and butcher's lick; another lady discreetly painted, whose fair hair was ruffled into a crest; the fat fair man I saw in the telegraph office, who said he had been a radio officer at Canterbury during the War; two natty young fellows just arrived from Kabul, who had taken a fortnight over the journey owing to the rains; and last of all a girl of fourteen, daughter of the painted lady, whose movements were beautiful to watch and who is destined to become a ballet dancer.

Judged by Russian standards, which differ from ours, the food was not really profuse; indeed how could it be? though they had bought, at considerable expense we discovered afterwards, the last sardines in the town. But it had that *air* of profusion which Russians always create about them, and as new guests kept wandering in, and new tables were brought, and new chairs, and the children hopped up on people's laps, the dishes kept pace and were still as full as ever of the sardines from India, paprika from Russia, fresh meat with onion salad, and bread. A decanter of yellow vodka, in which fruit was swimming, was endlessly replenished. The Russians, who gulped it off in cups, complained furiously of our slow sipping. But that was only at first.

The two young men from Kabul had been bringing a number of new English records that had been ordered from Peshawar; but they had all been spoilt in the wreck of their lorry by the storm at Haibak, and the loss was a tragic disappointment to this isolated community; though to hear them apologize for it, one might have thought the records had been ordered for us instead of them. As it was, tangos and jazz alternated with *Shehérezade*, *Boris Godunov*, and *Eugène Onyegin*. We danced, we sang, we sat down to eat, we danced again. Conversation was in Persian, and what made it odder, when talking to one's own kind, was the inevitable accompaniment of Persian gesture, the bowing of the head and fluttering of the eyelids, the hand on the heart, and the general assumption of self-deprecation. M. Bouriachenko and the man with the dove's voice addressed us as 'Sahib'. Perhaps they thought this sounded more equalitarian than the Persian Excellencies and Highnesses we used to them.

The hours fled, the decanter flowed, the telegraphist was carried out, I fell into a torpor, the Russians began to unload their emotions, and when I woke up I found Christopher gasping for breath under the souls of the whole community. It was two o'clock and time to go home. The hotel was only a few hundred yards away. But M. Bouriachenko, calling for the 'Consulski Vauxhall', insisted on driving us to it. This was an act of real friendship. For whether our walk was unsteady or not, it would have been unwise to run a risk of the Afghans observing it, a fact we appreciated when a sentry thrust his rifle into the window of the car.

This morning was painful beyond the usual run of next-mornings. We called at the Consulate after tea, bearing not flowers, but some boxes of cigars, and found them all sitting out in a sort of games court equipped with swings and parallel bars and a high net over which any number of people divided into two sides, can fist a soft football. A game was started for us, the party being increased now by three or four other men, proletarian savages, who are employed as chauffeurs and mechanics. The telegraphist looked older.

M. Bouriachenko told us that the only other Russians in this part of the country were four locust-fighters living in and about Khanabad. The locusts are a new plague here. They arrived from Morocco a few years ago, breed on the north slopes of the Hindu Kush, and thence descend on Russian Turkestan, where they menace the cotton crops.

Since there is a road from here to Khanabad, and another from there to Kabul which avoids the Haibak gorge, we have decided not to ride after all. This detour will take us 150 miles further east, to the edge of Badakshan, and the excuse for making it afforded by the blockage at Haibak is too good to miss. Christopher regrets the horse journey, but I think the detour will be more interesting.

Robat before Kunduz (1100 ft, 95 miles from Mazar-i-Sherif), 3 June Even before leaving Teheran, we had resolved not to sleep at Kunduz if we could help it. Moorcroft died of fever caught in these marches. There is a proverb which says a visit to Kunduz is tantamount to suicide. Here we are, therefore, lying in a mulberry grove beside a stagnant pool, both irresistible attractions to the fatal mosquito. Other pests abound. I pitched my bed near a wall. A wasps' nest was at once discovered in it, and anyhow, people warned me, it was full of scorpions. When I suggested removing to a neighbouring garden, they said that was full of snakes. We are lucky to have ordered those mosquito-nets in the bazaar at Mazar. I have draped mine over the camera tripod; Christopher had half a mulberry tree demolished to make him a framework. Frogs are blowing musical bubbles in the pool. On the south-east, a vast new range of snowy peaks has caught the first light of the moon. Our two guards are loading their rifles before going to sleep, and a cat assaults the morning's milk. For dinner we ate scrambled eggs and onions. Christopher thought of the onions, and had them ready cooked and chopped in the hotel so that they had only to be heated. A brilliant invention.

The day that brought us to this pass was complicated to start with by the after-effects of another Russian party. It was only a zakuska party this time; but again we danced, again the souls came out and fastened on us. M. Bouriachenko said that even if two great nations, like two mountains, were unable to approach each other, there was no reason why the individuals of those nations should not do so; for himself, he admired England and hoped for our sakes there would soon be a revolution there. He added that if only we would stay on at Mazar, instead of flying off in this absurd hurry, the Consul himself would be back in a few days with a supply of decent brandy; besides which he had every hope that our visas would be granted.

I had no such hope. But it struck me forcibly that the policy pursued by Russia and England of mutual exclusion from Turkestan and India is beginning to lose its sense. Looking at our hosts, quiet cultivated men and women who spent their money on classical music, it seemed to us preposterous that even transit visas through India should be denied them. And it dawned on us, moreover, that the interests of Russia and England in Asia, instead of conflicting as they used to do, have now become virtually the same, particularly with regard to the buffer states between them, whose purpose in foreign relations is to assert themselves by teasing their larger neighbours. If only the Russians would consent to dam up the trickle of money and doctrine which still percolates into India as a lip service to the Marxian creed of World Revolution, this identity of interest might emerge into the daylight. A conference between the Governor of Tashkent and the Viceroy, on Persia, Afghanistan, Sinkiang, and Tibet, would benefit both sides far more than do the maintenance of revolutionary propaganda on the one hand, and the fear of it on the other.

When we left, again in the Consulski Vauxhall, the whole party saw us to the gate, waving us goodbye and good journey.

Outside Mazar this morning we met a dragon. It was $3\frac{1}{2}$ feet long, yellow underneath, and rather high on its four little Chippendale legs. Lashing its tail furiously, it ran into a hole. Near by we found a sand-grouse's nest with three eggs in it.

At Tashkurgan, where the main road turns off to Haibak, we stopped for breakfast. I was taking a photograph of the castle, a Chinese-looking building above a mountain torrent, when the elder of our two guards, a motherly old fellow in a white frock coat crossed with big checks, said that photographing was 'unnecessary'. I answered that if he really thought that, he had better go back to Mazar; it was our lorry, and there was none too much room in it. Further on, as I was taking another picture of the Oxus plain from a convenient height, he again interfered, jogging my arm. This time I roared till his jaw and rifle dropped. When I next took out the camera, he was silent.

We wondered why the authorities at Mazar had given us two guards instead of one. Now the guards themselves have admitted it was to prevent us taking photographs. The poor creatures are rather distressed at not being allowed to do their duty. But we really can't help them.

*

The country was still bare, but a fiery opalescence now displaced the metallic drabness of the plain before Mazar. Such pasture as there was consisted of a dry prickly clover. There were no trees and little life. Every sixteen miles we passed a lonely robat. Once we saw a flock of vultures huddled in congress round a pool. Sometimes locusts went whirring by in small coveys. The foothills of the Shadian mountains, which bound the plain of Turkestan on the south, began to curve northward and we gradually ascended them. Suddenly, eighty-eight miles from Mazar, the ascent stopped and the road fell down a thousand feet. Beneath us, crawling up the hillside, bobbed a string of camels, each laden with a couple of wooden cots containing ladies. Beneath them unrolled the glinting marshes of Kunduz and the province of Kataghan. Far away, through the misty sunshine, rose the mountains of Badakshan, carrying my mind's eye on up the Wakhan to the Pamirs and China itself.

At the foot of the descent, another lorry was waiting on the threshold of a bridge made of poles and turf, which spanned a river in a cutting twelve feet deep. Our driver was about to pass, when the other lorry suddenly moved forward. The bridge quivered and sagged. In a cloud of dust and sticks, to the sound of screams and gasps and rending timbers, the lorry turned a slow side-somersault into the river, where it landed with its roof submerged and its chassis indecently exposed, while its wheels fluttered helplessly in the air. The passengers had dismounted, and the driver, whose cabin was tilted up by the opposite bank, climbed out unhurt. But someone shouted there were women inside, and with superfluous gallantry Christopher and I flung ourselves on the wreck, hacking away at the ropes that bound the outside and clearing out the bales from within, to discover there was no one there at all. As the bales were rescued from the current, the whole country grew gay with borders of herbaceous chintz, orchards of pink satin caps and swards of carpet, all laid to dry.

Already a swarm of half-naked men had sprung out of the fields to investigate the disaster. Now the Governor of Kunduz rode up on a fast grey pacer, an angry red-bearded man, who set about the population with his whip, bidding them haul the lorry out and mend the bridge before morning. Our luggage was put on to horses and taken across the river to a robat, which was so crowded that we have preferred to sleep in the open.

*

Among the passengers of the wreck was a tall man in a heavy black beard and lounge suit who spoke German. He said he was one of the king's secretaries, and was making this journey in order to write an Afghan travel book. There he sat on the river bank, industriously penning it from right to left. He looked suspiciously at our whisky, though we have now learnt the habit of calling it sherbet in public.

Khanabad (1300 ft, 27 miles from robat before Kunduz), 4 June
The bridge was mended by midday and our lorry crossed it safely. Seyid Jemal, our driver, turned out to be the other driver's brother. He linked our lorry to the wreck with a steel cable, and while the naked men levered with poles from below, gradually pulled it out the right way up. It had suffered no damage except to the paint, started at the first touch, and sailed off down the road in front of us.

A sandy track through high marsh reeds brought us to an open beach beside the river Kunduz, at a point where its flow of pinkish muddy snow-water, sixty yards wide, came sweeping round a bend on its way to the Oxus with the speed of an express train. The beach was crowded with people; a blazing heat rose from the shimmering sand; against the lucid pink-blue sky, a line of camels and a line of willows disarranged each other's silhouettes. As we arrived, the ferry was putting off from the opposite bank, crowded with men, horses, and merchandise. It consisted of two rough-hewn high-sterned barges, fastened together by a railed stage across the middle. The current caught it. Simultaneously a line of swimmers grasping a rush tow-rope struck out at right angles across the river, while a man in one of the sterns used a broad paddle as a rudder. At last, thanks to the bend, it hit our shore a quarter of a mile downstream. Further up, other swimmers were guiding horses and cattle across by themselves. When they landed, we saw that many of these professional mermen had large gourds tied to their backs. Their skins were dark brown with exposure, and some of their faces of a type which suggested the servile aboriginal; though no one could tell us if they belonged to a special race or not. Only our regard for the savage Afghan modesty prevented us from joining them on the return journey.

The ferry had now to be dragged upstream, to the top of the bend again, where our lorry mounted the railed stage. We approached the further bank at ten knots an hour, and I was preparing to swim for my life when, by an adroit twist, the impact was lessened and we grated into the low earth cliff. The excitement of the crowd equalled Putney on boat-race day: the dark-skinned naked swimmers, stately Uzbegs in flowered gowns, squat peering Turcomans in pointed fur caps, Hazaras in black turbans as broad as Ascot hats, and one or two men in fair beards whom we supposed to be Kaffirs, handed us up into the field above. Through them all stalked the red-bearded Governor of Kunduz, whip in hand, looking like a Scottish ghillie and conscientiously supervising the whole procedure.

A line of ramparts, white, weary, and old as the mounds of Balkh, announced Kunduz town. On the other side of it we struck across a rising green plain, which brought us nearer to the great snow-peaks on the south-east, so that we could distinguish faces and clefts of bare rock among the snow. Out in the pasture, which consisted of that curious prickly clover whose flowers are like clover flowers, cream with pink tips, while the leaves are more like holly, stood occasional kibitkas, rush-built and untidy, around which grazed herds of horses and cattle. A yellow asphodel* appeared, three or four feet high, singly at first, then in patches, at length transforming the whole prairie into a sea of deep daffodil yellow warmed by the golden blush of sunset.

The people of Khanabad call these yellow pokers 'sikh', and make a kind of thread from their green berries.

Under the mountains we joined the road from Kabul, whose double line of closely posted telephone wires had a new political meaning, if they stretch, as we supposed, to the mouth of the Wakhan Valley, that narrow salient of Afghanistan which separates the three great Asiatic states of Russia, China, and India. A sudden drop brought us into the town, where the Mudir-i-Kharija proved a youth of eighteen prematurely aged by appendicitis. The English words 'boots', 'programme', 'sugar', and 'motah-van' cropped up in his Persian vocabulary. He took us to drink tea in the Governor's audience chamber, a room ninety feet long adorned with the national arms in black and white on an orange curtain at one end of it.

Tired and dirty, we asked for rooms. But instead of the expected

* *Erymurus luteus.*

guest-house, which had recently fallen down, he led us to a grove of rustling plane trees as tall as elms, which dated, he said, 'from the days of the Mirs', in other words, from before the conquest of Badakshan by the Emir Dost Mohammad. Here tents had been pitched, carpets, tables, and chairs set out, and lamps lit for our reception. It would have been better done, he said, if he had known we were coming; but there was no telephone between here and Mazar to warn him.

We call our guards the Vicar and the Curate. Not knowing that a third tent in the background contained a newly dug latrine, I asked the Vicar where the lavatory was. At first he did not understand, though I used the ordinary Persian words. Then he guessed. 'Oh,' he said, 'you mean the *jawab-i-chai* – the answer-to-tea.'

A nice euphemism for that essential office.

Khanabad, 5 June This morning we saw the Governor, Shir Mohammad Khan, a sensible man, who answered our questions straightly without any pretence of being asleep all day.

'No,' he said in a low depressed voice, 'you can't go to Hazrat Imam, because it's near the river; and you can't go to see the hot springs at Chayab for the same reason; the river is the frontier, and it would be impolitic to allow you there. As for the Chitral road, the Durah pass will be closed by snow for another two months. And anyhow, in all three cases, you would have to get permission from Kabul.'

I regret Hazrat Imam, since the Mudir-i-Kharija has told us the shrine there has tiles on it.

Tomorrow, therefore, after ten months' travelling, we turn towards home.

There is little to interest us here, apart from our pleasant shady camp. The brick bridge over the river has been carried away by a flood. The Indian bean trees that scent the Governor's garden are said to come from Russia. They sell ice instead of snow in the bazaar.

Bamian (8400 ft, 195 miles from Khanabad), 8 June We had just embarked in the lorry at Khanabad the day before yesterday, when the Mudir-i-Kharija ran up and asked us to wait an hour, while he found two new attendants to go with us. At the prospect of losing the Vicar and the Curate, Christopher blew and roared, I stamped, the Vicar muttered in the Mudir-i-Kharija's ear that we were dangerous if thwarted, Seyid Jemal swore he would not wait another moment, and off we drove, kidnapping our own guards. They are pleased at the jaunt, having never seen the capital, but nervous of what may happen to them in Mazar when they return. I don't know why we set such store by their company; they are more comic than useful. The Vicar, whenever he is asked to do anything, repeats the request several times in a sing-song tone, utters a long eulogy on his inexhaustible desire to be of help, begs us to believe that his happiness and ours are one, and then doesn't do it. The Curate is avowedly lazy. He has to be galvanized into action by a forcible shake. But at least they no longer obstruct us from photographing or going where we want, which new guards might have done.

Eighteen miles from Khanabad, we rejoined the Kunduz as it entered the mountains, and are still beside a bit of it here at Bamian; in fact, but for this river it is difficult to see how a motor-road could ever have been made over the Hindu Kush. For the moment it proved a nuisance, or the parent of one. A small tributary, swollen with snow-water, brought us to a stop in the middle of the Baglan plain.

There was nothing to do but wait, marking the water by stones to see if it was rising or falling. Our only shade, as we nestled in the cool pasture, was from clumps of pampas grass. A little slug-shaped hill stood near, uplifting a few graves and a shrine to a view of the great snow-range on the east. After a time another lorry joined us, and its men organized a shooting match at a bit of tin, in which the Vicar and the Curate and Seyid Jemal joined. Christopher and I bathed; but the water was such that we had to clean our bodies afterwards with a clothes brush. When evening came we put out the beds beside the lorry. Mosquitoes the size of eagles collected as though to a dinner bell.

Early next morning I was lying in bed, when an old gentleman riding a bay horse arrived at the river. He was dressed in a faded chocolate gown flecked with roses and the end of his turban was wrapped round his face over an iron-grey beard. Across the saddle he carried a brown lamb. Behind him, on foot, came his son aged twelve, flapping along in a gown of geranium red and a white turban as big as himself, and holding a stick with which he directed the progress of a black ewe and her black lamb.

When the party had assembled at the ford, the process of crossing began. First the old man rode into the stream, with difficulty kept his horse's head against it, and deposited the brown lamb on the other side. While he was returning, the child caught the black lamb. This he gave to his father, who then re-entered the water dangling it by one leg so that it screamed. Bleating in sympathy, the ewe followed. But the current swept her away and landed her on the bank she had started from. Meanwhile her offspring, now safe on the further bank with the brown lamb, kept on crying. Again the old man returned, and helped his son drive the wet and shivering ewe a hundred yards up the bank above the ford. There the current caught her once more, and landed her neatly at the ford itself, this time on the further side, where she was warmly greeted by both lambs. Putting his foot on his father's boot, the little boy hopped up behind him and probed the stream with his pole as they crossed, to see if the bottom was firm. On the other bank he dismounted, restored the brown lamb to his father's saddle, set the ewe and the black lamb in motion, and launched into a swinging trot, with his geranium gown flying out behind him. The bay horse followed, and the procession was lost on the horizon.

It was now a question of whether we should go on by horse too. But the water had gone down $3\frac{1}{2}$ inches in the night, and Seyid Jemal resolved to make a bid to save his contract. Thirty men were collected from an invisible village, some to pull in front with ropes, others to push behind. The lorry reached the incline to the ford, flew headlong into the water, upset and all but killed the men in front, and in ten seconds had been carried too far down by the current to make the exit on the other side. It backed, turned its nose from the stream, and sailed along the river at thirty miles an hour, followed by a yelling mob of bearded torsos in skull-caps, who were just in time to give it a further shove on to dry land at a second ford further down. Not a drop of water had reached the vital parts of the engine.

Baglan itself was a congeries of villages at the south end of the plain, standing among fields where the corn was already reaped and lay drying in stooks. We crossed the Kunduz again by the Pul-i-Khomri, an old brick bridge of one arch, beside which I found a group of small white carnations on tall stalks. Henceforth the road was properly engineered with gentle gradients carried on embankments or passing through cuttings; but being still in the earth country, there was nothing to sustain these works and the rain had cut them like cheese. Almost every one, instead of being a convenience, necessitated a detour over ground where there was no road at all.

Now began the most beautiful part of the whole journey, which made us long to be on horses. The road left the river and started a frontal attack on the main Hindu Kush, climbing up their green bastions, not in twists, but by a succession of steeply sloping saddles leading from ridge to ridge. On all sides, below and above, as far as the eye could see, the escarpments of waving grass were spangled with an endless variety of flowers, yellow and white and purple and pink, growing with such art, neither too close nor too scattered nor too profuse in any one kind, that it seemed as if some princely gardener, some Oriental Bacon, had been at work over the whole mountain range. Blue chicory, tall pink hollyhock-mallows, clumps of lemon-coloured cornflowers on stout brown knobs, patches of low white spikes like jasmine, a big spotty-leaved saxifrage, a small flower of butter yellow with a brown inside like garden musk, bunches of blue and pink nettles with stingless leaves, and branching sprays of rose-pink lobster-blossoms, were only a few of those that winked at us from this vast enamelled lawn edged by the clouds above and the ever-receding waves of Turkestan below – winked at us, sometimes from under pistachio bushes, as we chugged and fumed, cursing our vandal truck, to the top of the Kampirak pass.

Scooting over the green uplands, we arrived at a narrow defile, two miles long, where the road became a torrent-bed of loose stones and the lorry could scarcely insinuate itself between the unloose boulders. When this opened out, the Kunduz was below us again; mighty snow-peaks rose from the other side of it. The river took us west now, cantering its white river-horses towards us down the valley, till darkness obliged us to stop at a village called Tala or Barfak or sometimes Tala-Barfak.

*

We woke up this morning to realize we had left Central Asia. Tribes from the south were moving northward, real Afghans, swarthy and half Indian in their dress, managing strings of two and three hundred camels. Ruined castles and fortified walls crowned the opposing heights. The river, as if enraged by its own shrinkage, ran foaming out of a gorge whose sheer rock walls rose hundreds of feet into the blue sky. This formation, interrupted by occasional cultivated valleys, lasted forty miles, and began by describing two-thirds of a circle. We crossed the river eight or nine times by wooden bridges. Pomegranate trees in scarlet flower and bushes of pink spiraea lined the water's edge. Eventually another bridge led us off the main road westward, into the valley of Bamian.

Since leaving the Oxus plain we had risen about 6000 feet, and the colours of this extraordinary valley with its cliffs of rhubarb red, its indigo peaks roofed in glittering snow and its new-sprung corn of harsh electric green, shone doubly brilliant in the clear mountain air. Up the side-valleys we caught sight of ruins and caves. The cliffs paled. And there suddenly, like an enormous wasps' nest, hung the myriad caves of the Buddhist monks, clustered about the two giant Buddhas.

A Frankish house with a tin roof beckoned to us from a bluff across the river. The Governor was away; but his deputy, an asthmatic porpoise in blue pyjamas, seemed perturbed by our arrival without notice and telephoned to Kabul to announce it. We walked out on to a balcony, looking down on the bright green fields, the grey-blue river lined with viridian poplars, and the red earth paths where the peasants were driving their animals – and then looking up to find the two Buddhas, a mile off, peering in at the balcony as if they were paying an afternoon call. A sheet of yellow-and-violet lightning fell from the clouds. A shiver ran down the valley, followed by a gust of rain. Then the tempest broke and shook the house for an hour. When it cleared, the indigo mountains were powdered with new snow.

Shibar (c. *9000 ft, 24 miles from Bamian), *9 June*   I should not like to stay long at Bamian. Its art is unfresh. When Huan Tsang came here, the Buddhas were gilded to resemble bronze, and 5000 monks swarmed in the labyrinths beside them. That was in 632; Mohammad died the same year, and the Arabs reached Bamian before the end of the century. But it was not until 150 years later that the monks were finally extirpated. One can imagine how the Arabs felt about them and their idols in this blood-red valley. Nadir Shah must have felt the same 1000 years later when he broke the legs of the larger Buddha.

That Buddha is 174 feet high, and the smaller 115; they stand a quarter of a mile apart. The larger bears traces of a plaster veneer, which was painted red, presumably as a groundwork for the gilt. Neither has any artistic value. But one could bear that; it is their negation of sense, the lack of any pride in their monstrous flaccid bulk, that sickens. Even their material is unbeautiful, for the cliff is made, not of stone, but of compressed gravel. A lot of monastic navvies were given picks and told to copy some frightful semi-Hellenistic image from India or China. The result has not even the dignity of labour.

The canopies of the niches which contain the two figures are plastered and painted. In the smaller hangs a triumph scene, red, yellow, and blue, in which Hackin, Herzfeld, and others have distinguished a Sasanian influence; but the clue to this idea comes from Masson, who saw a Pahlevi inscription here a hundred years ago. The paintings round the larger head are better preserved, and can be examined at close quarters by standing on the head itself. On either side of the niche, below the curve of the vault, hang five medallions about ten feet in diameter which contain Boddhisatvas. These figures are surrounded by horseshoe auras of white, yellow, and blue, and their hair is tinged with red. Between each medallion grows a triple-branched lotus; at least we supposed it to be that, though in other surroundings it might be taken for an ecclesiastical gas-bracket upholding three glass globes. The next zone above is occupied by a pavement in squares out of perspective, and the zone above that by a wainscot of Pompeian curtains finished with a border of peacocks' feathers. On top of this come two more rows of Boddhisatvas, seated against auras and thrones alternately, the thrones being decked with jewelled carpets. Between these stand large cups on stems, resembling Saxon fonts and sprouting cherubs. The topmost zone overhead is missing. The colours are the ordinary fresco colours, slate-grey, gamboge, a rusty chocolate-red, a dull grape-tint, and a bright harebell blue.

The subjects suggest that Persian, Indian, Chinese, and Hellenistic ideas all met at Bamian in the fifth and sixth centuries. It is interesting to have a record of this meeting. But the fruit of it is not pleasant. The only exception is the lower row of Boddhisatvas, which Hackin says are older than the rest. They achieve that air of repose, graceful but empty, which is the best one can expect of Buddhist iconography.

The chambers in the cliff preserve a similar record of contemporary architectural ideas. The monks were obliged to give some form to their ceremonial interiors. But of all conventions available to them, the inside of the Indian stone dome must surely have been the least suited to reproduction in monolith. Yet here they carved it, with its massive pendent brackets, its heavy criss-cross beams, and its inept little cupola. The Sasanian influence produced more sensible results. One spacious hall bears an extraordinary resemblance to the dome chambers at Firuzabad, and its mouldings, breaking into bows or something of the sort on top of the squinches, may tell how Sasanian stucco was originally applied. Other caves show domes resting on circular and octagonal walls, some elaborately carved, and one bearing an arabesque frieze which might be a prototype of that in the Friday Mosque at Kazvin, erected six centuries later. But the most remarkable connection with Mohammadan architecture, proving how directly it borrowed the inventions of the fire-worshipping past, is contained in a square cave where the dome rests on four squinches composed of five concentric arches each. This most unusual device, with the addition of another arch, reappears in a mausoleum at Kassan in Turkestan, which was built in the fourteenth century.

The French archaeologists have left the caves in good condition, repaired the painted plaster, added staircases where necessary, and put up sensible notices in French and Persian to guide those who have not had the chance of studying their published reports: 'Groupe C; Salle de Réunion', 'Group D; Sanctuaire, influences iraniennes', etc.

The Kabul road, after we rejoined it, still kept company with a last small tributary of the Kunduz, which led us up towards the Shibar pass, out on to bare hills where the corn was still but a sprinkle of green on the brown earth. There we met a man who said the road on the other side of the pass was blocked by a landslide. It was too late to reconnoitre it. We have therefore returned to the village of Shibar, a desolate group of houses under the naked peaks.

This morning at Bamian, Christopher was scrambling eggs with his dagger when the fire gave out, and he asked the Curate to fetch some more wood. He asked again. He then prodded the man with the dagger. Now at Shibar the Vicar and he wanted to share our room. We said it was not big enough. Unused to such treatment, the Curate gave us a lecture. No doubt, he said, we had our own Frankish customs. But in Afghanistan he begged us to realize, everything depended on friendship. If he did things for us, it was because we were his friends, not because we told him to do them. He was a guard in government employ, not our servant. For the rest of the journey he hoped we should be good friends, so that he *could* do things for us. And so on.

It is not our fault we have no servant. We have tried to engage one at every town since Herat, and in each case have been told by the authorities that the guards they supplied would act as servants. Thus in bullying the Curate we have only taken the authorities at their word. Nevertheless, his speech abashed us.

The villagers provided a concert after dinner.

'Only Afghanistan, Persia, England, and India make good music,' said the Vicar.

'What about Russia?' Christopher asked.

'Russia? Russian music is absolutely rotten.'

Charikar (5300 ft, 74 miles from Shibar), 10 June Not one landslide but a dozen prevented us from reaching Kabul tonight. We are only forty miles away, and already an iron bridge has announced the zone of civilization surrounding the capital. Here, in this caravanserai, we have dined off a table and sat on chairs, and have remembered, suddenly, that our journey is nearly over. The last week has been a busy one. The getting up at four, cooking porridge over a wood fire, ordering food for our meagre picnic outfit in its battered Persian tin, seeing the lamps are filled in case of a night in the open, jumping out to fill the water-bottles at every spring, cleaning our boots every other day, and rationing the men with cigarettes to keep them happy, have become an automatic routine;

and the thought that tomorrow it will cease leaves us flat and a little melancholy.

The Shibar pass is 10,000 feet high, and we were near the snow-line before we left the last trickle of the Kunduz, as it started on its long journey to the Oxus and the Sea of Aral. Five minutes later another trickle started on a journey to the Indus and the Indian Ocean. Geography has its excitements.

A mile beyond the pass we reached the first landslides, heaps of liquid mud and pebbles concealing large rocks. Here a gang of proper roadmen had been set to work. But at the second and more formidable set of obstacles, ten miles further on, I found only a few bewildered villagers puddling about like children, and had myself to act as foreman in order to put some method into their operations. The crops below the road, already half destroyed by the rivers of mud, were now menaced by a further spate, and poor frantic women rushed out from the village with sickles to save what remained for hay. The villagers regarded it as their duty to clear the road; but not so a party of muleteers who happened to come along and were greeted, on protesting against being forced into this labour, by a rain of blows from Seyid Jemal and by the sight of the Vicar aiming at them with his gun. They complied in terror.

The river, the new river, running down to India, was fringed with pink roses and white spiraea. The valleys grew richer. Groves of walnuts stood about the villages, where Indian merchants in tight gay turbans were sitting in their shops. And then, like a blow in the face, came the Charikar iron bridge.

Kabul (5900 ft, 36 miles from Charikar), 11 June From Herat to Kabul we have come 930 miles, of which forty-five were on horseback.

A winding hill-road brought us down from the Charikar plateau to a smaller plain inside a ring of mountains; running water and corrugated iron glinted among its trees. At the entrance to the capital the police deprived the Vicar and the Curate of their rifles, to their great distress; but being in turbans, no one would believe they were

266

government servants. We drove to the Foreign Office, where hot red English ramblers were climbing over iron railings; to the hotel, where there was writing-paper in each bedroom; to the Russian Legation, where they had had no answer to M. Bouriachenko's telegram; to the German shop, where they refused to sell us hock without a permit from the Minister of Trade; and finally to our Legation, where the Minister, Sir Richard Maconochie, has asked us to stay. It is a white house, dignified with pillars and furnished as it would be at home, without any mosquito-nets or fans to remind one of the Orient. Christopher says he finds it peculiar to be in a room whose walls aren't falling down.

Opinion at the Legation agrees on the silliness of refusing the Russian diplomats in Kabul transit visas through India. Even if they go as far towards the frontier as Jelallabad, the Government of India sends in official complaints. The result is a sort of gentlemen's agreement between the two Legations and the Afghan Government that the English shall not travel in the north of the country and the Russians in the south. That is why the authorities at Mazar could not allow us to the Oxus, though they would not admit such a reason lest it appear a limitation of their sovereignty. We were lucky to have got as close as we did, particularly as it appears that Haji Lal Mohammad, who bought the car, and our chauffeur Jamshyd Taroporevala, spread a tale that we were Secret Service agents engaged in map-making. Next time I do this kind of journey, I shall take lessons in spying beforehand. Since one has to put up with the disadvantages of the profession anyhow, one might as well reap some of its advantages, if there are any.

British diplomacy in Kabul just now hangs on the Minister's roses. At the King's birthday party, on 3 June, they were in full flower, and the Afghans, who are all rose-lovers, had never seen such big formal blooms. Next morning, visiting cards from the Minister of Court were fluttering from the finest trees; they had been left by his gardener in the night. Now all the other ministers want cuttings too, and are also in a turmoil over the peonies, which have been promised them for next year.

Magnificent as the formal roses are, I yet prefer an Afghan tree which stands by the gate in front. It is fifteen feet high and covered with such a profusion of white blossoms that hardly a leaf is visible.

Kabul, 14 June   Uneventful days.

The garden here is too pleasant to leave, full of sweet-williams, canterbury bells, and columbines, planted among the lawns and terraces and shady arbours; it might be England till one notices the purple mountain behind the big white house. The total establishment is ninety persons; at tennis this evening there were six uniformed ball-boys for one game. People complain, though I have never wanted to, that our embassies and legations, relying on Lord Salisbury's despatch, think it their duty not to help visitors. This legation might exist for no other purpose, for all the visitor can see. And not only the English visitor. Americans who come here generally get into trouble of some sort, and having no legation of their own, ask assistance of ours, which they receive.

Ghazni (7300 ft, 98 miles from Kabul), 15 June   The journey here occupied $4\frac{1}{2}$ hours, along a good hard road through the Desert of Top, which was carpeted with irises.

The famous 'Towers of Victory' stand 700 yards apart on the way to the village of Rozah: a pair of octagonal star-shaped stumps, each seventy feet high and now roofed with a tin hat to prevent further decay. Vigne, who sketched them in 1836, shows that their circular superstructures were more than twice as high again. They were built as minarets, commemorative rather than religious, for the ground gives no evidence that there was ever a mosque in the neighbourhood. It was a Sasanian habit to build such towers, and after the coming of Islam the Persians kept it up, till about the fourteenth century. The minarets at Damghan and Sabzevar, and many of those at Isfahan, are similarly isolated.

There has been a muddle over the founders of these towers. J. A. Rawlinson published the inscriptions on them in 1843, ascribing the larger and more splendid of the two to Mahmud, son of Sabaktagin, the maker of the Ghaznavide Empire and patron of Firdaussi and Avicenna. But Rawlinson must have mixed his notes;

for in 1925, when Flury the epigraphist obtained some photographs, he found that the inscription relating to Mahmud was actually on the smaller tower, while the larger bore the name of his descendant Masud III, son of Ibrahim. The smaller tower, therefore, must date from before 1030, the larger from between 1099 and 1114.

The difference between them is in breadth, the diameter of the larger, excluding the stone base, being about twenty-four feet, and that of the smaller about twenty-two. Both are built of a rich toffee brick tinged with red, and are adorned with carved terra-cotta of the same colour. In each case, each of the eight recesses between the star-points is divided into eight ornamental zones of varying depths. Between the third and fourth, fifth and sixth, and sixth and seventh zones, the brickwork is interrupted by wooden joists.

Apart from the zigzag patterns in which the bricks are set, the ornament of the smaller tower is confined to two narrow bands of terra-cotta in the middle, and to the sixteen panels of bold Kufic lettering at the top, which describe Mahmud as 'the august Sultan, King of Islam, trusted of society, Abul-Muzaffar, support of Mussulmans, help of the poor, Abulkasim Mahmud – may God illuminate his constancy – son of Sabaktagin Gazi . . . Commander of the Faithful'. The larger tower is richer, its bricks are closer set, and all eight zones are filled with elaborate ornament, sometimes bordered with lesser inscriptions. Another sixteen panels round the top proclaim the titles of Masud; their Kufic is taller and more graceful, standing out from a maze of pattern like soldiers from a crowd. Generally, when it is a question of comparing two buildings of similar design but different dates, the simplicity of the older is preferable. Here that is not so. The fineness of the larger's brickwork and the elaboration of its ornament have a functional propriety. They weight the tower to the earth, giving it that air of strength and cohesion which it needed to support the shaft above. An old photograph in the Legation at Kabul, taken about 1870, shows the detail of this shaft. The first twenty-five feet were plain and were probably hidden, when the tower was first built, by a wooden balcony. Thereafter it was divided into ornamental ribs, alternately curved and flat. These were surmounted by eight pairs of elongated niches and by a belt of carving which looks as if it contained a Kufic inscription.

It is interesting to remember that this minaret was built in the same century as the Gumbad-i-Kabus. Each is monumental, deserves the very palm of ostentation. But the difference between the ornateness of the one and the simplicity of the other shows that two separate ideas were at work in Persian architecture at that time. Seljuk architecture, which followed, was the fruit of these ideas, and inheriting the genius of both, attained a perfect balance between ornament and construction.

The Tomb of Sultan Mahmud, which lies in the village of Rozah half a mile off, has attracted the notice of more travellers than the towers. Ibn Battuta, in the middle of the fourteenth century, says it was surmounted by a hospice. Babur looked in of course, and saw the tombs of Sultans Ibrahim and Masud near by. Next came Vigne in 1836, and six years later an English army, which took away the doors of the tomb because some idiot of a historian – I believe it was Ferishta – had said they were the doors of the Hindu Temple of Somnath in Gujerat, which Mahmud had stolen when he sacked it. Prodigies of transport (they measure $16\frac{1}{2}$ feet by $13\frac{1}{2}$) were employed to bring them to Agra, while Lord Ellenborough requested the Princes of India to observe how worthy the British Government 'proves itself of your love, when, regarding your honour as its own, it asserts the power of its arms to restore to you the gates of the temple of Somnath, so long the memorial of your subjection to the Afghans'. The ridicule that greeted this announcement consigned the doors to permanent obscurity in the fort at Agra, where they still remain. Their wood is that of the Afghan deodar, and an inscription on the lintel invokes the forgiveness of God on Abulkasim Mahmud, son of Sabaktagin. Yet the legend of their Hindu origin still persists in school textbooks. The Government of India might well demolish it by returning them. Their rape has never even been justified by a published description of the carvings, which are unique in Mohammadan art.

After the War, when Niedermayer was here, the tomb lay open to the sky. We found it now beneath a spacious dome, approached through cloisters and a rose-garden.

Three old men were chanting from large Korans, while our guides leant over a wooden railing to take off the black pall, shaking the rose-petals that covered it into a heap at one end. There emerged an inverted stone cradle with triangular ends, five feet long and twenty inches high, and mounted on a broad plinth. The stone is marble, white and translucent. On the side facing Mecca runs a Kufic inscription in two lines begging 'a gracious reception from God for the noble Prince and Lord Nizam-ad-Din Abulkasim Mahmud ibn Sabaktagin'. On the other side, a small trefoil panel says: 'He died ... in the evening of Thursday when seven nights remained of the month of Rabiat II in the year 421.' That was 18 February 1030.

The virtue of the tomb as a work of art lies in the depth and fulness of the carving, in the glow of the marble where age has caressed it, and above all in the main inscription. Kufic lettering has a functional beauty; regarded as pure design, its extraordinary emphasis seems in itself a form of oratory, a transposition of speech from the audible to the visible. I have enjoyed many examples of it in the last ten months. But none can compare with these tall rhythmic ciphers, involved with dancing foliage, which mourn the loss of Mahmud, the conqueror of India, Persia, and Oxiana, nine centuries after his death, in the capital where he ruled.

The crowd that had followed us into the garden was excluded from the shrine while we were looking at the tomb, to the indignation of one man who wanted to say his prayers. 'Why do you allow those heretic clerks inside?' he shouted. 'It isn't clean.' The crowd took his side, and began to shout also, till our guards were threatened with a brawl. It was they who had suggested our visiting the tomb. The Foreign Minister had telegraphed from Kabul that we were to see everything.

Kabul, 17 June We solved a mystery on the way back from Ghazni.

Some small trees of the sallow type were growing along a stream near the road, and Seyid Jemal stopped to let his assistant pick a few branches from them, which he threw into the back of the lorry. As they fell at our feet, they gave out that same elusive smell which has pervaded the whole journey since we first met it at the Afghan frontier, and which now, in its overwhelming sweetness, brought the the minarets of Herat before my eyes again. It emanated from clusters of small yellow-green flowers,* which are unnoticeable from a distance, but which, if ever I smell them again, will remind me of Afghanistan as a cedar wardrobe reminds me of childhood.

Seyid Jemal has heard that soon after we crossed it, two lorries were

* The oleaster.

completely wrecked by the stream that delayed us on the Baglan plain, and that the Kunduz ferry has overturned and sunk, drowning five women.

We are now staying in the hotel here, which is run by Indians and is not uncivilized; they have just built an annexe and telegraphed for a German chef. Kabul for the most part has an easy unpretentious character, as of a Balkan town in the good sense of the term. It clusters round a few bare rocky hills which rise abruptly from the verdant plain and act as defences. Snow-mountains decorate the distance, the parliament sits in a cornfield, and long avenues shade the town's approaches. In winter, at a height of 6000 feet, the cold may be inconvenient. But at present the climate is perfect, hot yet always fresh. Cinemas and alcohol are forbidden. The Legation doctor has had to give up treating women at the instance of the Church; though they sometimes visit him disguised as boys. And the whole policy of forcible westernization is in abeyance. All the same, westernization is progressing by example, and one feels that perhaps the Afghans have struck the mean for which Asia is looking. Even the most nationalist of them makes a pleasant contrast with the mincing assertiveness of the modern Persian.

This morning at the Legation I met a Colonel Porter who asked what my share in the world's work was. I said I had been looking at Mohammadan architecture.

'Mind you,' he replied, 'I've seen a good deal of Mohammadan architecture one way and another, in Palestine, Egypt, and Persia, and I've given a good deal of thought to the matter. I can tell you the key to the problem if you like.'

'Really. What is it?'

'The whole thing's *phallic*,' he uttered in a ghoulish whisper.

I was surprised at first to note the influence of Freud on the North-West Frontier, but soon discovered that for Colonel Porter the universe itself was phallic.

In the afternoon Fletcher of the Legation drove us out to Dar-al-Aman and Paghman, the unfinished dreams of Amanullah. The former was to be a New Delhi, the latter a new Simla, created out of the British subsidies which Amanullah's father, Habibullah, accumulated year by year but never spent. Dar-al-Aman is joined to Kabul by one of the most beautiful avenues in the world, four miles long, dead straight, as broad as the Great West Road, and lined with tall white-stemmed poplars. In front of the poplars run streams confined by grass margins. Behind them are shady footwalks and a tangle of yellow and white roses, now in full flower and richly scented. And then at the end, O God, appears the turreted angle – not even the front – of a French municipal office, surrounded by a French municipal garden and entirely deserted. While below it, occupying the very centre of the whole four-mile vista, stands a German match factory in the ferro-concrete-farmhouse style.

Paghman, the Simla, spreads over a wooded slope two or three thousand feet above the plain, where grassy glades interrupt the poplars and walnuts, an orchestra plays of mountain streams, and the snows appear through the trees unexpectedly close. In each glade stands a house or office or theatre of such appalling aspect, so vilely reminiscent of a German Kurhaus and the back parts of Pimlico, that it is impossible to imagine where Amanullah could have found the architects to design them, even as a joke. But no; they are not a joke. Untenanted, shoddy, and obscene, they defile the woods and streams and the view of the plain beneath, where narrow shady lanes go winding among the irregular fields. The climax of this pseudo-civilization is a race-course, no larger than a cricket field, round whose hairpin corners elephants were forced to compete.

I bought some lapis this evening, not because it was cheap or a good colour, but because it comes from the famous mines near Ishkashim in Badakshan, and is therefore the authentic stone from which the old painters ground their blue. The sale of it is a Government monopoly and the whole export of the mines goes to Berlin.

Christopher has gone out to drink beer with a German schoolmaster, while I, Martha-like, have been packing and paying the bill. It is midnight.

INDIA: Peshawar (1200 ft, 189 miles from Kabul), 19 June The result of my virtue was that when Seyid Jemal drove up at five next morning expecting as usual to wait two hours, the luggage was ready on the doorstep and we reached Peshawar the same evenng. Even in a touring car the journey generally takes two days. It was a grim drive, down through the bare black-boned mountains into the steel haze of India. We were at Jelallabad by one, bought a melon, and hastened on towards the Khyber over a grey waste of pebbles dancing in the heat. At Dacca, a scattered hamlet containing a few shops, a petrol pump, and one stunted tree on a cliff above the now extensive river Kabul, the frontier formalities were quickly done with. The mountains closed on us. Seyid Jemal remarked with pride that he was an Afridi. Our passports were looked at again by a knot of Afghans sitting under two trees. And round the corner appeared an uplifted steel barrier, a sentry in a steel helmet, and a milestone announcing British India as if it were the local car-park. The new passport office was a bungalow in a garden of flowering shrubs. We sat on a bench and ate our last chicken salad out of the blue bowl from Isfahan, while the passport officer requested that as it was a quarter-past four, and therefore too late to allow Europeans through, we should say we had entered the pass at half-past three.

As passes go, the Khyber is invitingly mild. It is this which makes it the theatre of such stupendous works. The tracks of middle Asia, the single telephone wire on its stunted wooden posts, give place to communications of Roman exuberance. Not one, but two graded roads wind up and down the length of the defile: the one of asphalt, as smooth as Piccadilly and flanked by low battlements; the other, its predecessor, abandoned to camels, but still such a highway as we had not seen since Damascus. Intertwined with these comes a third and larger thoroughfare, a railway, leading to the head of the pass and soon to extend beyond it, glinting from tunnel to tunnel, whose black mouths, framed in pylons of red masonry, recede into the savage grey distance. Roads and railway are embanked on shelves of hewn stone linking mountain to mountain; iron viaducts carry them across the valleys and each other. Sheaves of telephone wires fastened to metal posts by gleaming white insulators, red and green signals jewelled in the torrid haze, drinking-troughs fashioned like antique sarcophaguses, and milestones proclaiming, at intervals of thirty yards, that the distance to L, J, and P – Landi Kotal, Jamrud, and Peshawar – has decreased, all complete the evidence of the neat grey blockhouses perched on every ledge and peak: that if the English must be bothered to defend India, it shall be with a minimum of personal inconvenience. This was our feeling. It was the spectacle of common sense that thrilled us amid the evil heat, the eyries of the tribesmen, and the immemorial associations of pilgrims and conquerors, a spectacle for complacent, boasting patriotism.

Seyid Jemal was in mad spirits. 'Sarakh bisyar harab! What an absolutely rotten road!' he shouted, grinning at its shiny complexion. 'Tonight you must be my guests in Khyber.' We passed Landi Kotal, where Hamber's regiment of Gurkhas was playing hockey, but saw no officers except those who whizzed by in tennis clothes and Morris cars, so that we could not deliver Hamber's messages. At Khyber village, a typical village of the pass, where every house was a fortified enclosure with its own watch-tower, Seyid Jemal stopped, and a crowd of scrofulous children leapt into the lorry, oblivious of our selves or luggage, to greet their father. The owner of the lorry, a walloping capitalist, rushed out of his house to see how his property had fared on the Afghan roads. Seyid Jemal's assistant, lifting the front seat, disclosed a secret hoard of Russian sugar purchased in Mazar. His relations arrived too, and the whole village was soon assembled in a ring to welcome the lost, after three months' absence.

We should have liked to accept Seyid Jemal's invitation. It would have been amusing to have walked over to the Landi Kotal barracks next day and revealed casually that we were staying down the road with our chauffeur. But even now we are not sure if we shall catch the *Maloja* at Bombay. With his usual good humour Seyid Jemal forsook his family and took us on. The hills opened out, disclosing the level tree-scattered eternity of India. At half-past seven we were drinking gin fizzes in the marble lounge of Dean's Hotel.

We said goodbye to Seyid Jemal with real regret. Between Mazar and Peshawar he had driven us altogether 840 miles. He was never ill-tempered or depressed by obstacles, but always calm and amused, punctual, polite, and efficient. During the whole journey, over the most difficult roads a motor could tackle, we did not once see the tool-box opened or a tyre changed.

The lorry was a Chevrolet.

The Frontier Mail, 21 June We stopped the night at Delhi, and next morning, before the sun was up, were standing beneath

Lutyens' memorial arch. A few novelties have been added since the Viceroy went into residence: Jagger's Assyrio-Cartier elephants, a plan of the city in gold on the base of the Jaipur Column, and statues of Irwin and Reading, which commonize the Great Palace. I suggested to Lord Irwin he should be done by Epstein. He answered, 'I thought you'd say that', and sat to Reid Dick. As for the gradient of the King's Way, it won't be my fault if Baker is not remembered for calculating malevolence.

It was curious at the Kutb to see ornament in the Seljuk style carved out of stone instead of stucco. The virtue goes out of it in this other material; it becomes Indian and painstaking, and loses its freedom.

This train left Peshawar only fifteen hours after we did, so that we had not much time.

SS Maloja, *1 June* A big boat of 20,000 tons, pitching through an inky sea. Clouds of spray; salt and sweat and boredom everywhere. The sound of retching and an empty dining-room.

After previous experience of a really cheery voyage by P. and O. in the crowded season, I came on board with dread. But that was four years ago, when Italian competition had only just begun. Now I detect a change for the better in manners and obligingness. Also the boat is only half full, so that we escape the communal life of a boarding-house. None the less it is an appalling penalty: a fortnight blotted out of one's life at great expense.

SS Maloja, *1 July* We have made friends with Mr and Mrs Chichester and Miss Wills. Seeing Christopher slopping about the deck in a pair of shorts and that red blouse he bought at Abbasabad, Miss Wills asked: 'Are you an explorer?'

'No,' answered Christopher, 'but I've been in Afghanistan.'

'Ah, Afghanistan,' said Chichester, 'that's in India, isn't it?'

Savernake, 8 July I left Christopher at Marseilles. He was going to Berlin to see Frau Wassmuss. England looked drab and ugly from